Taking Your iPad to the Max

Steve Sande

Michael Grothaus

Erica Sadun

Apress®

Taking Your iPad to the Max

ISBN-13 (pbk): 978-1-4302-3108-0

ISBN-13 (electronic): 978-1-4302-3109-7

Printed and bound in the United States of America 9 8 7 6 5 4 3 2 1

President and Publisher: Paul Manning
Lead Editor: Clay Andres
Development Editor: Douglas Pundick
Technical Reviewer: Erica Sadun
Editorial Board: Clay Andres, Steve Anglin, Mark Beckner, Ewan Buckingham, Gary Cornell, Jonathan Gennick, Jonathan Hassell, Michelle Lowman, Matthew Moodie, Duncan Parkes, Jeffrey Pepper, Frank Pohlmann, Douglas Pundick, Ben Renow-Clarke, Dominic Shakeshaft, Matt Wade, Tom Welsh
Coordinating Editor: Kelly Moritz
Copy Editor: Kim Wimpsett
Production Support: Patrick Cunningham
Indexer: John Collin
Artist: April Milne
Cover Designer: Anna Ishchenko

Distributed to the book trade worldwide by Springer Science+Business Media, LLC., 233 Spring Street, 6th Floor, New York, NY 10013. Phone 1-800-SPRINGER, fax (201) 348-4505, e-mail orders-ny@springer-sbm.com, or visit www.springeronline.com.

For information on translations, please e-mail rights@apress.com, or visit www.apress.com.

Apress and friends of ED books may be purchased in bulk for academic, corporate, or promotional use. eBook versions and licenses are also available for most titles. For more information, reference our Special Bulk Sales–eBook Licensing web page at www.apress.com/info/bulksales.

My work in this book is dedicated to my wife of 31 years, Barb. Without you, I wouldn't be able to realize my dreams.

–Steve Sande

To my brother Glenn, who is quickly becoming an Apple junkie.

–Michael Grothaus

Contents at a Glance

Contents

About the Authors

Steve Sande has been a loyal fan of Apple technology since buying his first Mac in 1984. Originally trained as a civil engineer, Steve's career as an IT professional blossomed in the 1990s. A longtime blogger, Steve is an editor at The Unofficial Apple Weblog (TUAW.com) and the author of three books about Apple's iWeb application. He lives with his wife of 31 years in Highlands Ranch, Colorado.

Michael Grothaus is an American novelist and journalist living in London. He was first introduced to Apple computers in film school and went on to use them for years to create award-winning films. After discovering many of Hollywood's dirty little secrets while working for 20th Century Fox, he left and spent five years with Apple as a consultant. Since then, he's moved to Europe and written his first novel. Currently, Michael is a staff writer for AOL's popular tech news site TUAW: The Unofficial Apple Weblog, where he regularly interviews tech CEOs and writes about all things Mac. When not writing, he spends his time traveling Europe, Northern Africa, and Asia. *Epiphany Jones*, a novel about trafficking and America's addiction to celebrity, is his latest book.

About the Technical Reviewer

Erica Sadun holds a PhD in computer science from the Georgia Institute of Technology. She has written, cowritten, and contributed to almost three dozen books about technology, particularly in the areas of programming, digital video, and digital photography. An unrepentant geek, Sadun has never met a gadget she didn't need. Her checkered past includes run-ins with NeXT, Newton, and a vast myriad of both successful and unsuccessful technologies. When not writing, she and her geek husband parent three adorable geeks-in-training, who regard their parents with restrained bemusement. *Eight Ways to Get the Most Out of Your Zune*, the O'Reilly Short Cut, and *Modding Mac OS X*, also with O'Reilly, are her latest books.

Acknowledgments

Steve Sande would like to thank Erica Sadun for being a good friend and a tireless mentor and for asking him along on this journey.

Michael Grothaus wishes to thank Erica, the awesome team at Apress, and the entire TUAW gang.

Introduction

Oh, how far we've come.

As we progress into the second decade of the 21st century, it's becoming increasingly obvious how the computers of the previous 30 years have begun to look not just old but archaic. The massive CRT monitors of the 1980s and 1990s have given way to pencil-thin displays of the 2000s. The PC's bulky and heavy beige box has been reduced to the size of a thick paperback, as with Apple's Mac Mini, or has even been assimilated into the display itself, as with Apple's iMac. This shrinking of the PC has also coincided with the computer becoming thousands of times more powerful—progress that shows no sign of abating. But although the minaturizing and the explosive growth in processing power are technological accomplishments that are nothing to scoff at, the iPad signals the beginning of a new era in technology—the era of the touch-based computer.

When you hold the iPad, you hold the future in your hands. Its Multi-Touch and gesture-based controls finally allow you to break the computer's digital/physical barrier. With the iPad, you can touch your movies, e-mail, and digital pictures; you can carry 10,000 books without increasing the weight in your bag; and you can flip through their pages with the swipe of your finger. Even the Web, something that has long been confined to a rigid desktop venue, becomes something akin to the magazine on your coffee table, yet with an infinite number of pages.

When the iPad was introduced, some said it was nothing more than a big iPhone. Indeed, the iPhone introduced the world to the Multi-Touch interface, and both devices do use the same OS. However, as you'll see, there are many minor and quite a few major differences. Using the iPad, your eyes are immediately enveloped by its large display; there's no squinting when you play games, navigate maps, and watch videos—all from your lap. Its full-size keyboard allows you to comfortably create documents, spreadsheets, and presentations with applications that rival those you find on older, traditional computers. No, the iPad isn't an over-grown iPhone; it's an evolution of the personal computer.

Taking your iPad to the Max introduces you to the iPad. Starting with helping you choose the iPad that's right for you, we walk you through purchase decisions and setting it up for the first time. You'll learn the gesture-based, Multi-Touch vocabulary that allows you to manipulate the iPad and its tens of thousands of apps. We'll show you how to connect to the Internet, browse the Web, touch your music and videos, and find and download apps from the App Store. You'll discover how to buy and navigate books using Apple's revolutionary iBooks app, view slide shows and photos, send e-mail, create notes and calendars, and even turn your iPad into a compass. You'll also discover that the iPad is not simply a new leisure device; it's a powerful office tool, and indeed can be a viable replacement to a traditional computer for many people. We walk you through creating rich documents, spreadsheets, and presentations. Finally, we show you some of our favorite third-party apps and ways we use the iPad as an artist's canvas, a teaching tool, and even a helper in the kitchen.

This book is written for anyone with an iPad or anyone who is thinking of getting one (you won't be sorry!). It doesn't matter whether you're a Mac or Windows user or, in fact, even if you've never used a computer at all. This book's thorough coverage and step-by-step discussions allow all iPad owners to learn about their device and come away with both the skills and the knowledge they need to use it to its fullest.

How you read the book is up to you. If you are totally new to the iPad (or computers in general), we suggest you read the book cover to cover, but you can also feel free to jump around from chapter to chapter if that works better for you. Above all, have fun while you're learning everything that the iPad can do. It's the future of computing, and it's a blast. Thanks for letting us show it to you.

Chapter 1

Bringing Your iPad Home

Purchasing your first iPad should be a fun and exciting experience for you. Compared to buying a full-fledged desktop or laptop computer, there aren't as many options to complicate matters. The price tag on an iPad isn't as daunting as that for an Apple MacBook Pro, so the impact to your wallet won't be outrageous even if you don't happen to make the perfect choice. In this chapter, you'll discover what decisions you should make before either heading to your local Apple retail outlet or ordering an iPad online. You'll learn what you need in addition to an iPad, what you can do if you're not pleased with your purchase or get a faulty unit, and how to get your iPad ready for everyday use. Here are all the basic facts you need to select, buy, and set up your iPad.

Picking Your iPad

Especially at this early stage of the life cycle of the iPad, you have a relatively easy decision to make regarding which model of the device to purchase. There are never that many iPad models available at any particular time, since Apple does a good job of keeping its product lines small and up-to-date. The big questions you'll have to ask yourself are whether you need 3G wireless capabilities and how much storage you want in your iPad. Let's look into these two questions in more detail.

Wi-Fi or Wi-Fi + 3G?

The iPad is an Internet-connected device. Sure, it can work as an electronic book reader or a gaming device without an Internet connection, but an iPad without Internet is like a Porsche with a flat tire. Apple gives you two choices: Wi-Fi (wireless network connectivity) models and Wi-Fi + 3G (wireless network plus 3G mobile data connectivity) models. If you ever want an Internet connection away from a Wi-Fi hotspot, you'll need to buy the Wi-Fi + 3G version of the iPad, because you cannot add the functionality to an iPad later.

The Wi-Fi + 3G models are slightly more expensive than the models with Wi-Fi only, to the tune of US$130 more than their Wi-Fi counterparts. What you're paying for is built-in 3G circuitry, a Global Positioning Satellite (GPS) receiver, and an antenna, which is a fancy way of saying that your iPad (with an optional subscription to a data plan with your local wireless carrier) can surf the Web, send and receive e-mail, and connect to the iBookstore from any location with 3G wireless service. Do you need 3G capabilities? Here are some questions you need to ask yourself:

- *Will you be using your iPad in places where there are no Wi-Fi hotspots?* If you plan on using your iPad around your Wi-Fi equipped home and office and if most of the locations that you visit (stores, libraries, coffee shops, airports, and hotels) provide free Wi-Fi, then you might not need the Wi-Fi + 3G model. However, if you often find yourself in need of an Internet connection when you're in your car, on a soccer field, or at some other location without Wi-Fi, then the Wi-Fi + 3G iPad may be the correct choice for you.

- *Do you have another way to connect to a 3G network?* You may already have a different method of accessing a wide-area wireless network. If you have a 3G router such as the Sierra Wireless Overdrive 3G/4G or Novatel MiFi for use with a laptop, then you can use it and your existing wireless data plan to connect to the Internet.

- *Are you willing to pay extra for both your iPad and the 3G data plan?* To begin with, a Wi-Fi + 3G iPad costs $130 more than the corresponding model without 3G. That's not the only additional cost you'll incur, since your wireless carrier is going to charge you for a data plan. In the United States, AT&T provides 3G data service without a contract for $14.99 per month for 250MB of data, or $29.99 monthly for unlimited data. International carriers offer similar plans, so check with your carrier for details about the cost and capacity of data plans in your country.

- *Do you need to use apps that are aware of the location of the iPad?* The Wi-Fi iPad has the ability to determine its location through something called the Wi-Fi Positioning System. This service, provided in North America by Skyhook Wireless, uses the known location of Wi-Fi access points to approximate the location of an iPad. Although this can provide location data to within 20 to 30 meters in crowded population centers in the United States and Canada, it doesn't work at all when the iPad is away from Wi-Fi. The Wi-Fi + 3G iPad contains a full Assisted GPS (A-GPS) receiver for pinpointing the location of the device using the GPS system. As a result, location can be determined almost anywhere on the planet provided that the Wi-Fi + 3G iPad can "see" the sky.

How Much Storage?

Once you've decided whether to purchase the Wi-Fi or Wi-Fi + 3G iPad, your next thought should be about the quantity of built-in storage you want in your iPad. Although the amount of working memory, or RAM, in the iPad is identical across the different models, the flash drives used for storing applications and data come in three different sizes: 16GB, 32GB, and 64GB. You cannot upgrade the flash drive in the iPad, so you're stuck with whatever you buy. Like any electronic device, the iPad will evolve over time, so larger storage capacities are likely in the future.

At the launch of the iPad, the difference between the 16GB and 32GB models was only $100, while maxing out the iPad's storage at 64GB was only $200 more than buying the base model. Before deciding how much storage you want to buy, consider these questions:

- *How big is your music library?* If your library is small and you want to listen to music on your iPad, no problem. If it's large, the extra space on the larger iPad models helps you store additional music and podcasts. Of course, if you already own a music device such as an iPod, you may want to continue using it for listening. iPods come in a variety of capacities and are much more portable than your iPad.

- *How many videos do you want to carry around?* A single two-hour movie may occupy more than a gigabyte of storage. If you travel a lot, especially on airplanes, you may want to pay more to store additional movies and TV shows with those extra gigabytes. In Chapter 7 of this book, we'll talk about using Handbrake to transfer video from DVDs to a format that your iPad can use. Although Handbrake does a great job of compressing video, movies can still be as large as 500MB to 1GB in size.

- *Do you plan to carry lots of pictures?* Although many digital pictures are pretty small (a typical photo is 300KB to 1.2MB in size), if you carry a few thousand of them around, they do add up to some serious storage. Do you laugh at carrying that many pictures around on your iPad? Apple's built-in support for the Mac iPhoto application makes it simple to put years of photo archives onto your iPad with a single synchronization option. Moving photos directly from a digital camera to your iPad is easy using the iPad Camera Connection Kit, so the idea of backing up a trip's worth of memories on your iPad while on vacation isn't entirely out of the question.

- *Do you need to carry lots of data?* You might not think of your iPad as a data storage device, but there are ways to use it (mostly involving e-mailing documents to yourself or using a third-party application) to bring data along with you on the road. If you think you might need to do this, maybe those extra gigabytes could be put to good use.

- *How long do you plan to use this iPad?* If you're an early adopter who plans to trade up at the earliest possible opportunity whenever Apple offers a new unit, you may want to save your pennies now in the hope that a better unit with more memory quickly debuts. If, instead, you want to get the most use out of the iPad for the longest period of time, paying more up front means you won't outgrow the memory quite as fast.

Considering System Requirements

iPads aren't like most other computers. At heart, they're similar to a large iPod touch. And, like an iPod touch, in order to effectively use one, you will need a computer with a USB 2.0 port and an Internet connection running iTunes 9.1 or newer. Although your iPad can receive app updates and synchronize data through a Wi-Fi or 3G connection, it still needs to be directly connected to your computer in order to receive system software updates. It's also much faster to transfer large amounts of music, movies, or photos through a direct USB 2.0 cable connection.

You won't be able to purchase apps, books, or music from your iPad until you successfully connect it to iTunes. That means you need either a Mac running OS X 10.5.8 or newer or a Windows computer running Windows XP (with Service Pack 3 or newer), Windows Vista, or Windows 7. This also means you need an iTunes Store account.

Before you decide to purchase an iPad, ask yourself whether you have a computer available that has all these features. If not, you might not be able to set up and use your iPad.

> **NOTE:** If you haven't yet put iTunes on your computer, you can get a free copy from www.apple.com/itunes. It's available for both Mac OS X and Windows systems and is quick and easy to install.

Buying Your iPad

After deciding among the available iPad models, you're probably ready to pull out your credit card and go buy that iPad (see Figure 1-1). Where should you go? To an Apple Store? To an authorized Apple retailer or Best Buy store? Or should you buy online? You might be surprised to learn that there are better and worse choices.

We recommend buying your iPad in person at a store. You can ask questions. You can make human connections. If something goes wrong with your purchase, you have a person who's there to help you work through it. This is not to say that calling Apple's support line is insufficient; it's just that being face to face with a real person makes solutions happen more readily.

The sad fact of the matter is that, on occasion, iPad purchases do not go smoothly. Some people end up with a screen flaw, such as dead screen pixels. It's not an uncommon problem, and if found soon after purchase, it may involve a trade-in for a new unit. Others may have problems connecting to Wi-Fi or 3G networks. The chances of resolving these issues increase significantly when you have a real person to talk to.

As for the question of Apple or other retailers, we lean slightly toward buying at an Apple Store. It's an Apple product you're buying, and the Apple staff members are simply more knowledgeable about that product.

Figure 1-1. *That nice shiny box contains the Apple of your eye, your iPad. Remember to keep all your packaging, receipts, and other purchase information just in case you need to return it to the store.*

Purchasing Your iPad Online

For a surprising number of people, there is no physical store nearby for picking up an iPad. In that case, the Apple Online Store is your best bet for getting your hands on an iPad as soon as possible.

> **NOTE:** There are two quick ways to buy your iPad online. First click the iPad tab at the top of the Apple website (www.apple.com), and then click the blue Buy Now button. The second way? Point your browser to the iPad page (http://store.apple.com/us/browse/home/shop_ipad/family/ipad) in the Apple Online Store. Be sure to have your credit card ready.

Apple makes it easy for you to purchase your iPad online. The individual models all have their own Select button, and a click brings you to a page that lets you choose which Apple accessories you want to add to your purchase. Adding those accessories to your purchase just requires a click of the radio button near each item, and when you are finally ready to check out, clicking the Add to Cart button displays the contents of your virtual shopping cart as well as a Check Out Now button. An estimate of the shipping date is displayed in your shopping cart next to each item so you know when to start waiting for the delivery truck driver to ring your doorbell.

Repairs, Returns, Warranties, AppleCare, and Insurance

In most situations, the iPad you buy will be in perfect working order, and you should never need to return it to Apple. However, if you do get an iPad that just isn't working properly or that fails during the first year of ownership, there is a tried-and-true process to follow.

First, visit the iPad Support web page (www.apple.com/support/ipad/) to see whether you have set up something improperly or whether there is a known issue and solution. If the online support does not resolve the problem, then it is time to either take the iPad to your Apple retailer or send the iPad to Apple.

For iPads that have been purchased at an Apple Store, the easiest thing to do is to grab your receipt, the iPad, the original box, and all the contents of that box, and then head to the store. The Apple Store staff may ask you to work with a person at the Genius Bar in an attempt to resolve the problem, in which case there may be a delay until they can fit you into their busy schedule.

At other Apple authorized retailers, the return policy may be different, so be sure to check that policy when you purchase your iPad.

iPads purchased online from Apple require a Return Material Authorization (RMA). To initiate the return process, call Apple's support phone number at 1-800-275-2273 and speak to an iPad support specialist. If that person determines that the iPad is faulty and is eligible for repair or replacement, they will issue an RMA to you.

> **NOTE:** Outside of the United States, you can refer to www.apple.com/support/contact/ phone_contacts.html for a list of international phone numbers for Apple Support.

In the first paragraph of this section, we called attention to "the first year of ownership." That's the complimentary warranty period for any iPad. If you want to extend that warranty for another year, you can purchase an AppleCare Protection Plan for iPad for $99. This extends your hardware repair coverage to two years. If interested, you can purchase this option online at the Apple Store (http://store.apple.com). Once the warranty expires, you'll have to pay the going rate for repairs or battery replacements. At time of publication, Apple has not set those prices.

American Express cardholders can double their iPad warranty simply by purchasing the device with their Amex card. This Extended Warranty program may be provided by other credit card companies, so be sure to check your card terms and conditions for details.

If you can, make sure to back up your iPad by syncing it to iTunes before bringing it in for service. Apple will usually restore your iPad to factory condition, which means you'll lose any data stored on the iPad during the repair and service process.

Is AppleCare worth buying? In our opinion, it is. In one case, AppleCare more than paid for the replacement of a logic board with a faulty FireWire port on an Apple PowerBook G4 almost three years into the plan.

You're entitled to complimentary phone support for 90 days after the purchase of your iPad. AppleCare extends that period to a full two years, and you can call Apple's experts as many times as you want to get your questions answered.

What about a situation where you find that an iPad isn't what you really needed, or what if you decide that you want the 64GB model instead of the 32GB iPad that you bought? Apple realizes that people change their minds or may be dissatisfied for one reason or another, so you have 14 calendar days to return your purchase. You must return the iPad in the original, unmarked packaging including any accessories (such as the power adapter), manuals, documentation, and registration that shipped with the product. There is a cost for this flexibility, because Apple assesses a 10 percent restocking fee on the return.

Apple does not offer an insurance plan for the iPad, and it's unlikely that the company will do so in the future. Instead, you'll need to call your renter's or home insurance carrier to see how much you'll have to pay for an iPad rider (a *rider* is placed on top of an existing policy, adding coverage for a specific item not covered under the standard plan).

Unboxing Your iPad

Once you arrive home with your iPad or it is delivered to your door, it's time to unpack it and set it up. iPad packaging (see Figure 1-2) is a small work of art. The iPad ships in a box that contains the device, a Dock Connector to USB cable, a 10-watt USB power adapter, and a packet of documentation. Each of these items is important and will help you in your day-to-day use.

- *Cable:* The USB cable attaches your iPad to either your computer or the AC adapter. Whether you're charging your iPad for another day of use or you are syncing with your computer to get the latest software update, the Dock Connector to USB cable is a crucial part of your iPad kit.

- *USB power adapter:* The AC power adapter included with your iPad plugs directly into the wall and allows you to charge your iPad (or any USB device, for that matter). It offers a single USB port. To use it, just connect your iPad to the adapter using the USB cable. It supplies the 5 volts required for powering USB devices.

Figure 1-2. *There's not much inside the iPad box: the iPad, a Dock Connector to USB cable, a 10-watt AC adapter, and some simple documentation.*

iPad Feature Overview

Once you've unpacked your iPad, take a few minutes to discover more about your new purchase. Figure 1-3 introduces the basic features on your iPad.

The top of the iPad houses a jack into which you can plug your earbuds, a built-in microphone, and a Sleep/Wake button that is used to power on and off certain features. If you purchased a Wi-Fi + 3G model, the top will also house a micro–Subscriber Identity Module (SIM) tray where your phone's micro-SIM card is stored. The bottom of your iPad has a built-in speaker and an indented slot for connecting to the Dock Connector to USB cable or a dock. The iPad's front has a large touch screen and a single Home button. You will not see this interactive screen until you have set up your iPad through iTunes.

On the right side of the iPad (as you look at it from the front), you'll find a volume rocker and an orientation lock slider.

Figure 1-3. *Feature breakdown displaying the buttons on the sides and front of the iPad. The dock connector port is on the bottom of the iPad near the Home button.*

Preparing for Setup

You have unpacked your iPad but haven't yet connected it to iTunes. Now is a good time to review the data on your computer. When your iPad is first set up, it will synchronize itself to iTunes and, depending on your computer, to your e-mail accounts, your calendars, and so forth. Before you go forward, here are some items you may want to review and clean up so your iPad starts out its life with the freshest possible data:

- *Contacts:* The iPad can sync with Outlook 2003 or 2007 on Windows, Address Book or Entourage on a Macintosh, and Yahoo! Address Book or Google Contacts on the Internet. To prepare for your first sync, review your existing contacts, and make sure they're up-to-date with current phone numbers and e-mail addresses. If you use another program to manage contacts, consider migrating your contacts to one of these solutions. If you'd rather not, that's OK too. You can add contact information directly to your iPad, although it's not as convenient as having the information automatically loaded for you.

- *Calendar:* Your iPad can synchronize with computer-based calendars just like it does with contacts. The iPad supports iCal and Entourage calendars on the Mac and Outlook calendars on Windows. Get your calendars into shape before your first synchronization, and you'll be ready to immediately manage your schedule both from your computer and from your iPad.

- *E-mail:* Your iPad works with most e-mail providers including Yahoo! Mail, Google Gmail, and AOL. If your e-mail provider uses the industry-standard POP3, IMAP, or Exchange services, your service will work with iPad. You may want to establish new accounts with these providers before you set up your iPad. That way, they'll load onto your unit the first time you synchronize. You can always add new e-mail accounts later, but it's nice to have them all set up and available for use right away.

- *Media:* Some iPad models offer relatively small storage space when compared to, for example, iPod Classic's generous 160GB hard drive. To make the most of this limited space, set up playlists for your favorite songs, TV shows, movies, and podcasts. Since, in all likelihood, you won't be able to synchronize your entire library to your new iPad, invest time now in weeding through your media to find those items you most want to have on hand.

- *Software and OS:* Update to iTunes 9.1 or newer before you attempt to set up your iPad. If you're using a Mac, make sure you've updated your OS to at least OS X 10.5.8. Windows computers must be running Windows 7, Windows Vista, or Windows XP Home or Professional with Service Pack 3 or newer. You can download the latest version of iTunes from Apple at www.itunes.com/download.

■ *iTunes Account:* Apple requires a current iTunes account in order to set up your iPad. If you do not already have one, you must sign up for an account with the iTunes Store. If you want to make purchases through the iTunes Store, App Store, or iBookstore, you'll need to have a valid address and credit card. Here are the steps you'll need to follow in order to create that new iTunes account:

1. Launch the iTunes application on your computer, and wait for it to load.

2. Locate iTunes Store in the column on the left side of the window. Click iTunes Store, and wait for the store window to load. You must be connected to the Internet for this to happen, because all the storefront information is stored at Apple.

3. Click the Sign In button at the top-right corner of the screen. iTunes opens the sign-in screen shown in Figure 1-4, which will allow you either to sign in with an existing account or to create a new one.

Figure 1-4. *The iTunes sign-in screen allows you to sign in to iTunes with your existing account or begin the process of creating a new account.*

4. Click Create New Account. The screen clears, and a message welcoming you to the iTunes Store displays.

5. Review the terms of service, and click Agree. A new window appears prompting you to create your account.

6. Enter your e-mail address and a password (you must enter the password twice for verification). Also enter a question and answer that will help verify your identity, as well as the month and day of your birth. Review the other options on the page, and adjust them as desired before clicking Continue. Again, the screen will clear, and you'll move on to the final account creation step.

7. Enter a valid credit card and the billing information for that credit card. These must match to finish creating your account. When you have entered the information, click Continue.

After following these steps, you will receive a confirmation e-mail at the address you specified while signing up. The e-mail welcomes you to the iTunes Store and provides you with the customer service web address (www.apple.com/support/itunes/store).

You don't need a credit card to get an iTunes App Store account. If you're planning on only downloading free apps and don't have a credit card, there's a way to create an iTunes App Store account from your iPad. The following instructions assume that you don't already have an account and that you've already unwrapped your iPad. Don't worry; you can always come back to these instructions later if you'd like to wait.

1. Launch the App Store app on your iPad by tapping its icon.

2. Scroll to the bottom of the page (either Featured or Top Charts), and tap the Sign In button.

3. Look for a free app. It can be anything, but just make sure that the price is listed as Free. Tap the Free button to start the "purchase" process; then tap Install App.

4. A dialog appears asking you to sign into the iTunes App Store. Tap the Create New Account button.

5. You'll be asked to choose a country or region for the store that matches the billing address for your payment method. Select one from the list that appears when you tap the country name next to the word *Store*; then tap the Next button.

6. Agree to the iTunes Store Terms & Conditions.

7. Now you're asked to enter new account information, including your e-mail address, a password, a secret question and answer, and your date of birth. When you've entered that info, tap Next.

8. On the Billing Information screen, tap the name next to the word *Credit Card*, and select None as your billing method. Enter a valid name and billing address, and then tap Next.

9. At this point, an Email Verification screen should appear. Tap Finish, and then open Mail on your iPad (that's assuming it's already set up; if not, you can do this part on another computer).

10. Open the e-mail from Apple, and tap the verification link. You're asked to sign in to complete the account creation.

11. Tap the Use Existing Account button, enter the user name (e-mail address) and password that you just created, and then tap OK.

12. You'll see a message telling you that your iTunes Store account has been successfully created. Tap the Done button, and then you can start downloading any free apps, books, music, or videos from iTunes, the App Store, or the iBookstore. Read more about these stores in Chapter 8.

Connecting Your iPad to the Computer

Once you've created an iTunes account on either your computer or your iPad, you should connect your iPad to your computer to back it up, check for software updates, and do an initial synchronization of data. If you haven't yet released your iPad from its box, here are the steps you need to take:

1. Remove the iPad from the box, and extract it from its factory wrapping. Also unwrap the included Dock Connector to USB cable.

2. Locate the two ends of the USB cable. One is thin and marked with a standard three-pronged USB symbol. The other is wide and marked with a rectangle with a line in it.

3. Connect the wide end of the cable to the Dock Connector port on the bottom of the iPad. Connect the thin end to a spare USB 2.0 port on your computer. iTunes will launch, and your iPad will chime softly.

If your iPad does not automatically power on and display either the white Apple or the Connect to iTunes message, press and hold the Sleep/Wake button. With the main screen facing toward you, you'll find it at the top right of the iPad. After a few seconds, the iPad should wake up and display the white Apple as it powers on. If the iPad does not respond and displays either the white Apple or the Connect to iTunes message, contact the store where you purchased the device or call Apple Support.

Syncing Your New iPad

Now you're ready to synchronize your iPad with your computer. This allows you to initialize your iPad's music, movies, podcasts, e-mail accounts, calendar, bookmarks, and so forth.

After connecting to your computer, iPad appears in the iTunes source list (the left column on the iTunes screen on your computer). If you own and use an iPhone, you're already familiar with iPad syncing. If not, here's a quick overview.

On your computer, click your iPad's name in the source list to open its preferences in the main iTunes window. The tabs along the top of the window allow you to set each of the options associated with your iPad.

> **TIP:** In iTunes on your Mac or PC, click your iPad's name a second time to open a text edit field that allows you to edit the name. You can name your iPad more creatively than "John Appleseed's iPad." Perhaps you could name your iPad "Bill Gates" for the laughs.

The Summary tab (see Figure 1-5) displays your iPad overview including the iPad's name, capacity, currently installed firmware version, serial number, and phone number. From this page, you can check for firmware updates and restore your iPad to a pristine factory-installed condition.

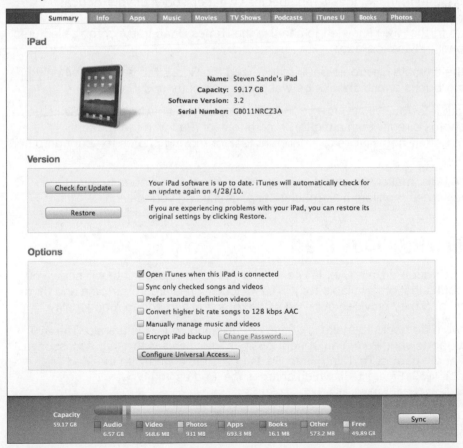

Figure 1-5. *iTunes allows you to manage the content loaded onto and synchronized with your iPad. Each tab offers a variety of controls, allowing you to choose what information gets loaded onto your iPad at each sync.*

The Info tab allows you to select which contacts, calendars, mail accounts, and bookmarks are synced to your phone. Select those items you want to sync by selecting check boxes, and click Apply. You can sync any POP3, Exchange, or IMAP e-mail account.

The Apps tab shows you the applications that have been installed on your iPad and can be used to organize what apps are on specific home screens. This tab is also used to share files between iPad apps and your computer.

The Music tab specifies which songs, playlists, and music videos you want to store on your iPad. If you own a large music library, you'll want to select just your favorite playlists or create smart playlists (covered later in this book) to establish an ever-changing collection. The Movies tab is similar to the Music tab but allows you to determine what movies you want to store on your iPad. Since movie files can be extremely large, you may want to move only a few at a time to your iPad for viewing.

TV fans who want to watch their favorite shows on iPad use the TV Shows tab to synchronize shows that were purchased in the iTunes Store. If your tastes lean more toward audio content, the Podcasts tab specifies what episodes of your podcast subscriptions are synced to your iPad. Students of all ages who use iTunes U courseware to further their knowledge can use the iTunes U tab to synchronize lectures and educational movies to iPads.

The iPad is the ultimate electronic book reader, and the Books tab is helpful when you want to sync e-books or audiobooks between your computer and iPad.

The Photos tab lets you synchronize your iPad photo collection with iPhoto. Since you can import photos directly from a digital camera to your iPad with the Camera Connection Kit, the Photos tab is an important tool for moving photos to your computer for backup purposes.

For any of the tabs, make your selections, and click Apply. The Capacity bar at the bottom of the screen monitors how much space remains on your device.

Accessorizing Your iPad

If you purchase your iPad in an Apple Store, your Apple sales associate will show you many accessories that are available for it. These accessories are from Apple and third-party sources, and they provide your iPad with protection and added functionality.

Apple sells two iPad docks to make charging and syncing your iPad a snap. The $29 iPad Dock supports your iPad in an upright position and works with other accessories and optional audio cables. Text entry into iPad apps is enhanced with the iPad Keyboard Dock ($69; Figure 1-6), which charges the iPad as you type.

Figure 1-6. *The iPad Keyboard Dock combines a comfortable keyboard with an iPad dock for fast text entry and battery charging at the same time.*

For protection, Apple provides the iPad Case ($39), which can also be folded into a variety of positions for supporting the iPad on flat surfaces. Many other Apple accessory manufacturers are getting into the iPad case market as well. Incase (`www.goincase.com`) has a variety of cases made with materials from rubberized plastic to neoprene, with prices from $39.95 to $59.95. If you like the texture and class of leather, Vaja Cases (`http://vajacases.com`) makes high-end iPad cases, sleeves, and bags ranging from $100 to $350.

Photographers will want to buy the iPad Camera Connection Kit ($29; Figure 1-7), which includes two adapters—one for connecting a camera through a USB 2.0 cable, the other for reading SD memory cards. The USB adapter can also be used to connect USB headsets and keyboards to the iPad.

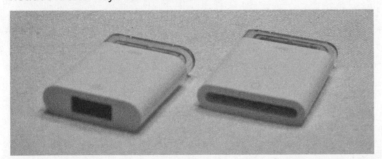

Figure 1-7. *The iPad Camera Connection Kit includes two adapters. The one on the left connects to a standard USB cable for direct connection to a digital camera, while the adapter on the right can be used to read or write SD memory cards.*

Since you might want to show slide shows or Keynote presentations from an iPad, Apple sells the iPad Dock Connector to VGA Adapter ($29). The VGA end of the adapter can be connected to external monitors, some TVs, and PC projectors. At publication time, the adapter worked only with Keynote, iTunes, and the iPad Videos application, severely limiting the usability of the iPad for making presentations.

The Apple Component AV Cable ($49) and Composite AV Cable ($49) also work with the iPad, providing two more methods of linking external monitors and projectors to the device. The same application limitations apply with these cables as well.

Finally, Apple's Wireless Keyboard ($69) and most other Bluetooth keyboards are iPad-compatible, providing an alternative way of entering text into iPad applications.

Summary

In this chapter, you learned how to select and purchase your iPad. You discovered what's involved in setting up your iPad before using it. To wind things up, here is a quick overview of some key points from this chapter:

- Your iPad choices come down to whether you want 3G connectivity and how much storage space you want.

- There are several venues for purchasing your iPad, but Apple Stores are our recommendation.

- Make sure your computer is compatible with iPad before you buy.

- Consider adding AppleCare to your iPad purchase for an additional year's coverage against hardware repairs.

- iPad technical support is free for 90 days, but you can call Apple's experts for up to two years with the purchase of AppleCare.

- Consider insuring your iPad against loss and damage by purchasing a policy rider from your insurance company.

Chapter 2

Putting Your Data and Media on Your iPad

So, you've unboxed your iPad and connected it to iTunes. Now what? In Chapter 1 we briefly touched on syncing your iPad with your music, movies, photos, and other data via iTunes. In this chapter, you will explore the options you have for syncing your data with your iPad.

The iPad iTunes Settings Pane

When your iPad is plugged into your computer, you'll see it automatically appear in your computer's iTunes source list under Devices. Click your iPad's name in the source list to open its settings pane in the main iTunes window (see Figure 2-1). You'll see a series of tabs along the top of the window; these allow you to set options associated with your iPad. The tabs you'll see (from left to right) are Summary, Info, Apps, Music, Movies, TV Shows, Podcasts, iTunes U, Books, and Photos. If you're an iPhone or iPod touch user, the iPad settings pane will look very familiar; however, you do have some options that are not available with the iPhone or iPod touch (including a new tab). If your iPad is your first Apple touch device, don't worry. You don't need any knowledge of the iPhone or iPod touch to navigate the tabs. After reading this chapter, you'll know all you need to know.

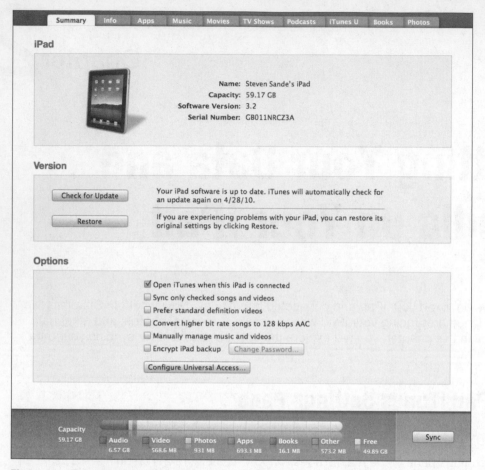

Figure 2-1. *iTunes allows you to manage the content loaded onto and synchronized with your iPad. Each tab running along the top of the settings pane offers a variety of controls, allowing you to choose what information gets loaded onto your iPad at each sync.*

Running along the bottom of the iPad settings pane, you'll see a long, colorful Capacity bar (see Figure 2-2). This bar will show no matter what tab you have selected. The bar shows you your iPad's total storage capacity and breaks down the amount of data you have on the iPad in color-coded squares along the Capacity bar. Blue is for audio, yellow is for photos, green is for apps, purple is for books, orange is for other stuff, and gray is for the remaining free space you have on your iPad.

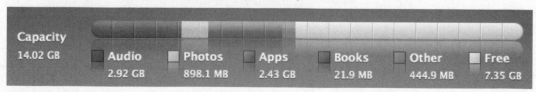

Figure 2-2. *The Capacity bar is a visual representation of the different types of files occupying space on your iPad.*

NOTE: The Capacity bar breakdown is pretty self-explanatory. Still, some people are thrown by orange—the color that represents "Other." What is "Other," exactly? This includes database files (which keep track of your music, video, and podcast libraries), which can be 100MB to 200MB in size; album artwork (which can be 500KB per track); and preference files for the applications you have on your iPad. Preference files let the apps remember in-app settings you've configured every time you launch them.

A Word on Syncing Your Data

The first-generation iPads hold 16GB, 32GB, or 64GB of data. But many of us have music or movie libraries that are far larger than even the greatest of the iPad's storage options. Apple devised these settings preferences to help organize and select your most important data and bring it to the iPad.

If you have a 16GB iPad and a 20GB music library, not only will you not be able to fit all your music, but even if you settle for 16GB of your music library, you'd still not have room for photos, movies, books, or apps. The following tabs that we discuss will help you select what to sync to your iPad.

Do note that although you most likely will not be able to fit all of your music, photos, and movies onto the iPad, you can keep changing up what you put on the iPad. For example, once you've watched a movie on your iPad, you can remove it and replace it with another one. Also, some files are larger than others. Movies are typically the largest, so don't worry about syncing your entire contacts, calendars, and book collections onto your iPad. These are all text-based files, and text takes up very little space.

Where Do You Get Media From?

The iPad is a great leisure device for consuming media. But where do you get that media? The easiest and most direct way to get movies, music, TV shows, and books onto your iPad is through the iTunes Store on your computer (see Figure 2-3). In the iTunes Store you can buy music by the song or album, rent or purchase movies, download your favorite TV shows by the episode, or subscribe to a Season Pass and download free podcasts and iTunes U content.

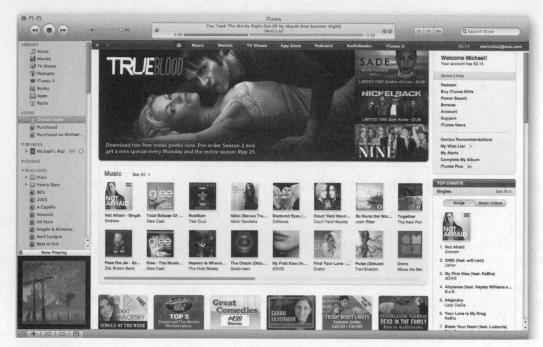

Figure 2-3. *The iTunes Store is the world's largest music store. You can also download movies, TV shows, apps, podcasts, and books from it.*

You can also import music and movies from your own collections. Importing music from CDs is straightforward using iTunes, and importing video isn't hard either. One way to get movies onto your iPad is to rip them from your DVD collection.

NOTE: *Ripping* a DVD means copying content from the disc into a format that's playable on other devices, including iPads. To load video from your DVDs onto your iPad, download a copy of HandBrake from `http://handbrake.m0k.org` (for both Windows and Mac) and convert your DVD content to an iPad-friendly format. HandBrake is free and easy to use. Insert your DVD into your computer, run the application, and follow the directions in the program. After your movie has finished ripping, you must then add it to iTunes by dragging and dropping the movie file onto your Movies library in the source list.

For applications, the only way you'll be getting them on your iPad is by using the iTunes App Store. You can easily browse for apps from the desktop version of iTunes or in the dedicated App Store app on the iPad (we'll talk about that app in Chapter 8).

There are several ways to get e-books for the iPad. Perhaps the easiest is to buy them through Apple's iBookstore (see Chapter 8 for details), which is part of the free iBooks app Apple offers for download. Another way is to download from the more than 30,000 free e-books at Project Gutenberg (`www.gutenberg.org`) and drag the books from your downloads folder into iTunes. There are also many e-book stores and even publishers

that sell e-books directly. For a good list of web sites that sell e-books, go to
www.epubbooks.com/buy-epub-books.

> **NOTE:** E-books come in many formats. The format compatible with the iPad's iBooks app is
> ePub. Make sure when buying an e-book outside the iBookstore that it is in ePub format, or
> else you'll need to find another app that reads the format your e-book is in. An example of this
> is books from Amazon's Kindle Store. Kindle books can be read on the iPad but not in the
> iBooks app. You need to download Amazon's Kindle app for the iPad to read e-books
> purchased from Amazon.

Remember to Apply Your Changes

After making any of the choices we discuss in the following sections, note that they do
not become finalized until you click the gray Apply button to the right of the Capacity bar
(see Figure 2-4). Don't worry if you forget to click it. iTunes will automatically remind you
before you navigate away from the iPad settings pane. Also, if you make a change in the
settings pane by mistake, don't panic! You can always click the Cancel button that sits
above the Apply button.

Figure 2-4. *The Cancel and Apply buttons allow you to accept or negate any of the changes you have made in
iTunes' iPad settings pane.*

The Tabs

The tabs (see Figure 2-5) running along the top of the iPad settings pane are how you
navigate all your iPad settings. There are ten tabs in total: Summary, Info, Apps, Music,
Movies, TV Shows, Podcasts, iTunes U, Books, and Photos. To begin configuring the
settings on any tab, just click the tab to select it.

Figure 2-5. *The tabs. Learn 'em, love 'em.*

The Summary Tab

The Summary tab (see Figure 2-6) is the first tab you'll see in the iPad settings pane. It
displays your iPad's overview including the iPad's name, capacity, currently installed
firmware version, serial number, and phone number. From this page, you can check for
firmware updates, restore your iPad to a pristine factory-installed condition, and set

options to help you manage the way your data is synced. The page is broken up into three boxes: iPad, Version, and Options.

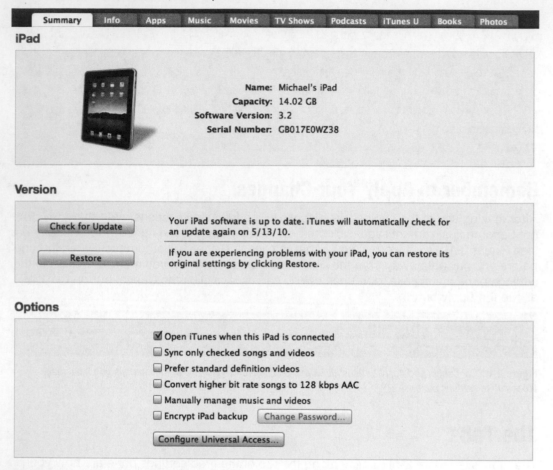

Figure 2-6. *The Summary tab provides an overview of your iPad's make and model.*

iPad Box

In this box an image of your iPad is displayed along with its name, capacity, software version, and serial number.

The only things that could ever change in this box are your iPad's software version number and your iPad's name. When you perform a software update on the iPad, its new version number will appear in this box. This is an easy way to tell what version of the iPad OS you are using. If you change the name of your iPad by double-clicking its name in the iTunes source list (see Figure 2-7), the name change will be updated here. Your iPad's capacity and serial number will never change.

Figure 2-7. *Double-click your iPad's name in the iTunes source list. You can rename it to anything you want. The name change will be reflected on the Summary tab.*

NOTE: You bought a 16GB iPad, but you notice that the capacity states your iPad has only 14.02GB of storage. What gives? Whenever you buy an electronics device that offers storage capacity, the advertised amount of storage will always be more than the actual storage available to you. Why? Several reasons. One is because the device's operating system must be stored on the same hard disk as your files. Without the OS, your device could not function. In this case, the iPad's OS takes up almost 2GB of space. Another, more technical reason, is because hard size can be measured in binary or decimal measurements. Binary says 1KB is equal to 1024 bytes, while decimal says 1KB is equal to 1000 bytes. When advertising storage space, companies choose to use the decimal measurement, which ends up showing more space than is actually available to you.

Version Box

The Version box allows you to manually check for iPad OS software updates by clicking the Check for Update button. Next to the button you will see text notifying you if your iPad software is up-to-date or if there is an update available. Sometimes iTunes will notify you that there is a software update available before you've even clicked the Check for Update button. It knows this because iTunes automatically checks for iPad OS updates once a week. You'll also see text to your right that tells you when the next time iTunes will automatically check for an update.

NOTE: If there is an iPad software update available, always install it. Sometimes updates provide new features; other times they provide simple bug fixes. Apple rigorously tests these updates before releasing them to the public, so it's always safe to assume the updates will make your device better (whether you notice it or not).

Below the Check for Update button is the Restore button. Clicking the Restore button allows you to restore your iPad to a factory-installed condition. You will rarely, if ever, use this feature. The only time to restore your iPad is if you are having technical difficulties with it or if you decide to sell the iPad or give it away and want to make sure all your personal data is removed from the device. Before the restore commences, you'll be shown a dialog box asking you to confirm the restore (see Figure 2-8).

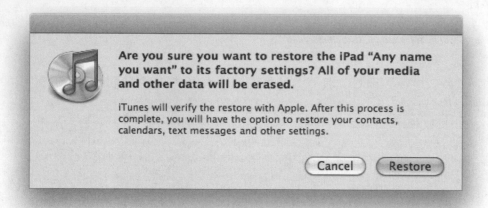

Figure 2-8. *After a restore, you'll have the option of putting back all your data on the iPad as it was before.*

Options Box

You have several preferences in the Options box. To enable or disable any of the features, simply select or deselect the check box next to it.

- *Open iTunes when this iPad is connected*: This option is selected by default. It tells your computer to open iTunes when it detects your iPad is connected via USB. If this option is deselected, iTunes will not open when you connect your iPad, and no data will be synced to your device until you manually open iTunes and click the Sync button next to the Capacity bar.

NOTE: Even though iTunes will not open or sync your data when this box is not selected, the iPad will still charge.

- *Sync only selected songs and videos*: When this option is selected, iTunes will only sync the songs in your library and playlists that have a check mark next to them in the iTunes library (see Figure 2-9).

  Let's say you have a Greatest Hits playlist set to sync with the iPad. In the playlist you have two copies of Michael Jackson's *Thriller* from two separate albums. You want to have only one copy of the song on the iPad, but you don't want to remove the extra copy from the playlist. If you deselect one version of *Thriller* in the playlist and have "Sync only selected songs and videos" selected, the playlist will sync to your iPad minus the extra *Thriller*, but the song will remain in your playlist in your iTunes library.

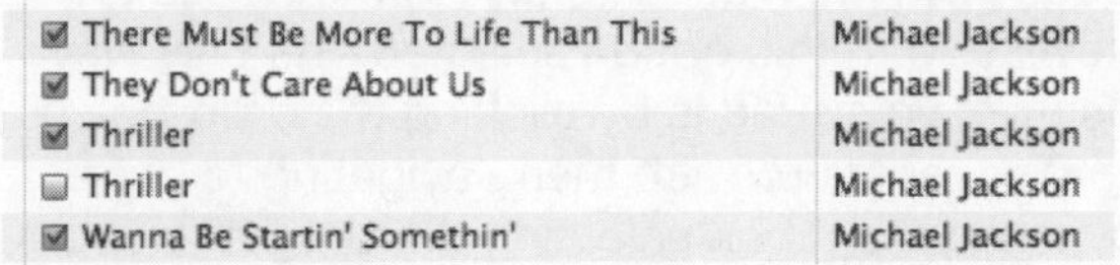

☑ There Must Be More To Life Than This	Michael Jackson
☑ They Don't Care About Us	Michael Jackson
☑ Thriller	Michael Jackson
☐ Thriller	Michael Jackson
☑ Wanna Be Startin' Somethin'	Michael Jackson

  Figure 2-9. *A selected song and an unselected song in iTunes*

- *Prefer standard definition videos*: With this selected, iTunes will sync only the standard-definition version of a video to your iPad if you have both the high-definition and standard-definition versions. You sometimes get both versions when you buy a movie or TV show from the iTunes Store. Choosing to sync only the standard-definition version will save you storage space on the iPad. HD is all the rage at the moment, and although the quality of HD video *is* superior to SD, if you're using your iPad to watch videos only occasionally and not as your main video consumption device, you might want to opt for the SD version. The quality is fine, and you'll be able to fit more video on your iPad for those long road trips.

- *Convert higher bit rate songs to 128 kbps AAC*: Digital music comes in many formats and sizes, with the most popular being MP3 and AAC. Depending on how you obtained your music, whether buying it from the iTunes store or ripping your collection from old CDs, your songs will likely have different encoding settings. A song encoded at 256KBps takes up twice the space as a song encoded at 128KBps. With the "Convert higher bit rate songs to 128 kbps AAC" option selected, any music synced to your iPad will be converted on the fly to 128KBps AAC files. The advantage of doing this is to save space on your iPad by reducing higher bit rate songs to a perfectly acceptable 128KBps.

NOTE: Unless you are an extreme audiophile with a gifted ear, most people will not notice a difference between a 128KBps AAC file and a 256KBps version of that file.

TIP: If you have an iPhone or iPod touch that you frequently carry around with you, you may want to opt to not put any music on your iPad. You'll save a lot of space, and you'll always have your music with you on your other device. Use that extra space on your iPad to fill it with video. Viewing a movie on the iPad's screen is much more enjoyable than on the iPhone's comparatively small screen.

- *Manually manage music and videos*: With this option selected, music and videos will never be automatically synced with your iPad. The only way to add music and videos on the iPad with this option is by dragging the songs or videos from the iTunes library onto the iPad in the iTunes source list. Likewise, with this option selected, the only way to remove music or videos from your iPad is by clicking the drop-down triangle next to the iPad in iTunes' source list; then navigating to your music, movies, or TV shows playlists; then selecting the song or video file; and finally pressing the Delete key on your computer's keyboard.

NOTE: Manually adding or removing music or video from your iPad does not affect the files on your computer. Whenever a file is added to or deleted from the iPad, it is just a copy of the file in your iTunes library. The original file will always reside in your iTunes library until you delete it from there.

- *Encrypt iPad backup*: Every time your iPad syncs to iTunes, a backup of all the files and settings on your iPad is created. This backup is handy if you ever need to restore your iPad. Once the restore is complete and you've synced your iPad to iTunes again, you have the option of restoring the iPad from this backup, which, once completed, will enable you to retain all your old settings and files on your newly restored iPad.

    With the "Encrypt iPad backup" option selected, your backups, and thus all your data, are encrypted and protected by a password. To back up from an encrypted data file, the user must know the password to the file. Next to this selection is a Change Password button. This allows you to change the password to your encrypted data at any time.

NOTE: Do not forget your password! If you encrypt your backups and you forget your password, your backup data will not be able to be restored, and you will have to resync all your data from scratch. You'll also have to reconfigure all the settings on your iPad to the way you had them, including rearranging the iPad's app icons. If you have lots of custom settings on your iPad, this can take a long time. Remember your passwords!

- *Configure Universal Access*: The last thing you will see on your Summary page is a Configure Universal Access button. Clicking this button opens a Universal Access box (see Figure 2-10) that allows you to set seeing and hearing device assistance options for people who are hard of sight or hearing.

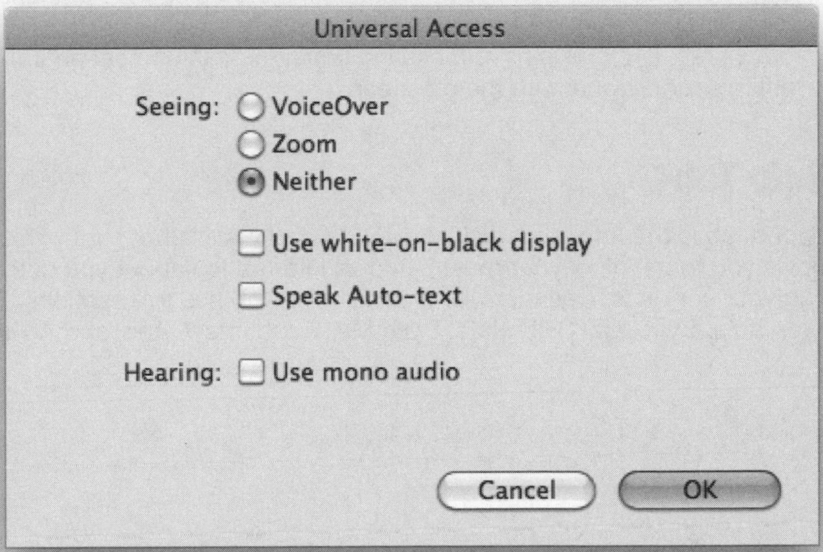

Universal Access

Seeing: ○ VoiceOver
○ Zoom
◉ Neither

☐ Use white–on–black display

☐ Speak Auto–text

Hearing: ☐ Use mono audio

Cancel   OK

Figure 2-10. *The Universal Access settings*

- *Seeing*: You have the option of selecting one of three radio buttons: Voice Over, Zoom, or Neither.

    - *Voice Over* will make your iPad speak the name of the button or its function when the user touches it.

    - *Zoom* will allow the user to zoom into parts of the screen that normally don't support a magnifying or zoom function. When this option is selected, the user can double tap any part of the iPad's screen with three fingers to automatically zoom in 200 percent. When zoomed in, you must drag or flick the screen with three fingers. Also, when you go to a new screen, zoom will always return to the top middle of the screen.

    - *Use white-on-black display*. Selecting this option will invert the colors of the iPad's screen so text appears white on a black background. The iPad's entire screen will look like a photograph negative.

- *Speak Auto-text*: With this option selected, any autocorrection text (such as the spell-check pop-ups that appear when you are typing) will be spoken aloud.

- *Hearing*: There is only one accessibility feature for the hearing impaired.

- *Use mono audio*: When this is selected, the stereo sounds of the left and right speakers will be combined into a mono (single) signal. This option lets users who have a hearing impairment in one ear hear the entire sound signal with the other ear.

The Info Tab

The second tab is the Info tab (see Figure 2-11), and it's all about you. This is the tab that allows you to get all of your most personal information about you onto the iPad including your contacts, calendars, and e-mail. This tab has five sections: Sync Address Book Contacts, Sync iCal Calendars, Sync Mail Accounts, Other, and Advanced.

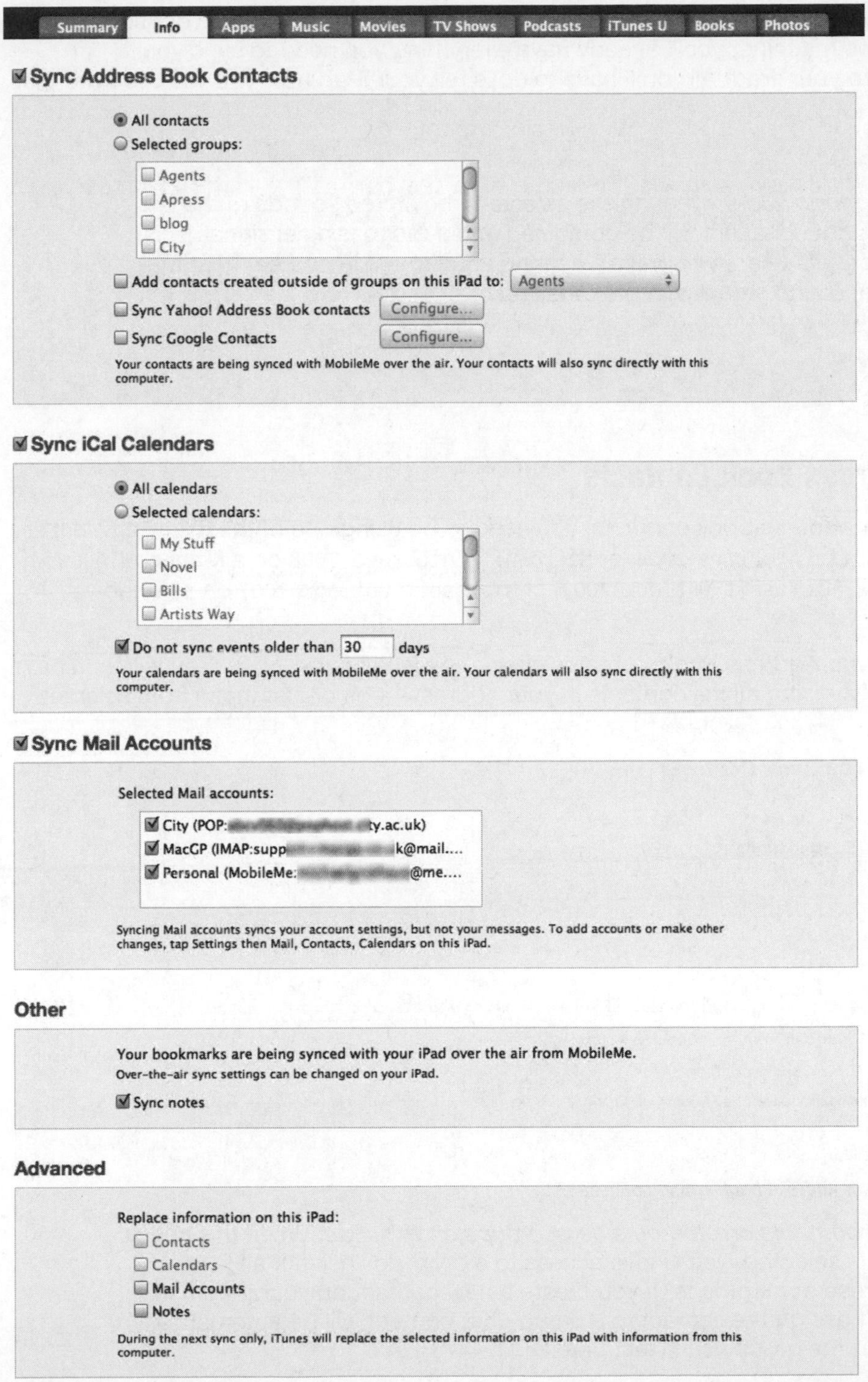

| Summary | **Info** | Apps | Music | Movies | TV Shows | Podcasts | iTunes U | Books | Photos |

☑ Sync Address Book Contacts

⦿ All contacts
◯ Selected groups:

☐ Agents
☐ Apress
☐ blog
☐ City

☐ Add contacts created outside of groups on this iPad to: [Agents   ⬍]
☐ Sync Yahoo! Address Book contacts   [Configure...]
☐ Sync Google Contacts   [Configure...]

Your contacts are being synced with MobileMe over the air. Your contacts will also sync directly with this computer.

☑ Sync iCal Calendars

⦿ All calendars
◯ Selected calendars:

☐ My Stuff
☐ Novel
☐ Bills
☐ Artists Way

☑ Do not sync events older than [30] days

Your calendars are being synced with MobileMe over the air. Your calendars will also sync directly with this computer.

☑ Sync Mail Accounts

Selected Mail accounts:

☑ City (POP: ⬛⬛⬛⬛⬛⬛ ty.ac.uk)
☑ MacGP (IMAP:supp⬛⬛⬛⬛⬛⬛ k@mail....
☑ Personal (MobileMe: ⬛⬛⬛⬛⬛ @me....

Syncing Mail accounts syncs your account settings, but not your messages. To add accounts or make other changes, tap Settings then Mail, Contacts, Calendars on this iPad.

Other

Your bookmarks are being synced with your iPad over the air from MobileMe.
Over-the-air sync settings can be changed on your iPad.
☑ Sync notes

Advanced

Replace information on this iPad:
☐ Contacts
☐ Calendars
☐ Mail Accounts
☐ Notes

During the next sync only, iTunes will replace the selected information on this iPad with information from this computer.

Figure 2-11. *The Info tab allows you to sync your mail accounts, contacts, calendars, bookmarks, and notes.*

As long as you have been using Mail, iCal, and Address Book on a Mac or using Outlook on a Windows machine, you'll already have everything you need to sync your information to your iPad. All you'll have to do is tell your iPad how you want to sync that information.

> **NOTE:** If you are using Apple's MobileMe service (www.me.com), after your first iPad sync, the Sync Address Book Contacts and Sync iCal Calendars options will always be deselected, and you'll see the explanation that your contacts and calendars are being synced over the air via MobileMe. *Over the air* syncing means you don't need to connect your iPad to your computer to update any changes you have made to contacts or calendars; the syncing is performed wirelessly.

Sync Address Book Contacts

To sync your address book contacts, you need to be using one of the following: Address Book, Microsoft Entourage 2004, or Microsoft Entourage 2008 on a Mac; or Windows Address Book, Microsoft Outlook 2003, or Microsoft Outlook 2007 on a Windows computer.

Select the Sync Address Book Contacts check box (see Figure 2-12). You will then have the option of syncing all the contacts in your address book or just those from selected groups.

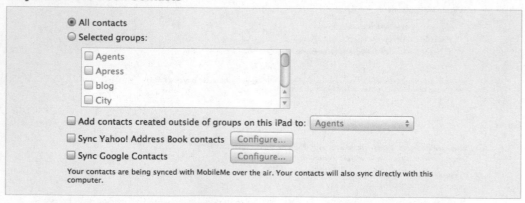

Figure 2-12. *Your address book syncing options*

- ■ *Add contacts created outside of groups on this iPad*: When this check box is selected, you'll have access to a drop-down list of all your address book groups. If you create a new contact on your iPad and don't assign the contact to a group, that contact will be automatically put in the group you select here.

- *Sync Yahoo! Address Book contacts*: When this is selected, you can automatically sync your Yahoo! Address Book contacts with your iPad address book. You will first have to agree to the pop-up box that asks you to acknowledge you are allowing your iPad to sync to your Yahoo! account. Next, you will be prompted to enter your Yahoo! ID and password. Once you've done this, your contacts are set to sync. Clicking the Configure button will allow you to enter a different Yahoo! ID.

- *Sync Google Contacts*: When this is selected, you can automatically sync your Google contacts with your iPad address book. You will first have to agree to the pop-up box that asks you to acknowledge you are allowing your iPad to sync to your Google account. Next, you will be prompted to enter your Google ID and password. Once you've done this, your contacts are set to sync. Clicking the Configure button will allow you to enter a different Google ID.

Sync iCal Calendars

To sync your calendars, you need to be using one of the following: iCal, Microsoft Entourage 2004, or Microsoft Entourage 2008 on a Mac; or Microsoft Outlook 2003 or Microsoft Outlook 2007 on a Windows machine.

To sync your calendars, select the Sync iCal Calendars check box (see Figure 2-13). Just like with contacts, you then have the option of syncing all your calendars or just selected ones.

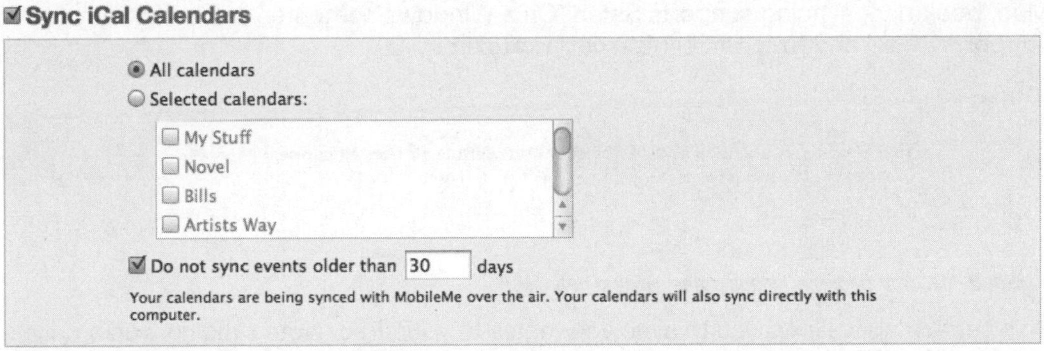

Figure 2-13. *Your calendar syncing options*

- *Do not sync events older than*: With this check box selected, events that are more than a certain number a days old will not be synced. The default number of days is 30, but you can enter anything up to 99,999 days.

NOTE: A great place to find premade calendars for holidays, school events, or your favorite sporting teams is at www.icalshare.com.

Sync Mail Accounts

All the mail accounts you have set up in Mac OS X's Mail or Microsoft's Outlook will appear here (Figure 2-14). You have the option of selecting or deselecting any of the accounts. Accounts not selected will not appear in the iPad's Mail app.

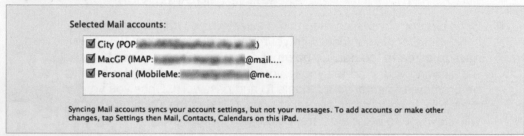

Figure 2-14. *Your e-mail account syncing options*

Other

Apple should really have named this section "Bookmark and Notes Syncing," but it opted for "Other." Here you can sync your web bookmarks from your browser on your computer to the Safari web browser on your iPad (see Figure 2-15). Again, if you have a MobileMe account, your bookmarks will be synced over the air. If not, select the Sync Bookmarks check box, and choose your browser from the drop-down menu. On the Mac, bookmark syncing supports Safari. On a Windows computer, bookmark syncing supports Safari and `Microsoft Internet Explorer`.

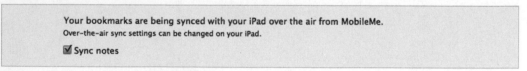

Figure 2-15. *Your bookmarks and notes syncing options*

This section also allows you to sync your notes to your iPad. Note syncing works only with the Mac OS X `Mail` application or, on a Windows machine, `Microsoft Outlook 2003` or `2007`. To enable note syncing, select the check box.

Advanced

This section, when selected, allows you to replace your contacts, calendars, mail accounts, and notes on the iPad with information from your computer (see Figure 2-16). This is a handy feature if your information gets out of sync and you want to make sure that everything you see on your computer matches with what's on the iPad.

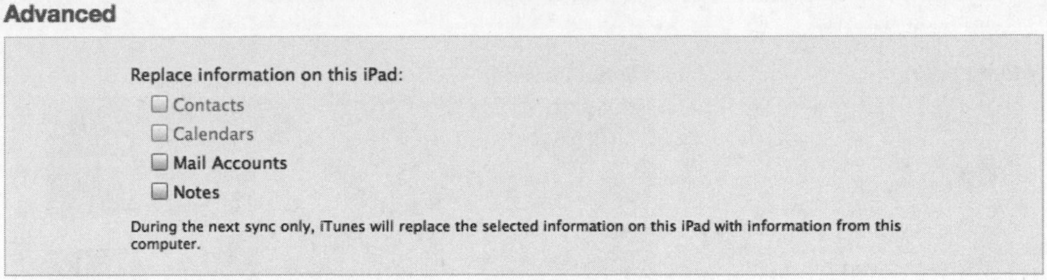

Advanced

Replace information on this iPad:

- ☐ Contacts
- ☐ Calendars
- ☑ Mail Accounts
- ☑ Notes

During the next sync only, iTunes will replace the selected information on this iPad with information from this computer.

Figure 2-16. *Your advanced syncing options*

When you select the respective check boxes, iTunes will replace the information on your iPad during the next sync only. After that sync, normal syncing will resume between your iPad and computer.

NOTE: If your calendars and contacts are being synced via MobileMe, you will not be able to select their check boxes in the Advanced section.

The Apps Tab

This is my favorite tab. It's the place where you get to decide which apps you want to put on your iPad and allows you to arrange them with drag-and-drop simplicity. This tab is composed of two main sections: Sync Apps (see Figure 2-17) and File Sharing (shown later in Figure 2-18). Let's get started.

Select applications to be installed on your iPad or drag to a specific home screen.
Drag to rearrange application icons or home screens.

Figure 2-17. *This is where you choose what apps to put on your iPad and in what order to arrange them in.*

Sync Apps

Under the Sync Apps heading, you'll see a scrollable list of all the applications you have in your apps library in iTunes. You can sort the list by name, by category, or by date downloaded. There's also a search box if you're one of those people who've downloaded thousands of apps and can't scroll through all of them quickly.

In the apps list, you'll see a check box on the left of the app's icon. To the right of the icon is the app's name, and below that are the app's category listing and the file size of the individual application. Any app that has a selected check box means the application is set to sync with the iPad.

> **NOTE:** Whenever you download a new app in iTunes, it will automatically sync with your iPad on the next sync. You can, of course, simply remove the app after the sync.

Next to the apps list you'll see a visual representation of your iPad desktop, and next to that you'll see one or more black screens with icons that are already on, or set to be synced with, your iPad. You'll also see a completely gray screen below the last black one.

The easiest way to get apps on your iPad is to find them in the apps list and simply drag them onto the virtual iPad screen. As soon as you do, the app's check box is automatically selected in the app list.

You can drag around the apps on your virtual iPad screen until you've arranged them in the order you like. You can also grab the smaller black screens and move them up or down in the list, rearranging entire pages of apps on your iPad. The black screen at the top of the list will be the home page on your iPad, and each one below that will be a subsequent swipe away. The gray screen at the bottom is an extra screen should you want to create a new screen with apps.

To remove an app, simply hover the mouse over the app, and you'll see a little X appear in the upper-left corner. Click the X, and the app disappears from the screen. On the next sync, the app will be removed from your iPad (don't worry, you can always get it back by re-dragging it to the virtual iPad screen).

NOTE: Apps shipped with the iPad cannot be removed from the device—they can only be repositioned.

Each screen can hold 20 apps in addition to the ones docked at the bottom of the screen. The Dock can hold up to six apps. Any apps you put in the Dock will show at the bottom of the iPad no matter what app screen you've swiped to. Since the docked apps will always appear at the bottom of any app page, it's best to put the one you use most frequently down there for quick access.

File Sharing

The iPad introduced an easy way to share files between your computer and itself. Beneath the File Sharing heading you'll see an Apps box and a Documents box (see Figure 2-18). Any apps that are currently on your iPad that support drag-and-drop file sharing will show up in the Apps list here. To get a file into the application, simply select the application in the Apps list, find the file on your computer you want to add, and drag it into the Documents list. You can also click the Add button at the bottom of the documents list to browse for the file on your computer.

File Sharing

The applications listed below can transfer documents between your iPad and this computer.

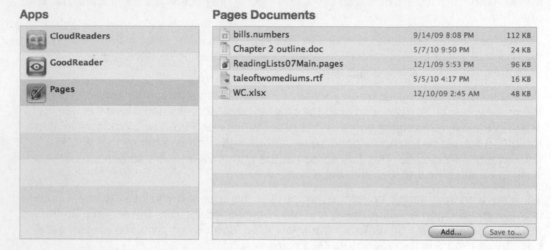

Figure 2-18. *Apps that support drag-and-drop file sharing and their enclosed documents*

If you've created a completely new file on your iPad, say in Apple's text editor Pages, and want to transfer that file to your computer, select the file in the Documents list, and click the "Save to…" button at the bottom and choose where you want to save the file on your computer. Alternately, you can simply drag the file from the Documents list to your desktop.

To delete a file from the app that contains it, simply select the file in the document list, and hit the Delete key on your keyboard. A pop-up window will appear asking if you really want to delete the file. Click Delete to complete the deletion.

As long as a file is shared inside an app, that file is always backed up as part of app backups when you sync your iPad to your computer.

> **NOTE:** Just because you can drag a file to an app's document box doesn't mean the app can open it. Apps are limited to working with files that the iPad supports. For example, the iPad does not support Microsoft's WMV video files. If you drag a WMV movie to an app, the app will contain it but will still not be able to play it. Apps are also limited to working with files they support. Pages wouldn't be able to open a movie document, for instance.

The Music Tab

The Music tab is pretty self-explanatory (see Figure 2-19). Make sure the Sync Music check box is selected at the top. In the box below it, you will see two radio buttons.

| Summary | Info | Apps | **Music** | Movies | TV Shows | Podcasts | iTunes U | Books | Photos |

☑ **Sync Music**

○ Entire music library
◉ Selected playlists, artists, and genres

☐ Include music videos
☐ Include voice memos
☐ Automatically fill free space with songs

Figure 2-19. *The Music tab allows you to select which songs, playlists, and artists you want to sync to your iPad.*

- *Entire music library*: When this is selected, your entire music library will be synced to your iPad. Note that your entire library will be synced only if you have the storage space available on your iPad. If you have more music than iPad storage capacity, the remainder of the music will stop syncing once the iPad is full.

- *Selected playlists, artists, and genres*: If you select this option, you will see three boxes appear listing all the playlists, artists, and genres you have in your iTunes library (see Figure 2-20). Go through and select the check boxes of the playlists, artists, and genres you want on your iPad.

- *Include music videos*: If you select this check box, any music videos associated with playlists, artists, or genres will be transferred to the iPad.

- *Include voice memos*: If you select this check box, any voice memos you have stored in your iTunes library will sync with your iPad.

- *Automatically fill free space with songs*: This check box appears only if you've selected the "Selected playlists, artists, and genres" radio button. If selected, once all your other files (movies, books, photos, and so on) have been synced to your iPad, any leftover free space will be filled with music until your iPad can't fit anything else on it. I don't recommend selecting this option. It severely limits your ability to create any new documents on your iPad since it won't have any space left to store them.

Figure 2-20. *Select the playlists, artists, and genres you want to sync with your iPad.*

The Movies Tab

The iTunes Store offers a large collection of movies available for rent or purchase that you can download and sync to your iPad. The Movies tab, shown in Figure 2-21, gives you several ways of getting your movies onto the iPad.

Figure 2-21. *The Movies tab allows you to select which movies you want to sync to your iPad.*

To sync your movies, first make sure the Sync Movies check box is selected. You'll see three boxes on the Movies tab:

- *Automatically include*: If this check box is selected, you'll be able to access a drop-down list of preset options to make your movie syncing experience easier. From the drop-down list, you can select to sync all your movies (not a good idea, because one hour of video can take up to half a gigabyte of space).

  If you'd like to go the space-saving route, select the 1, 3, 5, or 10 "most recent movies" preset. You also have the option of selecting the "all unwatched" movies preset, which will add all the movies in your library that you have not watched yet. Other preset options include syncing 1, 3, 5, or 10 of your "most recent unwatched movies" or 1, 3, 5, or 10 of your "least recent unwatched movies."

- *Movies*: If the "automatically include" check box is selected and set to anything but "all," you also have the option of selecting additional movies in your iTunes library in this box. With the "automatically include" check box deselected, you'll be able to manually select as many or as few of your movies as you want (see Figure 2-22).

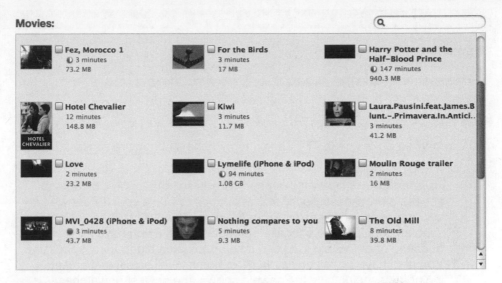

Figure 2-22. *The Movies check box allows you to select individual movies you want to sync to your iPad.*

- *Include Movies from Playlists*: This box, shown in Figure 2-23, gives you the option of including any movies found in your iTunes playlists.

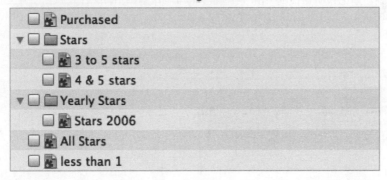

Figure 2-23. *This box allows you to sync any movies found in your iTunes playlists.*

The TV Shows Tab

As it does with movies, the iTunes Store offers large collections of TV shows available for purchase and download. All of these shows can be synchronized to and played back on your iPad. You can purchase episodes *à la carte* or buy a Season Pass. With this pass, you pay for the entire season at once, often at a slight discount, and the new shows automatically download as they become available.

To sync your TV shows, first make sure the Sync TV Shows check box is selected (see Figure 2-24).

Figure 2-24. *The TV Shows tab allows you to select which shows you want to sync to your iPad.*

You'll see three boxes on the TV Shows tab. These settings are similar to the Movies tab settings.

- *Automatically include*: If this check box is selected, you'll be able to access a drop-down list of preset options to make your TV show–syncing experience easier. From the drop-down list you can select to sync all your TV shows (again, not a good idea if you have a lot, because one hour of video can take up to half a gigabyte of space). You also have an "all unwatched" option as well as several presets including syncing only the newest shows, the newest unwatched shows, or the oldest unwatched shows. With all these options, you can apply the preset to all shows or just selected TV shows.

- *The Shows and Episodes boxes*: If the "automatically include" check box is selected and set to anything but "all," you also have the option of selecting additional TV shows from your iTunes library in this box (see Figure 2-25). With the "automatically include" check box deselected, you'll be able to manually select as many or as few of your TV shows as you want.

Figure 2-25. *The Shows check box allows you to select TV series to sync to your iPad. In the box to the left, you can select which episodes of the series to sync.*

- *Include Episodes from Playlists*: This box gives you the option of including any TV show episodes found in your iTunes playlists (see Figure 2-26).

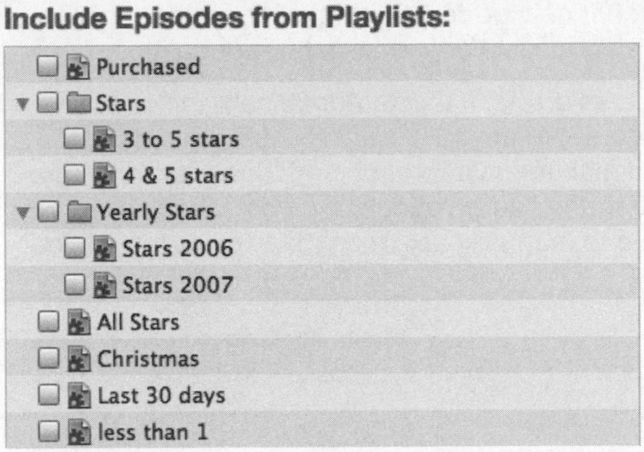
Include Episodes from Playlists:
Purchased
Stars
3 to 5 stars
4 & 5 stars
Yearly Stars
Stars 2006
Stars 2007
All Stars
Christmas
Last 30 days
less than 1

Figure 2-26. *This box allows you to sync any TV shows found in your iTunes playlists.*

The Podcasts Tab

Many people use iTunes to subscribe to their favorite podcasts. *Podcasts* are audio programs delivered over the Internet, much as TV shows are delivered over the airways. Numerous podcasts are available these days, including entertainment, advice, how-to shows, and much more. iTunes monitors your podcast subscriptions and can automatically download new shows when they become available. The Podcasts tab lets you control which shows are synchronized to your iPad.

The Podcasts tab, as shown in Figure 2-27, has a similar look and feel as the Movies and TV Shows tabs.

Summary
Info
Apps
Music
Movies
TV Shows
Podcasts
iTunes U
Books
Photos
Sync Podcasts
Automatically include
all unplayed
episodes of
all podcasts

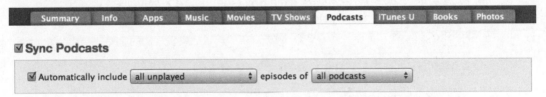

Figure 2-27. *The Podcasts tab allows you to select which podcasts you want to sync to your iPad.*

To sync your podcasts, first make sure the Sync Podcasts check box is selected. You'll see three boxes on the Podcasts tab:

- *Automatically include*: If this check box is selected, you'll be able to access a drop-down list of preset options to make your podcasts syncing experience easier. From the drop-down list you can select to sync all your podcasts. Syncing all your podcasts won't take up as much room as movies and TV shows will if the podcasts in question are audio-only. However, if you are downloading video podcasts, the same space requirements apply as with movies.

  In addition to the "all" option, you have an "all unplayed" and "all new" option as well as several presets including syncing only the newest podcasts, the most recent/least recent unplayed podcasts, or the most recent/least recent new podcasts. With all these options, you can apply the preset to all podcasts or just selected podcasts.

- *The Podcasts and Episodes boxes*: If the "automatically include" check box is selected and set to anything but "all," you also have the option of selecting additional podcasts from your iTunes library in this box (see Figure 2-28). With the "automatically include" check box unselected, you'll be able to manually select as many or as few of your podcasts as you want.

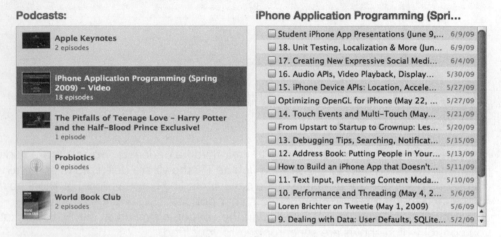

Figure 2-28. *The Podcasts check box allows you to select podcasts to sync to your iPad. In the box to the left, you can select which episodes of the podcast series to sync.*

- *Include Episodes from Playlists*: This box (see Figure 2-29) gives you the option of including any podcast episodes found in your iTunes playlists.

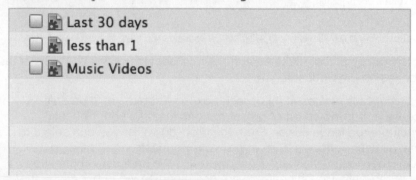

Figure 2-29. *This box allows you to sync any podcasts found in your iTunes playlists.*

The iTunes U Tab

iTunes U is a free service offered by Apple and educational institutions to disseminate educational tools such as class lectures and language courses. iTunes U operates much like podcasts, and getting them onto your iPad works in a similar function.

To sync your iTunes U items, first make sure the Sync iTunes U check box is selected (see Figure 2-30).

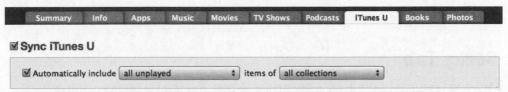

Figure 2-30. *The iTunes U tab allows you to select which iTunes U collections you want to sync to your iPad.*

You'll see three boxes on the iTunes U tab:

- *Automatically include*: If this check box is selected, you'll be able to access a drop-down list of preset options to make your iTunes U syncing experience easier. From the drop-down list you can choose to sync all your iTunes U items.

  In addition to the "all" option, you have "all unplayed" and "all new" options as well as several presets including syncing only the newest iTunes U items, the most recent/least recent unplayed items, or the most recent/least recent new items. With all these options you can apply the preset to all items or just selected items.

- *The Collections and Items boxes*: If the "automatically include" check box is selected and set to anything but "all," you also have the option of selecting additional items from your iTunes library in this box (see Figure 2-31). With the "automatically include" check box deselected, you'll be able to manually select as many or as few of your iTunes U items as you want.

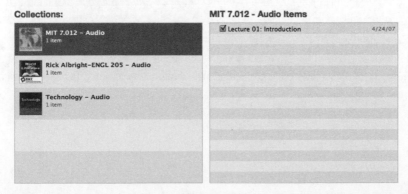

Figure 2-31. *The iTunes U check box allows you to select iTunes U collections to sync to your iPad. In the box to the left you can select which items of the iTunes U collections to sync.*

- *Include Items from Playlists*: This box (see Figure 2-32) gives you the option of including any iTunes U items found in your iTunes playlists.

Include Items from Playlists:

☐ 🎵 Last 30 days
☐ 🎵 Recently Added

Figure 2-32. *This box allows you to sync any iTunes U collections found in your iTunes playlists.*

The Books Tab

One of the big features of the iPad is the ability to buy and read e-books in the new iBooks app. We'll delve into the iBookstore and the iBooks app in Chapters 8 and 9, respectively; for now all you need to know is that the Books tab in the iPad settings pane is where you control what books get synced to your iPad (see Figure 2-33).

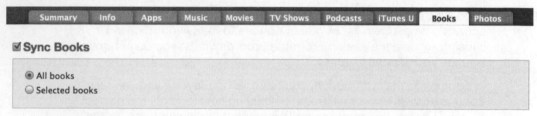

| Summary | Info | Apps | Music | Movies | TV Shows | Podcasts | iTunes U | **Books** | Photos |

☑ **Sync Books**

◉ All books
◯ Selected books

Figure 2-33. *The Books tab allows you to select which books you want to sync to your iPad.*

Make sure the Sync Books check box is selected at the top. In the box below it, you will see two radio buttons. "All books" syncs every book in your iTunes library. "Selected books" allows you to sync only the books you choose in the Books box further down the page (see Figure 2-34).

> **NOTE:** Even if you have 300 books in your iTunes library, you might as well sync them all.
> An e-book hardly takes up any space. As a matter of fact, *War and Peace*, one of the largest
> books out there (and also one of the greatest) takes up only 1.2MB of disk space. That's more
> than 50 percent less than a single 128KBps AAC music file. Of course, illustrated books will
> take up more space, but even then they still shouldn't take any more room than a few MP3s
> would. Don't worry about a cluttered library, either. You'll learn how to organize your books in
> Chapter 9.

Books:
Sort by Title
The Adventures of Tom Sawyer
Mark Twain
The Art of War
Sunzi 6th cent. B.C.
Common Sense
Thomas Paine
The Common Sense of Socialism
John Spargo
The Kingdom of God Is Within You
Leo Tolstoy
A Letter to a Hindu
Leo Tolstoy
Moby Dick, or, The Whale
Herman Melville
Personal Recollections of Joan of Arc — Volume 1
Mark Twain
Pride and Prejudice
Jane Austen

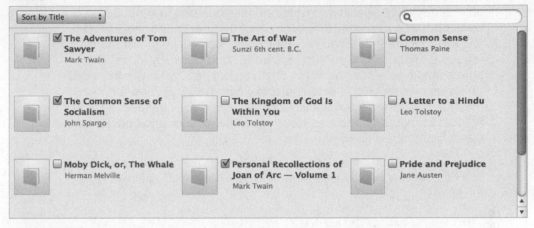

Figure 2-34. *The Books check box allows you to select individual books to sync to your iPad.*

Below the Books box you will see a Sync Audiobooks check box (see Figure 2-35). Again, there are two options: "All audiobooks" or "Selected audiobooks."

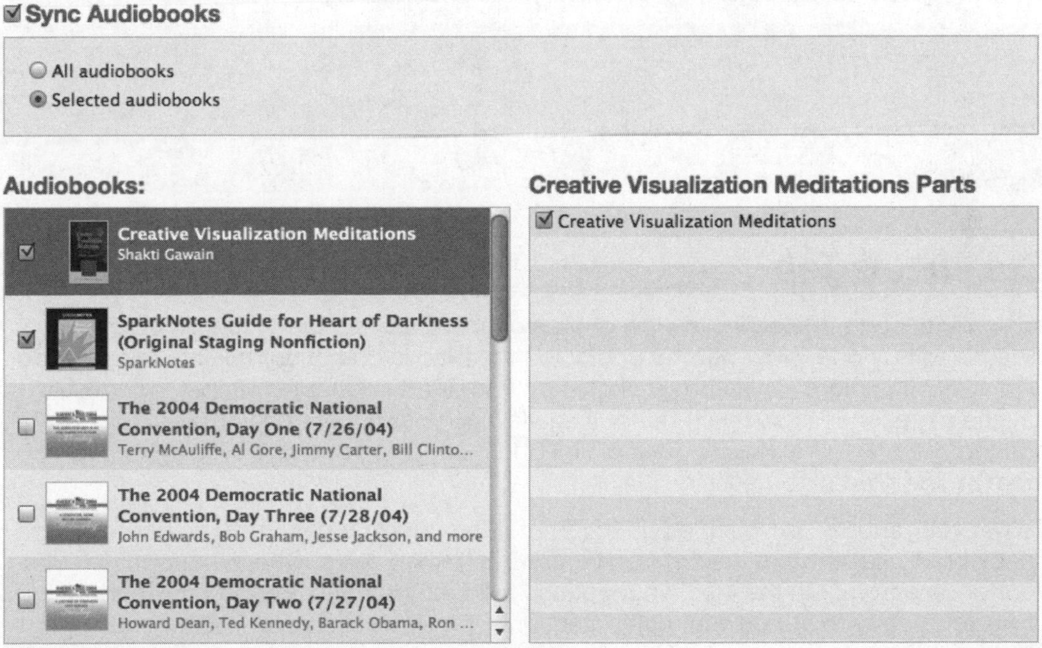

Sync Audiobooks
All audiobooks
Selected audiobooks
Audiobooks:
Creative Visualization Meditations
Shakti Gawain
SparkNotes Guide for Heart of Darkness (Original Staging Nonfiction)
SparkNotes
The 2004 Democratic National Convention, Day One (7/26/04)
Terry McAuliffe, Al Gore, Jimmy Carter, Bill Clinto...
The 2004 Democratic National Convention, Day Three (7/28/04)
John Edwards, Bob Graham, Jesse Jackson, and more
The 2004 Democratic National Convention, Day Two (7/27/04)
Howard Dean, Ted Kennedy, Barack Obama, Ron ...
Creative Visualization Meditations Parts
Creative Visualization Meditations

Figure 2-35. *The Sync Audiobooks interface*

With "All audiobooks" selected, any audiobooks you have in your iTunes library will be synced with your iPad. If you choose "Selected audiobooks," you'll be presented with the familiar layout you've seen on the other media tabs:

■ *The Audiobooks and Parts boxes*: In the Audiobooks box, you'll be able to manually select which audiobooks you want to sync. Some audiobooks have separate files, or *parts*, that designate chapters (as shown in Figure 2-35). You can select only the parts you want to sync for any audiobook in the Parts box. If the "automatically include" check box is selected and set to anything but "all," you also have the option of selecting additional audiobooks from your iTunes library in this box. With the "automatically include" check box unselected, you'll be able to manually select as many or as few of your audiobooks and their chapters as you want.

■ *Include Audiobooks from Playlists*: This box gives you the option of including any audiobooks found in your iTunes playlists (see Figure 2-36).

Include Audiobooks from Playlists:

Figure 2-36. *This box allows you to sync any audiobooks found in your iTunes playlists.*

NOTE: Unlike with e-books, audiobooks can be quite large since they are basically very long audio files. If you have dozens of audiobooks, you may want to transfer only a select few to save space.

The Photos Tab

Ironically enough, the ability to view photos on the iPad was pretty low on our list of reasons to buy one. Now viewing photos on the iPad is one of our favorite things to do with it. We'll explore viewing your photos on your iPad in Chapter 13, but for now we'll say the experience is so much better than viewing your photos on your desktop. There's nothing like physically holding your digital photos in your hand and swiping through them on the iPad's gorgeous display.

To get your photos on your iPad, in the Photos tab, make sure the "Sync Photos from" check box is selected at the top (see Figure 2-37); then select where you want to sync your photos from. On the Mac, your options will be iPhoto 4.0.3 or newer, Aperture 3.0.2 or newer, or any folder on your computer. On a Windows machine, your options will be Adobe Photoshop Elements 3.0 or newer or any folder on your computer.

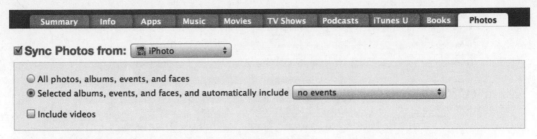

Figure 2-37. *The Photos tab allows you to select which photos you want to sync to your iPad.*

In the box below the check box, you have three options:

- *All photos, albums, events, and faces*: Selecting this option will sync every photo from your selected photo application or folder onto your iPad. Again, we recommend against this if your photo collections are as large as ours (one of us has somewhere around 80GB of travel photos on a Mac). If you have only a few thousand photos, load 'em up!

> **NOTE:** The first-generation iPads do not have a built-in camera, but you can still add photos to your iPad via the Camera Connection Kit. The $29 kit (available at www.store.apple.com) includes two adapters—one for connecting a camera through a USB 2.0 cable, the other for reading SD memory cards.

- *Selected albums, events, and faces, and automatically include*: Selecting this option displays album, events, and faces boxes further down the page (see Figure 2-38). From these boxes you can choose which iPhoto photo albums and events to sync. You can also choose if you want to sync your friends' faces. Faces is a feature in iPhoto that uses facial software recognition to create collections of photos in which a certain person appears.

  When you select any of the check boxes next to a certain album, event, or face, you'll see the photo count of that selection displayed to the right. With the "Selected albums, events, and faces, and automatically include" option selected, you'll be presented with a drop-down list of options allowing you to select all, none, or a preset date-specific range of iPhoto photos, even collections.

- *Include video*: When this check box is selected, any video files that you took with your digital camera that appear in any of your selected albums will also transfer to the iPad. Keep in mind that video can quickly use up storage space.

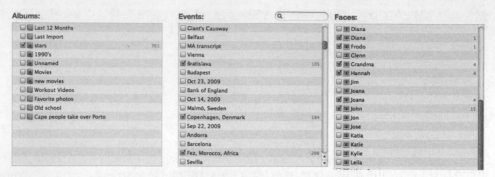

Figure 2-38. *Choose which iPhoto photo albums, events, and faces to sync.*

iTunes Device Settings

iTunes has several preferences for the iPad. To access these, open iTunes and choose iTunes ➤ Preferences from the menu bar on a Mac, or choose Edit ➤ Preferences from the menu bar if you are on a Windows machine. The iTunes preferences window will pop up with a series of icons running along the top. The only one you are interested in for the iPad is the Devices icon. Click the Devices icon (it looks like an iPhone), and you'll be presented with the Devices settings pane, as shown in Figure 2-39.

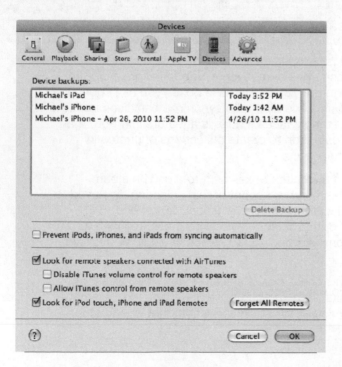

Figure 2-39. The iTunes device settings window

Here you'll find settings for devices that interact with iTunes. These devices can include iPads, iPods, iPhones, and AirPort Express devices.

- *Device backups*: Any time you sync your iPad, iTunes creates a backup of its contents. Any backup of iPods, iPhones, or iPads can be seen here. You'll see the name of the device along with the date it was last backed up. Hover your mouse over the name of the iPad to be presented with its serial number.

  iTunes will keep only one backup of your device at a time, but you can choose to save backups of your backups by navigating to them on your computer and storing them on an external hard drive. iTunes places the backup files in the following locations:

  Mac: ~/Library/Application Support/MobileSync/Backup/

  Windows XP: \Documents and Settings\(username)\Application Data\ Apple Computer\MobileSync\Backup\

  Windows Vista: \Users\(username)\AppData\Roaming\Apple Computer\ MobileSync\Backup\

  The list of information iTunes backs up is a long one:

  - Safari bookmarks, cookies, history, and currently open pages
  - Map bookmarks, recent searches, and the current location displayed in Maps
  - Application settings, preferences, and data
  - Contacts
  - Calendars
  - CalDAV and subscribed calendar accounts
  - YouTube favorites
  - Wallpapers
  - Notes
  - Mail accounts
  - Autocorrect dictionaries
  - Camera roll
  - Home screen layout and web clips
  - Network settings (saved Wi-Fi hotspots, VPN settings, network preferences)
  - Paired Bluetooth devices (which can be used only if restored to the same iPad that did the backup)

- Keychain (This includes e-mail account passwords, Wi-Fi passwords, and passwords you enter into web sites and some other applications. The keychain can be restored only from backup to the same iPad. If you are restoring to a new device, you will need to fill in these passwords again.)

- Managed configurations/profiles

- MobileMe and Microsoft Exchange account configurations

- App Store application data (except the application itself, its tmp and Caches folders)

- Per-app preferences allowing use of location services

- Offline web application cache/database

- Autofill for web pages

- Trusted hosts that have certificates that cannot be verified

- Web sites approved to get the location of the device

- In-app purchases

To delete an iPad backup, select the backup from the device backups list, and click the Delete Backup button. Confirm the deletion by clicking the Delete Backup button in the window that pops up.

- *Prevent iPods, iPhones, and iPads from syncing automatically*: Select this box if you want to disable automatic syncing when you plug your iPad into your computer. To sync, you'll need to manually click the Sync button at the bottom of the iPad's iTunes settings pane.

The only other option relevant to the iPad in the device settings window is the "Look for iPod touch, iPhone, and iPad Remotes" check box. Apple makes an iPhone app called Remote. This app allows you to use your iPod touch, iPhone, or iPad as a remote control for your home computer's music library. In other words, you can be sitting on your couch and navigating your entire iTunes library on your Mac or Windows computer right from your iPad. All you need is the free Remote app, the iPad, and your computer to be on the same Wi-Fi network. If this box is deselected, your iPad will not be able to pair with your iTunes library. Clicking the Forget All Remotes button will make iTunes unpair with every iPod touch, iPhone, or iPad that it allowed to be used as a remote.

Restoring

If you are ever experiencing problems with your iPad, you can choose to restore it. You have two options of restoring: you can restore to the factory defaults, or you can restore from a backup. The factory default method will restore your iPad to its original factory settings—as if you've just turned it on for the first time. Restoring from backup will restore the iPad from its last saved backup file.

To restore to factory settings, in iTunes on your computer select the iPad from the devices list, select the Summary tab, and click Restore (this deletes all the data on the iPad and restores it to the factory settings). When prompted by iTunes, select the option to restore your settings.

To restore from backup, in iTunes on your computer right-click (or Control-click) on the iPad in the devices list, and choose Restore from Backup. The iPad will then be restored from the backup listed in the "Device backups" list.

> **NOTE:** If you've set up password encryption on your iPad backups (discussed earlier in this chapter), you will not be able to restore from the encrypted backup if you forget the password. Be sure to write it down!

Summary

In this chapter, you've explored the options you have for syncing your media and data with your iPad. You've discovered where to get your media and how to make sure your iPad/iTunes sync preferences stick. To wind things up, here is a quick overview of some key points from this chapter:

- The way your iPad connects with iTunes and the settings pane you are presented with will be familiar to you if you've used an iPhone or iPod touch; however, there are some important differences with the iPad.

- The Capacity bar will always be visible in the iPad settings pane and is an easy indicator to see how much space you have left on your iPad.

- No change you make to your iPad preference window is complete until you click the Apply button. Likewise, if you accidentally make a change you don't want, you can always click the Cancel button.

- It is important to manage what data you sync with your iPad. If you sync all your music, you might not have room left over for syncing your photos and videos.

- Syncing apps can be fun and easy using the visual representation of your iPad on the Apps tab. However, sometimes app syncing can be a slow process if you have a lot of apps. Waiting can be a pain, but it's best never to interrupt a sync.

- Syncing your movies, music, TV shows, podcasts, iTunes U items, books, and photos is pretty straightforward, and once you've mastered how to sync one form of media, the rest of the forms are a cinch.

Chapter 3

Exploring the iPad Hardware

Now that you've purchased your iPad and have had a chance to sync it with iTunes, you'll get a bit more familiar with the actual hardware. In this chapter, we'll talk about the various hardware controls on your iPad and how to use them. We'll discuss the care and maintenance of your new device, and we'll explore the details of some of the more widely used Apple accessories for iPad. Grab that iPad, any Apple accessories you may have purchased, and perhaps a refreshing beverage, and let's take a quick tour of the hardware.

The Bits and Pieces of an iPad

In Chapter 1, you were briefly introduced to the names and locations of some of the switches and ports that decorate the outside of your iPad. In this chapter, *how* those switches and ports are used is the important information.

Sleep/Wake Button

On the top-right corner of the iPad is one of the more important buttons on this little slab of glass and aluminum—the Sleep/Wake button (Figure 3-1). That's kind of an odd name for a button, but it describes the function quite clearly.

When your iPad has been totally powered down, you'll need to press and hold this button for about three seconds to turn it back on. A white Apple logo will appear, followed shortly by either the Home screen of your iPad or the Passcode Lock screen.

Figure 3-1. *The Sleep/Wake button is used for powering the iPad on or off and for putting it to sleep when it's not being used.*

If you don't plan on using your iPad for a few hours, you have your choice of either waiting for it to automatically lock and go to sleep (if that option has been turned on in Settings) or manually putting it to sleep. To do the latter, give the button a quick, firm press, and the screen goes dark. When the sound on your iPad is turned up, you'll even hear a click as an audible verification that the device has been put to sleep.

You can wake up the iPad either by giving the Sleep/Wake button another quick press or by pressing the Home button. Once again, if you have enabled a passcode lock, you need to enter that passcode correctly before you can use the iPad.

Occasionally, you may want to shut off your iPad completely. This means, of course, that it won't be magically picking up e-mail, waking to display alarms, or doing anything else. It will be totally shut down. This is handy when you're not going to be using the iPad for a long time (for example, you leave it home while on a trip) and don't want the battery to discharge.

To shut off the iPad, simply hold down the Sleep/Wake button for about five seconds. The iPad will display a black screen with a Cancel button at the bottom in case you really don't want to shut it off and a red button near the top labeled "Slide to power off." Sliding your button to the right with your finger shuts off power to the device.

This trick can be useful on those rare occasions where an iPad app simply won't respond to your touch and the entire device is locked up. To turn it back on, press the Sleep/Wake button one more time.

Screen Rotation Lock

Moving to the right side of the iPad (as oriented with the Home button and Dock Connector port at the bottom and the screen facing you), the next switch is the screen rotation lock (Figure 3-2). New iPad users can sometimes get frustrated when they're reading or playing a game, tilt the iPad a little too far in one direction or another, and have the screen change its orientation from portrait to landscape, or vice versa.

Figure 3-2. *The screen rotation lock (the small switch) and the volume toggle (the larger button)*

That's where the screen rotation lock comes in handy. For example, if you're reading a book in iBooks and find that you prefer the book-like feel of reading in portrait mode, then you might want to lock the screen orientation in portrait mode. To lock the screen in portrait mode, orient the display by tilting the bottom of the iPad down. When the display is in the proper orientation, slide the screen rotation lock button down.

An icon showing a circular arrow with a lock in the middle of it (Figure 3-3) appears on the screen momentarily. The same icon in miniature form appears in the right corner of the status bar at the top of the screen. Now you can turn the iPad any way you want, and the screen always stays in the same orientation.

Figure 3-3. *No matter how your iPad is oriented, the display will remain in the same orientation if the screen rotation lock is enabled.*

To turn the screen rotation lock off, just slide the lock button upward toward the top of the screen. The lock in the center of the icon disappears, showing that the screen rotation is now unlocked.

Volume Toggle

Continuing our tour around the perimeter of the iPad, the next button encountered is the volume toggle. As the name implies, it is used to turn the volume up or down or to shut off sound completely. You can see where the volume toggle is located in Figure 3-2.

Increasing the volume of the speaker in the iPad (or any headphones attached through the headphone jack) just requires a push on the top part of the toggle. One push brings the volume up a notch; holding down on the toggle quickly takes the iPad to top volume.

Bringing the volume down requires pushing on the other end of the volume toggle. If you push and hold the volume toggle on its lower end, your iPad's sound is shut off. That's handy for those situations where you need to quickly turn off the volume on Pandora when the phone rings.

Whenever you touch the volume toggle, a visual indication of volume appears in the center of the iPad display (Figure 3-4). If you have a set of Apple headphones with a volume switch on the cord plugged into your iPad, you can use that switch in a similar manner to adjust volume without touching the iPad.

Figure 3-4. *This transparent icon appears when you adjust the volume on your iPad with either the volume toggle or the headphones with a volume switch.*

Speaker

Speaking of sound volume, the next item on the iPad tour is the speaker. It's hidden on the bottom of the iPad (Figure 3-5) and blasts out various system beeps, music, and movie soundtracks through a set of three tiny oblong openings behind mesh grills.

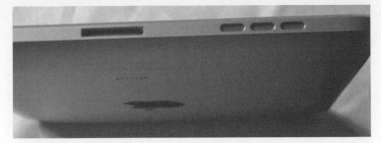

Figure 3-5. *The iPad speaker openings (right) and Dock Connector port (left)*

There's not much to say about the speaker, other than if you're purchasing or making a case for your iPad, be sure that it has an opening in the proper location so that the sound isn't muffled.

Dock Connector Port

The Dock Connector port is the iPad's high-speed connection to the world. Through the port, your iPad connects to your Mac or Windows machine for syncing, can capture photos through the Camera Connection Kit, and can use a variety of docks or cables for charging the battery.

We'll be talking about many of those accessories later in this chapter, but for now, we're going to just talk about using the Dock Connector port with the included Dock Connector to USB cable.

You can find instructions on how to plug the cable into the Dock Connector port in Chapter 1. When plugging the cable into your iPad, be sure to have the side with the small gray icon (it's a rectangle with a line in it) facing up, and also make sure that you push the cable in squarely. In other words, don't have the cable connector angled up, down, or sideways because that can cause undue wear on the Dock Connector port.

Home Button

To quote Dorothy in *The Wizard of Oz*, "There's no place like home." The Home button (Figure 3-6) is undoubtedly the most heavily used physical button on the iPad.

Figure 3-6. *The Home button, centered on the bottom of the fingerprint-smeared iPad in this figure, has many uses.*

It is used for a number of actions:

- Quitting an application that is in use and returning to the Home screen.

- Turning on a sleeping iPad.

- Returning to the main Home screen by clicking the Home button twice in quick succession. This feature can be changed in the General ➤ Home settings to make the double-click enable search or the iPod app.

- Switching to the iPad search function. Click the Home button once if you're on the main Home screen, or click three times in quick succession if you're on another pane of the Home screen.

One fascinating thing about the iPad is that depending on how you're holding it, the Home button can be on the top, bottom, left, or right side of the display. In most situations, however, it is in the standard bottom side of the screen.

Headphone Jack

On top of the iPad on the left side is the headphone jack (Figure 3-7).

The headphone jack accommodates any standard 3.5mm stereo headphone connector, so you have thousands of choices for headphones to enhance your listening pleasure. Apple sells two headphones: the Apple Earphones with Remote and Mic and the Apple In-Ear Headphones with Remote and Mic. Both of these headphones provide a way for you to control music volume as well as play, pause, rewind, advance, or skip through music or video.

Figure 3-7. *The headphone jack is the larger of the two circles at the top, while the microphone is that tiny dot below.*

There's a little known secret about the headphone jack on the iPad that you should know. In that jack is a small liquid sensor. If you ever get your iPad wet, the liquid sensor changes color. This indicates to any Apple technician who is disassembling your iPad that the iPad was wet at one point or another, and it voids your warranty. Unfortunately, some people have found that the liquid sensor may show "water damage" even if the iPad has just been exposed to extremely humid conditions.

If this happens to you, it's within your rights as a consumer to insist on having the technician open the iPad, because there is a second internal sensor that is less susceptible to humidity.

Microphone

The iPad's microphone is probably the most invisible piece of equipment on the device. Located right next to the headphone jack, it's a tiny hole.

If you're using an iPad application to record a lecture or conversation, you can enhance the sound recording slightly by orienting the mic directly toward the person(s) speaking. When you're recording your own voice, either of the Apple headphones with microphones discussed in the previous section provides clear reproduction of your speech without picking up a lot of background noise.

USB headsets also work well for listening to and recording on the iPad when connected through the USB adapter that is part of the iPad Camera Connection Kit. We'll discuss the Camera Connection Kit later in this chapter.

Micro-SIM Port (Wi-Fi + 3G iPad Only)

There's one more port on the Wi-Fi + 3G iPad that doesn't exist on the Wi-Fi model: the micro-SIM port (Figure 3-8).

Every device that is connected to a GSM-based mobile phone system anywhere in the world uses a small card called a *subscriber identity module* (SIM) card. Your 3G iPad cannot access the Internet through a 3G network without an SIM card, so each 3G iPad comes with one pre-installed. Apple uses a smaller SIM card form factor in the iPad called *micro-SIM*.

On occasion, SIM cards may be defective and require replacement. For that purpose, there is a tiny door on the left side of the 3G iPad. That door has a miniscule hole in it, which you can think of as the lock for the door.

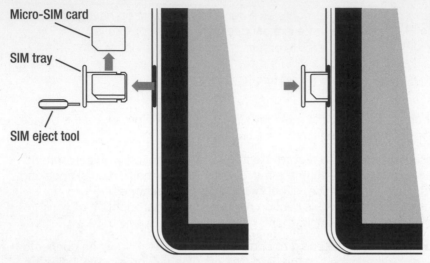

Micro-SIM card

SIM tray

SIM eject tool

Figure 3-8. *The micro-SIM card, the SIM tray, and the SIM eject tool are found only on the Wi-Fi + 3G iPad.*

The 3G-enabled iPad also comes with a SIM eject tool, which is a small oblong aluminum piece with a small protrusion on one end. To open the SIM door, take the SIM eject tool and put the protruding piece into the hole in the door. Apply pressure to the tool, and the door will pop up from the surface. It is quite easy to lose the SIM eject tool, so in a pinch you can use a small paper clip bent to resemble the tool.

Grasping the top of the door with your fingers, pull the micro-SIM out of the iPad. It rests in a small tray, and it can be popped out and replaced with a new micro-SIM. To put the new SIM into the iPad, simply push the tray back into the iPad until the door is flush with the side of your device.

Care and Maintenance of Your iPad

Although an iPad isn't as expensive as MacBook Pro, you'll still want to keep it around as long as possible. With a little loving care, your iPad can serve you for many years to come. In this section of Chapter 3, we'll tell you how to maintain your iPad for long life and years of loyal service.

Cases

As with the iPhone before it, the iPad is creating its own economy with a plethora of accessories being produced for it. Some of the hottest products for iPad are cases that protect the device from scratches, water, dirt, and accidental drops. Although we're not going to list every possible case in this section, we'll talk about the different types of cases and who they're for.

Sleeves

An iPad sleeve (Figure 3-9) is usually made of a soft material with a nonscratch lining. The iPad is placed into the sleeve, and then it's commonly put into another carrying case—a backpack, a purse, a briefcase, or a laptop bag.

Figure 3-9. *An iPad sleeve by Booq. Image courtesy of Booq.*

More than anything, sleeves are designed to protect the iPad from scratches when it is placed into another bag. They can be made of a variety of materials (there are sleeves made of fleece, cork, neoprene, nylon, and hemp, for example), and prices are also all over the map.

Examples of sleeves are products from ColcaSac (www.colcasac.com) and Booq (http://booqbags.com).

Bags

iPad bags (Figure 3-10) are meant to not only protect the iPad but be the primary form of transportation for it as well. As such, they're usually equipped with a handle or strap of some sort for easy carrying. Price-wise, bags are usually more expensive than sleeves, but they also provide more protection. Often there's some sort of padding provided, as well as a stiff insert to protect the screen.

Figure 3-10. *The attractive and functional Ristretto bag from Tom Bihn. Image courtesy of Tom Bihn.*

Several classy bags are made by Booq and Tom Bihn (www.tombihn.com).

Skins

If you want to protect the surfaces of your iPad without a lot of extra weight, consider a skin. These are usually made of a thin material that might not protect your iPad against a drop but will keep scratches away. Skins can be made of thin plastic material (such as Zagg's Invisible Shield for iPad; www.zagg.com) or rubber (Incase Grip Protective Cover; www.goincase.com).

Book-Style Cases

The iPad is an excellent electronic book reader, so why not make it look like a book? Apple's iPad Case is the best example of this type of case, with a cover that flips over to protect the screen. It also has a slot on the back into which the edge of the cover can be placed to prop the iPad up for easy viewing (see Figure 3-11).

Figure 3-11. *The Apple iPad Case not only protects your iPad but also serves as a useful wedge for typing or a frame for showing pictures.*

Other manufacturers are making similar cases, including Incase with the Convertible Book Jacket and the beautiful Dodocase (www.dodocase.com).

Caring for the Battery

One great thing about the iPad is the battery life. It's not uncommon to go for days without charging the battery, and the thought of being far from a power outlet will no longer cause you to panic. A good rule of thumb is that for normal usage the battery level drops about 10 percent for each hour of use. If you're playing games with some heavy graphic and sound demands, your battery may not last as long on a charge. On the other hand, if you're reading an e-book, the iPad battery may last longer.

However, your iPad battery won't last forever without a charge, so you'll want to charge it on a regular basis. You do this by connecting the iPad to a power outlet using the Dock Connector to USB cable and the 10W USB power adapter or by connecting the cable to a high-power USB 2.0 port.

What do we mean by high-power USB? Generally, that means plugging either directly into a port on your computer or into a powered USB hub. Plugging your iPad into a port on a USB keyboard or into an unpowered USB hub won't charge it. Instead, you'll see the message "Not Charging" in the status bar next to the battery icon. We recommend plugging the iPad into the power adapter every night to receive a full charge.

If your iPad is *very* low on power, you may see one of the images in Figure 3-12 on the screen. These mean that the device needs to be charged for at least ten minutes before you can use it. If the battery is extremely low or completely drained, you may not see these images for up to two minutes after plugging the iPad into a power source.

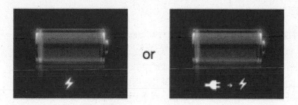

Figure 3-12. *If you see either of these symbols on your iPad screen, stop using it, and plug it into a power source as soon as possible.*

With constant usage, your iPad battery may eventually get to the point that its capacity to hold a charge has depleted 50 percent or more from the original specification. You'll be able to tell this is the case if your iPad is constantly running out of power or if it never shows that it is completely recharged after being plugged in for a long time. In this case, you may need to have your battery replaced by an Apple-authorized service provider. If you purchased an AppleCare Protection Plan for your iPad and you've owned it for less than two years, you may be able to have Apple replace the battery at no cost.

There are some simple steps you can take to stretch your battery life that can be useful in situations (international flights, for example) where you cannot readily recharge your battery:

■ *Turn off push notifications*: Some apps use Apple Push Notifications to provide alerts. These tend to decrease battery life when frequently used, so you can disable push notifications by going to Settings ➤ Notifications and turning Notifications to Off.

■ *Turn off Wi-Fi*: When you're not using Wi-Fi, turn it off to save power. Go to Settings ➤ Wi-Fi and set Wi-Fi to Off.

■ *Have a Wi-Fi + 3G iPad?* Using 3G networks tends to drain battery power faster than connecting via Wi-Fi. If you're in a zone with low or no 3G coverage, turn off 3G to improve your battery life. There are two ways to do this. First, choose Settings ➤ Cellular, and set Cellular Data to Off. The second method is to simply turn on Airplane Mode, which is accomplished by going into Settings and setting Airplane Mode to On.

■ *Minimize use of location services*: iPads can determine where they are by two methods: by Wi-Fi location through Skyhook Wireless's database of Wi-Fi hotspot locations or by Assisted GPS (A-GPS) on Wi-Fi + 3G iPads. Both of these methods can reduce battery life. If you don't need to know where you are or where you're going, disable location services. Go to Settings ➤ General ➤ Location Services and slide the Location Services switch to Off.

■ *Adjust the brightness of your screen*: The iPad normally has Auto-Brightness turned on, which means that it will brighten the screen in bright ambient light conditions and darken it in darker rooms. You may want to adjust brightness yourself by going to Settings ➤ Brightness & Wallpaper and dragging the slider to the left to lower the default screen brightness. Less brightness results in better battery life.

■ *Know your downloaded applications*: Some apps that you run on your iPad may be eating your battery life. Games that prevent the screen from dimming automatically are a common culprit, as are apps that need to run continuously for location updates. Geotracking apps that poll the GPS position of a Wi-Fi + 3G iPad are known to pull the battery life down quickly.

■ *Keep your iPad out of temperature extremes*: Apple recommends keeping your iPad out of direct sun and hot cars. Extreme heat can cause decreased battery life and may also result in other issues we'll discuss shortly. Apple's recommended temperature ranges for the iPad are 32° to 95° F (0° to 35° C) in operation and -4° to 113° F (-20° to 45° C) when it is turned off.

■ Set your iPad to turn off after a short amount of inactivity. The Auto-Lock feature, which can be set by going to Settings ➤ General ➤ Auto-Lock, will automatically turn off your screen after a preset amount of time. For best battery life, set the interval to a short time like one or two minutes.

Caring for the Screen

Unlike the easily scratched displays on early mobile devices like the Apple Newton MessagePad or Palm Pilot, the iPad's screen is made of a very durable and extremely hard glass. Although it will resist most scratches, eventually something may scratch the screen. Except in extreme situations, this should not harm the screen, and you should still be able to use your iPad with no difficulties.

Probably the biggest issue you'll have with an iPad display is that it tends to pick up fingerprints. The iPad screen has an oleophobic (oil-repelling) coating on it, but it still picks up smears and fingerprints quite easily. How easily? Take a look at Figure 3-6, which shows an iPad after a few days of regular usage.

Cleaning fingerprints and smears off of your iPad screen can get to be a bit of an obsession. Fortunately, about the only time that they're readily visible is when the iPad is turned off, so you shouldn't need to get obsessive about fingerprints. On those occasions where the smearing is really interfering with your iPad use, Apple recommends turning off the iPad completely, unplugging all cables, and then using a soft, slightly damp, lint-free cloth. We recommend using a RadTech ScreenSavrz cleaning cloth (`www.radtech.us`), dampening the cloth slightly with water, and then squeezing it until almost all the water is gone.

Some iPad users claim that baby wipes work well to clean the iPad screen. They're inexpensive, convenient, and easy to use. After cleaning the screen, just wipe any remaining dust or liquid residue with a soft cloth.

Next, use the cloth to wipe the screen. Make sure that you avoid any openings on the iPad, such as the headphone jack, Dock Connector port, and speaker.

Never use window cleaners, liquid eyeglass cleaners, household cleaning sprays, alcohol, ammonia, or any abrasives to clean the iPad, because they may damage the screen.

Heat: The iPad's Worst Enemy

In the previous section about battery life, we mentioned Apple's recommendation that you keep the iPad out of hot conditions in order to optimize battery life. There's another good reason to make sure that you keep your iPad cool—it may shut off if it gets too hot.

Apple designed the iPad without a built-in cooling fan so that you wouldn't be bothered by the noise and power consumption of a fan. Unfortunately, that means that the only way your iPad can keep itself cool is by transferring heat to the surroundings through conduction.

Some iPad early adopters have reported that when their device experiences conditions with a high ambient temperature, a warning appears on the screen and the iPad shuts down. To bring your iPad "back to life," it's necessary to bring it into a cool place out of direct sun until it can cool down. This seems to be a more common occurrence during summer and when the iPad is being used in direct sunlight.

Apple Accessories for iPad

When this book was being written shortly after the release of the iPad, there were already thousands of third-party accessories available. For many iPad buyers who will be making their purchase from a nearby Apple Store or through the Apple Online Store, Apple accessories may be their first choice.

In this section, we'll describe the iPad accessories made by Apple and how they can be used to enhance your user experience. You've already been introduced to these accessories in Chapter 1; here, we provide more details about how each of these items can be used with your iPad.

iPad Case

We mentioned the Apple iPad Case earlier in this chapter as a way to protect your device from scratches. The iPad Case is useful in many other ways as well.

The iPad Case is made of a slightly rubbery material, which means that when your iPad is inserted into it and being carried around, it is easier to grip. We find the "naked" iPad to be somewhat slippery, so having the iPad Case has probably kept us from dropping the iPad at least once.

The iPad is actually held in the case by friction. You insert the iPad into the case through a thin slot that is about the thickness of the iPad. Once it is in the case, there's a small border of the case material that extends over the front of the iPad to hold the iPad in place. Another flap of material is tucked behind the iPad to cover the slot where you inserted the iPad.

Our favorite feature of the iPad case is not that it protects the screen so well but that it can be folded into a handy stand, as shown in Figure 3-11. There's a small flap on the back of the case that grips the edge of the cover. When the cover is tucked into this flap, it turns the iPad case into a wedge that facilitates onscreen typing in landscape mode. You can also stand up the iPad in the iPad case, which is perfect for reading recipes in the kitchen.

iPad Keyboard Dock

Although the onscreen virtual keyboard of the iPad makes it easy, at least in landscape mode, to touch-type, many iPad owners find that they miss the tactile feedback of a traditional keyboard.

Apple realized this and developed the iPad Keyboard Dock, which is a mashup of an Apple keyboard and an iPad dock. Simply stated, there's a dock for charging your iPad and a keyboard that has special keys for activating iPad-specific features. The iPad Keyboard Dock has an Apple-standard Dock Connector port, so you can hook up any iPad accessories that use the port. There's also an audio line-out port for connecting your docked iPad to a stereo or powered speakers, although you'll have to supply your own audio cable.

Some negatives about the iPad Keyboard Dock? It holds the iPad only in one configuration, and the angle of the screen can't be adjusted. It also can't be used in landscape (sideways) mode, and there's no way of distancing the keyboard from the screen. That's fine, because Apple also makes the iPad Dock.

Any Bluetooth keyboard can be used with your iPad, so you don't need to buy the iPad Keyboard Dock—or any dock, for that matter. Just prop up your iPad so that the screen is easily visible, pair a Bluetooth keyboard with the iPad, and you're in business with a "real" keyboard instead of the iPad's virtual one.

iPad Dock

If you don't like the Keyboard Dock, there's always the plain iPad Dock, which does away with the keyboard and just provides a docking base for charging and syncing your iPad (Figure 3-13).

Figure 3-13. *The Apple iPad Dock is plain, functional, and less expensive than the Apple Keyboard Dock.*

Like the Keyboard Dock, the iPad Dock provides access to a Dock Connector port and an audio line-out port. It also has the same issue of holding your iPad at one fixed angle, so there's no way to adjust the angle. However, if you decide to use the iPad with the Wireless Keyboard (discusses in a moment), you do have the option of moving the keyboard around rather than having it fixed in one place as with the Keyboard Dock.

iPad Camera Connection Kit

For photographers, a very useful accessory from Apple is the iPad Camera Connection Kit (Figure 3-14). The kit consists of two separate connectors that plug into the iPad's Dock Connector port. The first has a slot for a Secure Digital (SD) memory card like those used in many digital cameras and camcorders. When you want to move photos or movies from your camera to your iPad for sharing or touch-up, you simply plug in the Camera Connection Kit's SD adapter, remove the SD card from your camera, and insert it into the SD slot on the Camera Connection Kit.

Figure 3-14. *The iPad Camera Connection Kit consists of a USB adapter (left) and an SD memory card reader (right).*

Even more useful is the second connector, which provides the iPad with a USB port. What can you connect to the USB port? A digital camera or camcorder, of course, but you can also attach most USB keyboards, USB headsets, and even an iPhone or iPod touch.

The ability to add a USB headset to an iPad makes it a great portable workstation for Skype voice chats, and if you have a favorite USB keyboard that you just can't part with, you'll now be able to use it with your iPad.

iPad 10W USB Power Adapter

The iPad comes with a 10W USB power adapter for charging, but you may want a second adapter for travel or so you can charge up both at home and at work. The iPad 10W USB Power Adapter has one additional piece that's not included with the standard adapter that you get with your iPad—it's a 6-foot-long power cord, so you don't need to be right next to the power outlet to get a charge.

iPad Dock Connector to VGA Adapter

When Steve Jobs announced on the iPad on January 27, 2010, he also announced the availability of iWork for iPad. iWork consists of three powerful apps: Pages, Keynote, and Numbers.

Apple's Keynote is presentation software, so for those of us who give presentations as part of our work life, this was exciting news. What we needed, however, was some way to get the image from the iPad to a standard PC projector or large monitor.

Minutes later, Jobs announced the iPad Dock Connector to VGA Adapter (Figure 3-15), which provides exactly that capability. Before you get too excited and think that you can display everything on your iPad screen to an audience using this adapter, we should tell you that it only works with applications that have been written to include a set of special drivers for the VGA Adapter. That number is growing daily, but you should check for compatibility with the VGA Adapter before buying an app with video-out in mind.

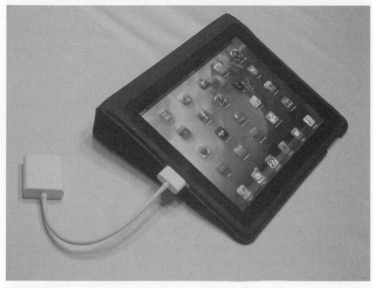

Figure 3-15. *The iPad Dock Connector to VGA Adapter is useful for displaying Keynote presentations on an external monitor or PC projector.*

Still, this adapter is a godsend for presenters who don't want to lug a laptop around. With Keynote for iPad, the adapter, your iPad, and a PC projector, you're ready to wow the crowd with your presentation.

Apple Composite AV Cable

Not every PC projector or TV uses the VGA standard for input of video signals, so Apple made sure that the Apple Component AV cable worked with the iPad. This cable was actually designed for use with the iPod Classic so that movies stored on the iPod could be displayed on a TV or home theater system.

Once again, the cable works only with applications that have been written to take advantage of the video-out capabilities of the iPad. We hope more iPad programmers will support video-out in their applications in the future.

Apple Component AV Cable

Like the Composite AV cable, the Apple Component AV cable is a former iPod product that has found new life with the iPad. If your TV or home theater system has component video and audio inputs, you can display Keynote presentations and videos on the big screen.

Apple Wireless Keyboard

The Apple Wireless Keyboard is another Apple product that can be used with the iPad. This diminutive keyboard is comfortable and has good tactile feedback for touch-typing.

The keyboard uses Bluetooth wireless connectivity to converse with the iPad and has two AA batteries that provide power to it. If you have an existing Apple Wireless Keyboard and want to use it with your iPad, you will need to pair the keyboard with the iPad only—you cannot use it for both your Mac and your iPad unless you go through the pairing process each time you want to use it.

The best thing about the keyboard is that it is not attached to anything, so you can use it in front of your iPad, in your lap, or up to 30 feet away from the iPad. The Wireless Keyboard does not have the iPad-specific keys that are included on the Keyboard Dock.

As we mentioned earlier, just about any third-party Bluetooth keyboard will work with the iPad. For the ultimate in portability, you might want to consider a folding Bluetooth keyboard like the Matias Bluetooth Folding Keyboard (http://matias.ca/foldingkeyboard/index.php).

Apple Earphones with Remote and Mic

Although the iPad essentially uses the same operating system software as an iPhone, it's not designed to make or receive phone calls. Even the iPad Wi-Fi + 3G can't make voice calls except by using Voice over IP (VoIP) software like Skype (http://skype.com) or Line2 (www.line2.com).

Even though you can't make phone calls with your iPad like you can on any iPhone, you'll still want to listen to music, watch movies, or even take part in the occasional VoIP chat. For that reason, you may want a good set of headphones. The Apple Earphones with Remote and Mic have a small switch on one of the earphone cables that acts as a remote control for iTunes. If you need to fast-forward to the next song, pause, turn the volume up or down, or rewind, you can do it with the remote.

The remote switch also includes one important component—a small directional microphone for picking up your voice. Since these are the same headphones that are included with each iPhone, you can use them with your iPad by simply plugging them into the headphone jack.

Apple In-Ear Headphones with Remote and Mic

The last Apple accessory for the iPad that we'll discuss is another headphone. The Apple In-Ear Headphones with Remote and Mic are virtually identical to the previous entry, but with one important difference. These headphones actually fit inside your ear canal so that you get better sound quality and isolation from outside noises.

Summary

This chapter introduced you to the user-controllable hardware of your iPad by taking you on a tour of the various switches and ports you'll use on a daily basis. You also became familiar with the care and maintenance of your iPad and found out more about the iPad accessories that you can purchase from Apple.

Here are some key points from this chapter:

- For ease of use, the iPad has very few physical switches and toggles. Most interaction with an iPad is done through the touch screen. The true buttons and switches consist of the Sleep/Wake button, the Home button, the volume toggle, and the screen rotation lock.

- There are many ways to extend the battery life of your iPad for those rare occasions where you'll be away from a power outlet for a long time. On those long international flights, consider dimming the screen, lowering the volume, and turning off all wireless services (Wi-Fi, 3G, and Bluetooth).

- Extreme temperatures are the enemy of your iPad. Chances are if you're feeling uncomfortable, your iPad is too! Keep it at a temperature you'd feel comfortable at, and you shouldn't run into any problems.

- Never get liquids into any of the ports on your iPad, especially the headphone jack. Exposure to liquids can void the iPad warranty.

- If you plan on using any of the Apple cables or adapters to connect your iPad to a projector, TV, or home theater system, understand that not all apps may support those cables.

Chapter 4

Interacting with Your iPad

For those of you who have used an iPhone or iPod touch, you'll already have some idea of how to interact with your iPad. However, because of the iPad's large screen, you'll find some subtle differences between the iPhone and your iPad. Never used an iPod touch or iPhone before? That's OK too, because you are absolutely going to be blown away by the iPad's Multi-Touch screen. The iPad responds to the language of your touch. Its vocabulary includes *taps*, *drags*, *pinches*, and *flicks*. With these actions, you control your iPad as easily as using a mouse to control your personal computer. And there's a lot more to interaction than just drags and double-clicks. Your iPad offers Multi-Touch technology. That means it can recognize and respond to more than one touch at a time.

In this chapter, you'll discover all the different ways you can interact with your iPad—from zooming into and out of pictures to using the iPad's large built-in keyboard to setting Accessibility options. Let's get started.

Interaction Basics

Personal computers have mice. Personal digital assistants (PDAs) have styluses. The iPad has your fingers. It does not work with mice or styluses. It requires real finger contact. Your iPad does not just sense pressure points. It detects the small electrical charge transferred from your fingers. That means you can use your iPad with your fingers, your knuckles, or even—if you're feeling up to it—your nose, but you cannot use it with pencil erasers, Q-Tips, or those PDA styluses. The electrical charges in your touch make it possible for the iPad to detect and respond to one or more contacts at a time, that is, to use Multi-Touch technology.

TIP: If you're feeling really adventurous, you can use a frozen hotdog in place of your finger. Korean winters are very cold, and people were getting frostbite on their fingers from removing their gloves to use their iPhones outside. Some enterprising people in Korea discovered that you could use a frozen hotdog in lieu of your finger and still be able to interact with the iPhone's touch screen, all while keeping their gloves on. Theoretically, a frozen hotdog should work with the iPad's screen as well.

The iPad Language

How you touch your iPad's screen provides your communication vocabulary. Here's a quick rundown of the basic ways you can speak to your iPad:

Pressing the Home button. The Home button lives below the touch screen and is marked with a white square. Press this button at any time while in an app to return to your Home screen with its list of applications. Double-pressing the Home button while on another page of apps will instantly return you to your Home screen.

Tapping. Tap your iPad by touching your finger to the screen and removing it quickly. Tapping allows you to select web links, activate buttons, and launch applications. When typing text, you may want to tap with your forefinger or, if it's more comfortable, your thumb.

Double-tapping. Double-tapping means tapping your screen twice in quick succession. Double-clicking may be important on your personal computer, but double-tapping is not actually used all that much on your iPad. You can double-tap in Safari (the web browser that ships on your iPad) to zoom into columns and double-tap again to zoom back out. In Photos (the iPad's built-in photo viewer), use double-tapping to zoom into and out from pictures.

Two-fingered tapping and dragging. The iPad's Multi-Touch technology means you can tap the screen with more than one finger at a time. A few applications respond to two-fingered gestures. To do this, separate your forefinger and middle finger and tap or drag the screen with both fingers at once. For example, in Safari, a double-fingered drag allows you to scroll within a web frame without affecting the page as a whole.

Holding. At times, you'll want to put your finger on the screen and leave it there until something happens. For example, holding brings up the spyglass while you're typing, and in Safari, it brings up URL previews.

Dragging. Drag your finger by pressing it to the screen and moving it in any direction before lifting it. Use dragging to scroll up and down in Safari and iPod (the application that plays your iTunes songs). Some applications offer an index on the right side, like the one shown for the iPod app in Figure 4-1. To use this index, drag along it until the item you want comes into view.

Figure 4-1. *The index bar (boxed) to the right of the iPod app*

Flicking. When you're dealing with long lists, you can give the list a quick flick. Place your finger onto the screen, and move it rapidly in one direction—up, down, left, or right. The display responds by scrolling quickly in the direction you've indicated. Use flicking to move quickly through your e-mail contacts list, for example.

> **TIP:** Flicking and dragging will not choose or activate items on the iPad's display. Try this yourself by dragging and flicking on the Home screen.

Stopping. During a scroll, press and hold your finger to the screen to stop scrolling. Apple's legal text provides a great place to practice flicking, dragging, and stopping. To get there, select Settings ➤ General ➤ About ➤ Legal. Have fun with its endless content of legalese that you can flick, drag, and stop to your heart's content. If you don't want to stop a scroll, just wait. The scroll will slow and stop by itself.

Swiping. To swipe your iPad, drag a finger from the left side of the screen toward the right. Swiping is used to unlock your iPad and to indicate you want to delete list items.

Pinching. On the iPad, you pinch by placing your thumb and forefinger on the screen with a space between them. Then, with your fingers touching the screen, move them together, as if you were pinching the screen. Pinching allows you to zoom out in many iPad programs, including Photos and Safari.

Unpinching: To unpinch, perform the pinch in reverse. Start with your thumb and forefinger placed together on your screen and, with the fingers touching the screen, spread them apart. Unpinching allows you to zoom into those same iPad applications where pinching zooms out.

Orientation

In most images of the iPad, you'll notice it's in portrait orientation with the physical Home button on the bottom bezel. However, there's actually no "right" way to hold the iPad. Apple designed the iPad as an orientation-agnostic device. What this means is you can hold the iPad in portrait or landscape mode and still interact with the device (Figure 4-2). As a matter of fact, you could completely flip the iPad upside down and still see what's on your screen as right side up.

Figure 4-2. *The iPad in portrait and landscape modes*

Although there's no right way to hold your iPad, some apps do offer additional features when you flip the iPad into landscape or portrait mode. For instance, if you are in Mail in portrait mode, you will see only the currently selected e-mail on your screen. To see a list of other e-mails, you need to select the inbox in a drop-down menu in the header bar. If, however, you rotate your iPad to landscape orientation, you'll be presented with a list of all your e-mails alongside the currently selected e-mail. We'll discuss orientation-specific features of various apps later in the book.

> **NOTE:** Although most apps will display in either orientation, some will not. Many games force you to use the iPad in landscape mode.

The Lock Screen

If you've just turned on your iPad or when your iPad has been idle for a while, it automatically locks, and the screen goes dark. When this happens, press the Home button. The locked iPad screen appears, as shown in Figure 4-3. To unlock your iPad, swipe the slider from the left to the right. The locked screen clears, and the Home screen springs into place.

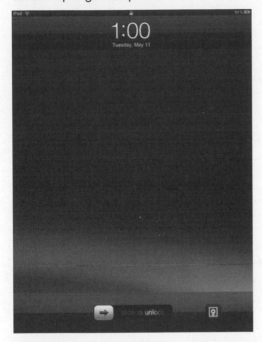

Figure 4-3. *The iPad lock screen*

You can set how long the iPad should wait before locking itself. Go to Settings ➤ General ➤ Auto-Lock, and choose the number of minutes you want your iPad to wait before locking. To disable autolocking, choose Never—and make sure you have a good power source available nearby. Autolocking is a power-saving feature. Disabling it means your iPad runs through its battery more rapidly.

For security, you can assign a passcode for your iPad. A *passcode* is just like a password except with numbers. Go to Settings ➤ General, and tap Passcode Lock and then Turn Passcode On to establish a new passcode. Your iPad prompts you to enter a four-number code, as shown in Figure 4-4.

Figure 4-4. *Setting your passcode*

Enter a code, or tap Cancel to quit without entering a code. After you enter the code, the iPad prompts you to reenter it and then enables further Passcode Lock settings. Those settings include setting how long the iPad needs to be idle before it's locked down, setting whether the picture frame will be displayed while the iPad is locked (more on the picture frame in Chapter 13), and setting whether all the data on the iPad should be erased after ten failed passcode attempts.

To test your passcode, click the Sleep/Wake button once (to put your iPad to sleep) and again (to wake it up). The passcode challenge screen greets you, as shown in Figure 4-5. Enter your passcode, and your iPad unlocks.

Figure 4-5. *The passcode lock screen*

To remove the passcode from your iPad, go back to the Passcode Lock settings screen (Figure 4-4). Choose Turn Passcode Off, and reenter the passcode one more time to confirm that it's really you making this request.

So, what happens if you lose your passcode or a mean-spirited colleague adds one to your iPad without telling you? You'll need to connect the iPad to your home computer and use iTunes to restore the iPad software. You can restore your iPad by selecting the Summary tab in iTunes and clicking Restore. For more information about restoring your iPad, see Chapter 2.

On the lock screen, to the right of the Slide to Unlock bar, you'll notice there is a small icon of a flower inside a box (see Figure 4-3). This is the Picture Frame button. Tap this to turn your iPad into a digital picture frame. The iPad will display your photographs one after the other on the screen until you choose to stop it by tapping the screen and tapping the Picture Frame button again or sliding the Slide to Unlock bar. You'll learn more about the picture frame function of the iPad and its settings in Chapter 13.

The lock screen can also perform one last function: controls for the iPad's music player. If music is playing on the iPad when the screen is locked, you can double-press the Home button to display music controls at the top of the screen. You'll learn more about these controls in Chapter 7.

The Home Screen

As discussed, when you turn on your iPad, you'll be presented with a lock screen. Depending on whether you have a passcode set on your iPad, either you'll swipe the Slide to Unlock bar and be presented with a numeric keypad or you'll be immediately taken to your iPad Home screen.

The iPad Home screen (see Figure 4-6) is the first page of apps you have on your iPad. Depending on how many apps you have, you may have several pages that will show in subsequent order when you swipe to the left.

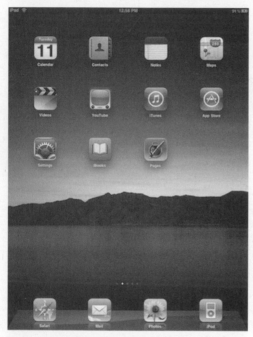

Figure 4-6. *The iPad Home screen*

TIP: Since the Home screen will be the first page you're taken to when you unlock your iPad, it makes sense to keep your most frequently used apps on the Home screen for easy access.

From the top of the screen down, you'll see the following elements:

Status bar. A thin, black bar runs along the top of your iPad Home screen. This status bar, shown in Figure 4-7, will display on every page of your iPad Home screen.

iPad 📶	12:58 PM	91 % 🔋

Figure 4-7. *The status bar*

The status bar can show many icons, but the standard layout you'll most likely see is the following: in the upper-left corner, you'll see the word *iPad* or *iPad 3G* (depending on which model you have), next to a Wi-Fi icon. The Wi-Fi icon shows you that you are connected to a wireless hotspot and also tells you the strength of your wireless signal. If you have an iPad 3G, you'll also be presented with the name of your 3G service carrier. In the middle of the status bar, you'll be presented with the current time. On the right corner of the status bar, you'll see a battery meter icon, next to the percentage of the battery remaining.

The status bar can also show other status icons. These include the following:

> *Airplane mode*: This is available on iPad Wi-Fi + 3G only. With airplane mode, you can't access the Internet or use Bluetooth. Other functions of your iPad are available.

> *E*: This stands for EDGE, a cellular data network that's slower than 3G. Many times E will appear when you are outside your 3G network. You can connect to the Internet using EDGE; just keep in mind it's slower than 3G (available on iPad Wi-Fi + 3G only).

> *o*: This little symbol stands for GPRS. If 3G is a race car and EDGE is a bicycle, GPRS is a turtle. Think 1994 dial-up slow (available on iPad Wi-Fi + 3G only).

> *Activity*: You'll see this icon whenever network activity (such as downloading data) is occurring on your iPad.

> *VPN*: This shows you are connected to a virtual private network (VPN). Many companies use VPNs so you can log in securely to their e-mail systems or private networks from your home.

> *Lock*: This padlock tells you your iPad is locked. You'll only ever see this icon on the lock screen.

> *Screen Rotation Lock*: This signifies that the screen rotation is locked. See Chapter 3 for more details.

> *Play*: This icon tells you a song, podcast, or audiobook is playing.

Apps page: Below the black status bar you'll see a series of app icons (see Figure 4-8). Each page can hold up to 20 apps in addition to the ones found in the Dock. As we'll discuss shortly, apps can be deleted and rearranged without the need to plug your iPad into iTunes.

Figure 4-8. *A page full of apps*

Page dots: Just above the app icons in the Dock, you'll see a series of small, white dots (see Figure 4-9). This series of dots begins with a tiny magnifying glass. We'll get to the magnifying glass shortly. The dots next to the magnifying glass signify the number of pages of apps you have on your Home screen. If you see five dots, that means you have five pages of apps. The dot that is the brightest signifies the location of the page you are currently on among all your pages of apps.

Figure 4-9. *The dots signify how many pages of apps you have.*

The dock: At the bottom of every page of the Home screen is a long, gray slate known as the *Dock* (see Figure 4-10). The Dock can contain up to six apps. No matter what page of apps you swipe to, the Dock will always show the same apps. The advantage of this is that if you have ten pages of apps but frequently check your e-mail, no matter what page of apps you're on, you'll always have quick access to your Mail app if you've placed it in the Dock.

Figure 4-10. *The Dock can hold between zero and six apps.*

NOTE: Unlike with some apps, no matter if you are holding your iPad vertically or horizontally, all the elements of the Home screen, including how you interact with it, always remain the same.

Manipulating the Home Screen

There are several ways you can interact with your iPad Home screen.

Navigating the apps pages: If you are on your first page of apps, swipe your finger to the left to reveal the next page of apps. Keep swiping your finger to the left to proceed navigating through all your app pages. To go back to the previous page of apps, simply swipe your finger to the right. Alternately, you can drag your finger to the left or right to go for the slow reveal of the next page of apps.

NOTE: The pages of the Home screen move only left or right. Unlike in many apps, they do not move up or down.

Launching apps: To launch an app, simply tap its icon. To return to the Home screen, press the round, physical Home button on the iPad's bezel.

Manipulating app icons: This is fun. Let's say you want to rearrange the icons on your Home screen but aren't near your computer to do it through the iPad's iTunes preferences page that we discussed in Chapter 2. Simply touch and hold any icon on the Home screen. After a few seconds, you see all the icons on the page start to jiggle like they're little mounds of Jell-O (see Figure 4-11). You can now remove your finger from the app. The icons will continue to jiggle. While jiggling, you can touch and hold any app icon and then simply drag it to a new position on the page. You can also drag icons to and from the Dock.

Figure 4-11. *Jiggling icons. In this example, the app Super 7 icon is being moved.*

You can go ahead and swipe to a new page of apps while they are all jiggling and rearrange the apps on that page. You can also transfer apps between pages. Simply touch and hold the app you'd like to move to a different page and drag it toward the side of the screen where the page is located. After a brief pause, the next page will automatically swipe over, and you can drop the app anywhere you want it. If that page is already full of 20 apps, the app in the lower-right corner will be pushed to the next page automatically.

> **NOTE:** If your Dock already has six apps on it, you must remove an app first before adding a new one to the Dock. Unlike with home pages, apps in the Dock will not automatically be pushed to a new page if you try to add a new app to a full Dock.

Removing apps: In Chapter 2 we told you how to remove apps from your iPad using iTunes. You can also remove an app from the iPad right on the iPad. To do this, simply touch and hold any icon on the Home screen and wait for them all to begin jiggling like they did when you were rearranging apps (see Figure 4-12).

Figure 4-12. *While an app is jiggling, tap the X to remove it.*

Notice how some of the apps have a little black and white *X* in their upper-left corner? Tapping that *X* will delete the app. Don't worry if you accidentally delete an app from your iPad. The apps are always store in your iTunes library, and you can reinstall them at any time.

> **NOTE:** You cannot delete any Apple apps that were factory installed on your iPad. You can, however, delete Apple apps that you installed yourself, such as Pages, iBooks, Numbers, and Keynote.

To delete an app, simply touch the *X*. A pop-up will appear on the screen asking if you want to delete the selected application. You'll also see a note saying deleting the app "will also delete all of its data," as shown in Figure 4-13. *This is important!* If you've created a new document inside the app or achieved a new high score on a game and delete the app before syncing it to iTunes, any new data associated with that app will be deleted. So, if you've created a new documents in Pages and decide to delete the Pages app, you new document will be forever lost if you don't sync your iPad before deleting Pages. Any documents the Pages app contained before the last sync will be available to you again if you resync the Pages app from iTunes.

Figure 4-13. *The deletion ratings and warning pop-ups*

> **NOTE:** If you delete an app accidentally and need it back right away but are not near your computer, you can simply use the iPad's built-in App Store app to download the app again. If it was a paid application, don't worry; you won't be charged a second time. Your iTunes account will know you've already paid for it.

If you are sure you want to delete an app, go ahead and tap the Delete button. If you've changed your mind, tap Cancel. If you tap Delete, you'll be presented with one last pop-up asking you to rate the app. You can touch to give it between one and five stars, or you can simply tap the No Thanks button. If you rate the app, your rating will appear along everyone else's in the iTunes Store.

When an app is deleted, all the other apps on the page will shift one position to fill the space of the deleted app.

Force Quitting an App

The iPad's Home screen allows you to launch any application with a single tap. When in an app, press the iPad's Home button to return to the Home screen at any time. If, for some reason, a program hangs and your iPad becomes unresponsive, you can press and hold the Home button for six to ten seconds to quit that program and return to the Home screen.

> **TIP:** A Back button appears in the upper-left corner of many iPad screens while inside an app. Tap this button to return to the previous screen in the app. This is different from pressing the Home button. The Back button moves you between screens within an app. The Home button leaves an app and returns you to the Home screen.

Spotlight Search

At this point, you've explored everything the iPad Home screen offers save one important feature. Earlier we mentioned a small gray magnifying glass icon next to the row of dots that represent the pages of apps that you have (see Figure 4-14). This magnifying glass icon represents the iPad's powerful search feature, named Spotlight.

Figure 4-14. *The Spotlight magnifying glass icon (circled) at the bottom of every home page*

To access Spotlight, simply swipe to the right of the first page of your Home screen. You'll be taken to a page that displays a small, white search field at the top with the words *Search iPad* in it. At the bottom of the page, you'll be presented with the built-in keyboard.

Simply begin typing any search query into the search field and the space between the search field, and the keyboard will begin populating with results (see Figure 4-15).

Figure 4-15. *The Spotlight search results page*

At this time, Spotlight isn't as powerful as it could be. If you own a Mac, you'll know that Spotlight is capable of searching in documents, not just by a document's file name. Currently, Spotlight is capable of searching only the following:

> *Contacts*: First, last, and company names.

> *Mail*: To, From, and Subject fields.

> *Calendar:* Event titles, invites, and locations.

> *iPod:* Song names, artists, and albums. Podcast and audiobook titles and names.

> *Notes:* Interestingly, although Spotlight can't search the text in the body of an e-mail message, it can search the text in a note from the Notes app.

To select a result, simply tap it, and you'll automatically be taken to the document or file in the app it's found in.

NOTE: If you have dozens and dozens of apps, instead of swiping through all the Home screen pages, you can simply go to Spotlight and search for the name of the app. When its icon appears, simply tap it to launch it.

Spotlight Settings

Go to Settings ➤ General ➤ Home, and you'll find a few options for Spotlight. Here you can choose to change a double-click of the iPad's Home button to automatically take you to the Spotlight search screen. Also, tapping the Search Results button will take you to a list of apps that Spotlight searches through. You can deselect apps to eliminate them from Spotlight search (for example, tap Music to deselect it, and names of songs won't show up when you're searching). You can also use the grip icon to the right of the screen to rearrange the order that search groupings appear in.

iPad Settings

The iPad has myriad settings allowing you to customize how your iPad works and looks. You can find all of these settings in the Settings app on your iPad Home screen (Figure 4-16).

Figure 4-16. *The Settings app icon*

Tap the Settings app, and on the left side of the screen, you'll see a list of settings for the iPad and any Apple iPad apps that shipped with the iPad (see Figure 4-17). Below those, you'll see an Apps heading. Any apps you've downloaded from the iTunes Store will appear here if they have customizable settings. To select an app's setting, tap the name of the app.

Figure 4-17. *The general settings selections*

Although we'll go into greater depth about Apple's built-in app's individual settings throughout the book, for now let's get acquainted with the iPad's General settings.

About: This shows you how many songs, videos, photos, and applications you have on your iPad. It also shows you your iPad's total storage capacity and how much you have left. Your iPad's OS version number, model, and serial numbers can be found here, along with your Wi-Fi and Bluetooth IDs. At the very bottom, you'll see links to Apple's legal and regulatory documentation.

Sounds: This area gives you a slider to adjust the volume on your iPad and also enables you to turn on or off sounds for e-mail, calendar alerts, lock sounds, and keyboard clicks.

Network: This displays your network settings. See Chapter 3 for details.

Bluetooth: This allows you to turn the iPad's Bluetooth signal on or off. If you aren't using any Bluetooth devices with your iPad, keep Bluetooth turned off. It'll save you battery life.

Location Services: If this is turned on, any apps that can automatically find your location (like the Maps app) will be able to do so.

Auto-Lock and Passcode Lock: As we talked about earlier, this is where you configure your lock settings.

Restrictions: If you share your iPad among your family or buy one for your children, you may want to limit what they can do on it. The Restrictions settings will let you limit access to Safari, YouTube, and the iTunes Store app. In addition, you can restrict users from installing new apps and using location services. You can also choose what content you want allowed on the iPad. Settings include restricting In-App purchases and limiting access to movies, music, TV shows, and apps that surpass your chosen ratings.

Home: The settings under Home allow you to choose whether double-clicking the iPad's Home button will take you to the Home screen, Spotlight search, or the iPod app. You can also choose whether to show iPod controls while playing music. This is also where you choose Spotlight settings that we mentioned earlier.

Date & Time: This allows you to select a 24-hour clock as well as set your time zone and set the date and time manually.

Keyboard: This is where you control all your keyboard settings. We'll go through them in the next section.

International: Use this settings pane to select your preferred language and region formatting for addresses and phone numbers.

Accessibility: This is where the settings for the sight and hearing impaired are. We'll go into these in detail later in the chapter.

Battery Percentage: Choose whether to display the percentage of battery power you have left next to the icon of the battery in the status bar.

Reset: Reset All Settings lets you set your iPad's settings to factory default. Erase All Content and Settings works like Reset All Settings but also erases all your personal data. This section also allows you to reset your network, keyboard, Home screen layout, and location settings to the iPad's factory defaults.

The Keyboard

Like the touch keyboard on your iPhone? You haven't seen anything yet. Using the iPad's keyboard for the first time is nothing short of an epiphany when you realize what a large-screen, Multi-Touch device is capable of.

The keyboard, shown in Figure 4-18, will display automatically when you are in any app that needs to have text input. It is important to note that the software keyboard will not display if the iPad is paired to an external Bluetooth keyboard. (Refer to Chapter 3 for Bluetooth pairing.)

Figure 4-18. *The iPad's Multi-Touch keyboard*

For this section, we'll look at using the onscreen keyboard in Apple's Notes app that comes on every iPad.

Open Notes, and click the + button in the upper-right corner to create a new note. At the bottom of your iPad's screen, you'll see the keyboard automatically appear (see Figure 4-19).

Figure 4-19. *The keyboard appears at the bottom of the iPad's screen.*

NOTE: Using the keyboard in portrait orientation gives you a smaller keyboard but more space to see what you're typing onscreen. If you switch to landscape orientation, you'll have a larger keyboard but less space to see what you've typed. Play around to see what works best for you.

Though Apple has outdone itself in designing the iPad's keyboard, many people still think it's the hardest thing to get used to on their new iPad. Making the switch to a touch screen keyboard can be difficult, but it does get much better over a relatively short amount of time. The keyboard gets easier to use the more you use it, not just because you get used to it, but because it has a secret.

The secret is that the keyboard, shown in Figure 4-18, is smart—so smart that it corrects for a lot of typos and misaligned fingers. It automatically capitalizes the start of sentences. It suggests corrections for misspelled words. It uses predictive technology to make it easier to hit the right keys. So, within a few weeks, you'll master the keyboard's quirks. You can also use Apple's iPad case (mentioned in Chapter 1) to give the iPad a better angle for typing. A flap folds out from the back of the case and forms a wedge that tilts the iPad at a comfortable angle so you can type and look at the screen above the keyboard at the same time. The angle of the case makes it easier to avoid mistakes touch-typists make on the iPad's onscreen keyboard, namely, resting palms and fingers on the screen.

Here are some of the key technologies that make the iPad keyboard work:

Dictionary. The iPad has a built-in dictionary that learns frequently used words as you type (see Figure 4-20). It also picks up names and spellings from your address book. This means it gets better at guessing your intentions as it builds its data.

> The iPad knew I wanted to spell my friend's rather uncommon name because she is in my address book. Her name is priy|
> > Priyanka ×

Figure 4-20. *An example of the iPad learning words and names from your contacts*

Automatic correction. As you type, the iPad looks for words similar to what you're typing and guesses them, placing the guess just below the word you're typing (see Figure 4-21). To accept the suggestion, just tap the spacebar, and the full word is inserted.

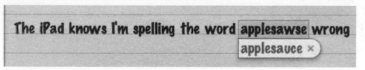

> The iPad knows I'm spelling the word applesawse wrong
> > applesauce ×

Figure 4-21. *An example of the iPad's autocorrection features*

Spell check. If you do spell a word wrong or the iPad doesn't recognize it, you'll see a red line appear below the word. When you tap the word, one or more alternate spellings will appear above it (see Figure 4-22). Simply tap the right word, and it inserts itself into the text.

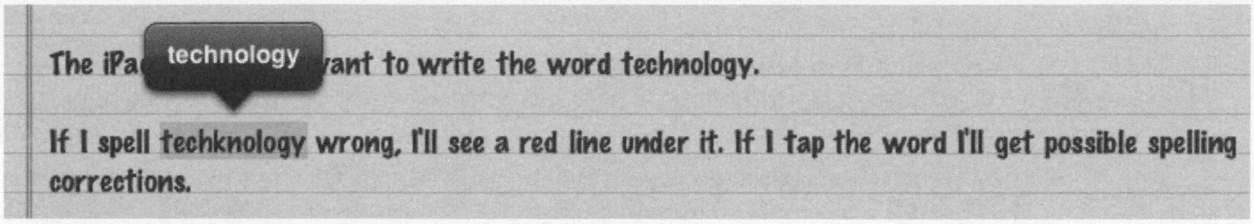

The iPad technology want to write the word technology.

If I spell techknology wrong, I'll see a red line under it. If I tap the word I'll get possible spelling corrections.

Figure 4-22. *An example of the iPad's spell-check feature*

Predictive mapping. The iPad uses its dictionary to predict which word you're about to type. It then readjusts the keyboard response zones to make it easier for you to hit the right letters. Likely letters get bigger tap zones; unlikely letters get smaller ones.

More Keyboards

Thought the iPad had only one keyboard? Think again. It has more than a dozen (in different languages). It also has two other keyboards you'll frequently access from the primary keyboard on your screen.

On the primary keyboard (shown earlier in Figure 4-18), you'll notice the comma, exclamation point, question mark, and period next to the Shift key. Below that is the *.?123 key* (in some applications it's the @123 key). Tapping the .?123 key automatically switches your QWERTY keyboard into a numeric keyboard with further punctuation symbols, an "undo" option, and another keyboard modifier key labeled *#+=* (see Figure 4-23).

TIP: You don't need to use the "undo" button to undo something. You can simply shake your iPad. (Not too hard! You don't want to look like you've lost your marbles!) An undo pop-up will appear on the screen giving you the option of undoing your last action or canceling the undo.

Figure 4-23. *The.?123 keyboard*

Tapping the #+= key takes you to a third keyboard with more punctuation and a "redo" button (see Figure 4-24). Redo, if the app supports it, will repeat the last action performed. So if you've copied and pasted text, tapping the redo button will paste the text again.

Figure 4-24. *The #+= keyboard*

Getting Started

When you're new to the iPad, start by typing slowly. Typing with the iPad in your hands can be difficult because of the device's size. For optimal typing experience, place the iPad on a table or prop it in your lap. At first, you may be typing by using your index fingers on each hand, but the more you use it, the more you'll typing as you do on a physical keyboard. Whatever method you use, make sure to go at a pace that allows you to keep track of what you're typing and make corrections as you go. Here are a few typing how-tos:

Summoning the keyboard: To open the keyboard, tap in any editable text area.

Dismissing the keyboard: To make the iPad's keyboard go away, tap the bottom-right key (you can see the key in Figures 4-18, 4-23, and 4-24). It's the button with the picture of a keyboard and a down arrow on it. To get the keyboard back, simply tap in any editable text area again.

Accepting or rejecting automatic corrections: The iPad displays suggested corrections just below the word you're typing, as shown earlier in Figure 4-21. To accept the suggestion, tap the spacebar. (You don't need to finish typing the word; the iPad puts it in there for you.) To decline the correction, tap the word itself. The iPad will not make a substitution, even when you press the spacebar.

Using the spyglass: While you're typing, you can adjust the cursor by using the iPad's built-in spyglass feature, as shown in Figure 4-25. Hold your finger somewhere in the text area until the spyglass appears. Then use the magnified view to drag the cursor exactly where you need it.

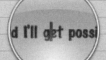

Priyanka is my friend.

The iPad can guess I want to write the word technology.

If I spell techknology wrong, I'll see a red line under it. If I tap the word I'll get possible spelling corrections.

Figure 4-25. *The spyglass gives you pinpoint precision for cursor placement.*

NOTE: If you are going to be doing a lot of typing on your iPad (like writing a book, for instance), you may want to look into getting the iPad Keyboard Dock or the Apple Bluetooth keyboard we told you about in Chapter 3. A physical keyboard turns the iPad into more of a traditional computer that you are used to. Plus, if you are a touch-typist, you'll probably type much faster on a physical keyboard because you can feel its presses and hear its clicks. You aren't limited to an Apple Bluetooth keyboard either. Several third-party keyboards work with the iPad. Contact the manufacturer to find out what their Bluetooth keyboards do.

iPad Typing Tricks

Once you get the hang of the keyboard, the iPad offers several other ways to make typing easier. This section describes a few of these handy iPad typing tricks.

Contractions

When you want to type a contraction like *can't* or *shouldn't*, don't bother putting in the apostrophe. The iPad is smart enough to guess that *cant* is *can't* (Figure 4-26). Of course, if you're typing about the British Thieves' language, make sure to tap the word to decline the change from the noun to the contraction.

When you're typing in a word like *we'll*, where the uncontracted *well* is a common word, add an extra *l*. The iPad corrects *welll* to *we'll* and *shelll* to *she'll*.

Figure 4-26. *"Cant" becomes "Can't."*

TIP: Other contraction tricks include *itsa*, which gets corrected to *it's*, and *weree*, which gets corrected to *we're*.

Punctuation

When at the end of a sentence, tap the punctuation key, then tap the item you want to use (such as a question mark or period), and finally tap the spacebar. The iPad is smart enough to recognize the end of a sentence and put you back in alphabet mode. During normal typing, you can also double-tap the spacebar to add a period followed by a space. This double-tap trick is controlled in your settings via Settings ➤ General ➤ Keyboard ➤ "." Shortcut.

Accents

Tap and hold any keyboard letter to view inflected versions of that letter. For example, tapping and holding *e* presents the options of adding e, é, or ê (among other accents), as shown in Figure 4-27. This shortcut makes it much easier to type foreign words. To select a non-English keyboard, go to Settings ➤ General ➤ International ➤ Keyboards and choose from your iPad's long list of foreign-language variations.

NOTE: At the time of writing, there are no right-to-left settings for Arabic or Hebrew. However, there is a $0.99 app called Hebrew Keyboard II for the iPad that allows you to type into a text entry field using a Hebrew software keyboard. You can then copy and paste the text into any other app on the iPad. Sure, it's an extra step, but until Apple gets around to supporting right-to-left languages, it's better than nothing.

Figure 4-27. *iPad handles accents like a pro.*

Caps Lock

To enable the Caps Lock function, go to Settings ➤ General ➤ Keyboard Preferences. When this function is enabled, you can double-tap the Shift key to toggle the lock on and off.

Word Deletion

When you press and hold the Delete key, the iPad starts off by deleting one letter and then the next. But if you hold it for longer than about a line of text, it switches to word deletion and starts removing entire words at a time.

Autocapitalization

Autocapitalization means the iPad automatically capitalizes the word at the beginning of a sentence. So, you can type *the day has begun*, and the iPad is smart enough to capitalize *the*, as in *The day has begun*. This means you don't need to worry about pressing the Shift key at the beginning of every sentence or even when you type *i*, because *i went to the park* becomes *I went to the park*. Enable or disable autocapitalization in Settings ➤ General ➤ Keyboard Preferences.

Copy and Paste

Apple has created an easy and intuitive way to select a word or block of words, copy them, and then paste them into another location.

Let's copy some text from a web page in iPad's Safari web browser. Before you can copy a word, you'll need to select it. To do that, press and hold your finger over a word. A black contextual menu will pop up that gives you the Select and Select All options. Select will highlight just the single word. Select All will highlight all the words on the page. No matter which you choose, you'll be presented with a grab point at the beginning and end of the selected text (see Figure 4-28). These grab points allow you to adjust which text is selected.

Figure 4-28. *Grab points allow you to select a single word, a sentence, or a whole paragraph to be copied.*

> **NOTE:** If you've selected text to copy in an editable document, you'll see a contextual menu that says Cut, Copy, or Paste. Selecting Cut will remove the text. Selecting Copy will copy it, and if you already have text copied, you'll be able to paste it over your current selection.

Once you have selected your text, you'll see another contextual menu that says Copy. Tapping Copy will copy the text and make it available in any app that support text input.

Now let's go back to the note in the Notes app. To paste the text you copied from Safari into your note, simply press and hold your finger on the screen until the spyglass pops up. Use the spyglass to adjust the cursor to the location where you want to insert the copied text and let go. You'll see another contextual menu pop up that gives you three options: Select, Select All, and Paste. Tap Paste, and your copied text will be instantly inserted (Figure 4-29).

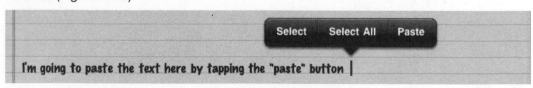

Figure 4-29. *Simply tap Paste, and your text is inserted automatically.*

Undo and Redo

As mentioned earlier, the iPad's keyboard sports undo and redo buttons. Tapping the undo button undoes the last action you performed. So if you've copied and pasted text, tapping the undo button will unpaste the text but leave it copied on your clipboard. Remember that you can also shake your iPad to display an undo pop-up that will ask you whether you want to undo the last action you performed.

Redo, if the app supports it, will repeat the last action performed. So if you've copied and pasted text, tapping the redo buttoniPad typing tricks.

 will paste the text again.

Accessibility

Apple wanted to make sure everyone could use the iPad as easily as possible. To that end, Apple offers accessibility features to help people with disabilities use the iPad. We briefly touched on the iPad's accessibility options in the iPad iTunes settings pane in Chapter 2. The iPad features more accessibility options than the ones you see in the settings pane, however. To see all the accessibility options, tap the Settings icon on the iPad's Home screen. Under General settings, tap Accessibility. You'll see the Accessibility settings slide onto the screen (see Figure 4-30). Let's go through these settings one by one.

Figure 4-30. *The Accessibility settings*

VoiceOver

With VoiceOver turned on, the user can simply touch the screen to hear a description of what is beneath his finger. They can then double-tap to select the item. With VoiceOver enabled, the iPad will speak when the user has a new e-mail message and can even read the e-mail to the user.

Zoom

Zoom allows those hard of seeing to magnify their entire screen. This is different from the standard pinch and zoom features of the iPad's regular software. Accessibility Zoom will magnify everything on the screen, allowing the user to zoom into even the smallest of buttons. When this option is selected, the user can double-tap any part of the iPad's screen with three fingers to automatically zoom in 200 percent. When the screen is zoomed in, you must drag or flick it with three fingers. Also, when you go to a new screen, zoom will always return to the top middle of the screen.

White on Black

For some people with seeing difficulties, inverting the color of a computer screen so it resembles a photographic negative allows them to read text better. Turning White on Black does this.

Mono Audio

With Mono Audio selected, the stereo sounds of the left and right speakers will be combined into a mono (single) signal. This option lets users who have a hearing impairment in one ear hear the entire sound signal with the other ear.

Speak Auto-Text

With this option selected, any autocorrection text (like the spell-check pop-ups that appear when you are typing) will be spoken aloud.

Triple-Click Home

If you are sharing an iPad in a house with someone with disabilities, selecting this option will allow users, by triple-clicking the iPad's physical Home button, to quickly toggle VoiceOver or White on Black on or off (Figure 4-31). You can also set it so triple-clicking the Home button causes a pop-up to appear onscreen asking what accessibility feature to turn on.

Figure 4-31. *The Accessibility Options pop-up window*

NOTE: With the exception of the triple-click Home feature, all of these accessibility settings can also be configured from within the iPad iTunes settings pane on the Summary tab (see Chapter 2).

Summary

This chapter explored all the ways you can interact with your iPad, from taps to buttons to pinches. You read about the touch screen and how you can communicate with it. You discovered how to access your Home screen, how to lock it, and how to rearrange its icons. You explored your iPad's General settings, and you learned tips and tricks to using the iPad's virtual keyboard and setting accessibility options. In short, you were introduced to all the basic ways you and your iPad can communicate with each other. Here are a few key lessons for you to carry away with you:

- Build up your working iPad interaction vocabulary. You will be surprised how often one of the rarer gestures, like the two-fingered tap, can prove useful.

- If you are using your iPad in an area where your data's security is an issue, be sure to set a passcode lock.

- Spotlight is a powerful search tool on the iPad and offers you another way to quickly launch your apps.

- The iPad supports more than a dozen keyboard languages as well as physical hardware keyboards.

- Don't worry about typing perfectly on the iPad. Its smart keyboard will correct most of your mistakes automatically.

- Just because you have a disability doesn't mean you can't use the iPad. The iPad has many accessibility features to help the those with sight or hearing issues.

Chapter 5

Connecting to the Internet

Although your iPad could theoretically be used as an unconnected computer with no links to the outside world, it's really designed to be an Internet tool. It has built-in Wi-Fi or Wi-Fi + 3G connectivity, and most of the default apps are useless without having an Internet connection of some sort.

Without the Internet, you'd have no need for Mail to send and receive messages, and there would be no reason for the Safari web browser. You wouldn't be able to pull up maps, YouTube would just be a bland icon taking up space on your Home screen, and you couldn't buy apps from the App Store, books from the iBookstore, or music, movies, and videos from iTunes. Facebook and Twitter? Forget about them without that Internet connection.

Fortunately, Apple makes it simple for you to connect to the Internet. In this chapter, we'll tell you how to make and troubleshoot Internet connections through Wi-Fi and 3G and discuss an alternative to the built-in 3G.

Connecting with Wi-Fi

Wi-Fi is the common name for wireless networking based on the IEEE 802.11 standard. Although Wi-Fi has its roots in the early 1990s, it has really taken off in the past ten years, with Wi-Fi access points now available in many public places such as hotels, libraries, restaurants, and even buses and airplanes.

For many people, Wi-Fi access points were a godsend for home networking because it meant that computers and printers could be connected to each other without the expense and inconvenience of installing cabling. In most cases, a Wi-Fi router is attached directly to a home cable or DSL Internet modem to provide wireless Internet to any computer within range.

Your iPad supports Wi-Fi connections under the 802.11a/b/g/n standards. It's not necessary to know what each of these standards means, other than the maximum raw data rate (the speed at which data is pumped to your iPad) increases with each successive standard. The iPad and Wi-Fi router will communicate with each other based on the highest common standard, so if your Wi-Fi router supports only 802.11b, the rate at which the two devices will talk will be limited to 802.11b speeds. Likewise, if you have one of the newest Apple AirPort Extreme Wi-Fi routers, your iPad communicates with it using the fast 802.11n standard.

Authentication and Encryption

One important factor for all Wi-Fi networks is the use of encryption. Encrypted networks require that a password or passphrase be entered when joining the network for the first time. The password not only authenticates your iPad to the network, essentially making sure that you are allowed to use that network, but is used as a key to encrypt any data that is transferred between your iPad and the router.

Both authentication and encryption are important for any wireless network. Setting up authentication on your home or office network ensures that no unauthorized person can use your wireless network without your permission. This is important, since providing access to your Internet connection to anyone who happens to be in the area can be considered a breach of the terms of service with many Internet service providers. In addition, if anyone commits a crime from a computer connected to your wireless network with or without your knowledge, you can be held accountable.

Likewise, encryption makes it difficult for hackers to intercept and decode transactions between your iPad and any other computer. This is extremely important when you're performing monetary transactions. There are three major types of encryption that are in place on most home, office, and public Wi-Fi networks at this time: WEP, WPA, and WPA2. WPA2 is the successor to the WPA encryption standard and is considered (when used with a strong passphrase) to be extremely secure.

Why are we discussing authentication and encryption in a book about iPads? Well, if you're unfamiliar with Wi-Fi networks, the topic will definitely come up when you try to connect your iPad to the networks.

Setting Up Wi-Fi

Your iPad isn't going to automatically connect to the Internet the moment you turn it on. Why? Apple wants you to set up syncing with iTunes first, and that's always done through a USB connection to another computer. Once you've completed the setup, you're free to get connected, and for most people, that initial connection is done with Wi-Fi.

You'll need to know your network password or passphrase, as well as the name of the network to which you want to connect. Knowing the name can be very important if you live in an apartment building where there are many wireless networks within range. A pop-up appears on the screen asking you to enter the network password, and once you've entered it correctly, you are connected to the network.

In Figure 5-1, there is only one network named Rubyshouse that is within range of the iPad. The lock icon signifies that you need to enter a password or passphrase before you can connect to the network, while the AirPort icon (the fan-shaped icon to the right of the lock) indicates the relative signal strength of the network.

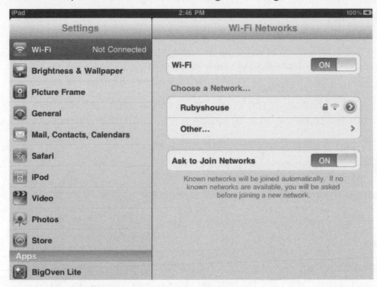

Figure 5-1. *In the Settings app on an iPad with Wi-Fi only, the top button is for changing your Wi-Fi settings.*

To enter the password and join the network, tap the network name, and a password screen appears. Type in your password or phrase, and then tap the Join button on the iPad's virtual keyboard. If you've entered the password correctly, the network name turns blue, and a check mark appears next to it indicating that it is the selected network. If you didn't enter the correct password, you'll see an error message similar to the one in Figure 5-2. Tap the Dismiss button, and try again.

Figure 5-2. *It looks like somebody mistyped the password here. Tap Dismiss to try it again.*

If your iPad Wi-Fi is not enabled, you can turn it on by going to Settings ➤ Wi-Fi and sliding the button marked Off so that it displays On.

Your iPad remembers networks that you've joined so that you don't have to reenter network information every time you move to a new wireless network. If there is no known network nearby, either you have to manually select the new network or you'll be asked if you want to join a new network. What's the difference? It all depends on whether the Ask to Join Networks button is set to On. If it isn't, you have to manually select the network, and if it is, your iPad will ask you whether you want to join the new network.

When you are connected to a Wi-Fi network, the Wi-Fi icon in the status bar displays your connection strength. More full bars (up to five) indicate a stronger connection.

Troubleshooting Wi-Fi Connection Issues

There are some common issues that new iPad owners may run into, so we'll discuss them here.

No Network Name Displayed

In this case, the network may be closed or private, meaning that the service set identifier (SSID) or network name has been set as hidden. To connect to the network, you'll need to tap the Other button shown earlier in Figure 5-1, which displays the screen in Figure 5-3.

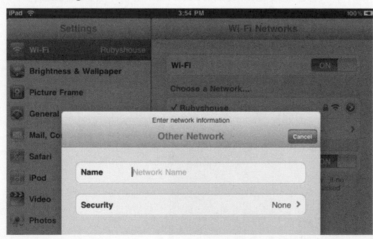

Figure 5-3. *Entering information about hidden networks is useful when using iPads in corporate environments.*

Ask your network administrator the name of the network, and enter that in the Name field. It's also a good idea to ask them what type of security has been set up on the network, since you'll need to choose that by tapping the Security button (Figure 5-4).

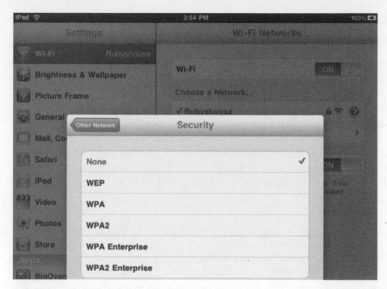

Figure 5-4. *The iPad uses settings to define the type and level of encryption used to keep your data from prying eyes.*

Once you've entered the network name and security type, you'll be asked for the password or passphrase and can continue to connect to the network.

What do these acronyms stand for? Wired Equivalent Privacy (WEP) is an aging method of securing wireless networks. Then why is WEP available on the nice, new iPad? It exists primarily for the benefit of people who haven't upgraded their Wi-Fi access points to newer, more secure technology.

WPA stands for Wi-Fi Protected Access, another aging security technology. WPA Enterprise was a standard encryption algorithm with additions that made it more "bulletproof" for corporate use.

If at all possible, you should use WPA2 or WPA2 Enterprise security to ensure that your data is protected in transit. WPA2 is the most secure existing Wi-Fi security method at this time. It's recommended that you use a truly random passphrase of 13 or more characters for even better security, although it may be more useful to just use a longer—but more memorable—passphrase.

What do we mean by memorable? Something that *you* can easily remember but would be very difficult for someone else to guess. For example, a passphrase of "ilovemydogfredandhesmyfavoritepet" is much easier to remember than "X1F39%@233.abc$@#@."

The Join Button in the Enter Password Screen Is Grayed Out

This means that the password you're entering is too short for the type of security enabled on the network. Make sure you have right password, and then try again.

You've Just Set Up the Wi-Fi Router and Don't Know the Password

Some Wi-Fi routers have default passwords. Either contact the manufacturer's web site to find out what the default password is or change the password to something you can remember. The latter solution is recommended in order to maintain security on your network.

There's Only a Single Bar of Signal Strength, or You Can't See Your Wi-Fi Network

Wi-Fi access points and routers have a limited amount of range, particularly when there are concrete walls, walls with a lot of wiring or piping in them, or microwave ovens nearby. Either move closer to the Wi-Fi access point or try to avoid the sources of interference.

You're at a Public Spot and a Web Page Is Asking You to Sign On to the Network

This is quite normal with public Wi-Fi networks, including the AT&T wireless hotspots in U.S. Starbucks locations. If you're in a location that requires you to pay for Wi-Fi, a login screen may appear into which you'll have to enter subscription information or purchase access time. If it does not appear, open the Safari web browser on your iPad, and the screen should appear.

Your Wi-Fi Connection Is Showing Five Bars, but You're Not Connecting to the Internet

Make sure that you are connecting to the correct Wi-Fi network and not another one nearby. If you are trying to connect to the proper Wi-Fi network, then the connection from your Wi-Fi access point or router to your cable or DSL modem may be down. If that connection looks fine, then your Internet service provider may be having issues. You can test this by checking other computers at your location to see whether they're able to use the Internet.

All the Wi-Fi Networks Have the Same Name

This is more common than you'd imagine. Many people purchase Wi-Fi access points or routers and never change the name from the factory-set one. In heavily populated areas, it's not uncommon to see a number of networks named "Linksys." If you're in this situation, contact the router manufacturer for information on uniquely naming your Wi-Fi network.

None of These Solutions Have Worked

It may be time to reset the network settings on your iPad. To reset network settings, tap Settings ➤ General ➤ Reset ➤ Reset Network Settings. This will restart your iPad, and when it comes back up, all saved networks, Wi-Fi passwords, and other settings will be gone. Try to locate and join the network again.

If you can't connect to your network, then try to see whether your iPad can connect to a publicly available network. For instance, if you have an Apple Store close by, try connecting to their network. At least if that doesn't work, you can always confer with the Apple Genius Bar at the store.

Special Wi-Fi Settings

For most people, the default Wi-Fi settings work perfectly. However, there may be situations where you are connecting to a network that requires special settings. In this case, you may be asked to change those settings on your iPad.

You can access special Wi-Fi settings by going to Settings ➤ Wi-Fi and then tapping the blue arrow icon to the right of the network name. A much more detailed listing of network settings appears (Figure 5-5).

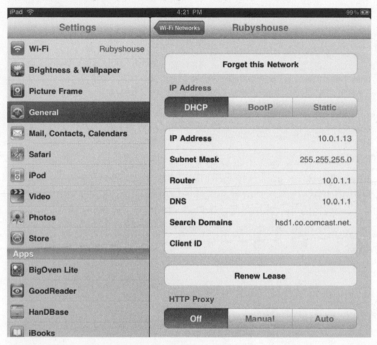

Figure 5-5. *You may never need to change or view your network settings. This is where you can control those settings in those cases where it's necessary.*

The first thing you may be asked to change is the way in which your iPad receives an Internet Protocol (IP) address. Most of the time, that's done through something called Dynamic Host Configuration Protocol (DHCP). When your iPad is set up to get a network address using DHCP, it asks for an address when it joins a network and is then given a "lease" that lasts a certain amount of time. That lease usually renews automatically. If you ever need to renew the DHCP lease manually, there's a button on the DHCP settings screen you can tap to do that (Renew Lease).

Another way to get an IP address is through Bootstrap Protocol, or BootP (Figure 5-6). The BootP tab shows information that may need to be changed for your iPad to receive an address from a pool of addresses registered on a configuration server.

Figure 5-6. *The BootP configuration display*

Finally, some networks require a fixed, or *static*, IP address (Figure 5-7). In this case, you're usually given a static IP address, a subnet mask, and router and DNS server addresses to enter into the appropriate fields in order to connect to the network.

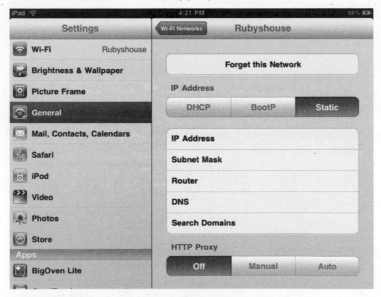

Figure 5-7. *Static IP settings on the iPad*

On all the screens shown previously, there are three buttons for HTTP Proxy. A *proxy server* is a computer system that acts as an intermediary between your computer and some other server. Many companies, for instance, require all web traffic from computers to pass through a proxy server to log or audit usage.

Connecting with 3G

Earlier in this book, we described the difference between the two primary models of iPad: Wi-Fi only and Wi-Fi + 3G. In this section, we'll show how to set up a connection to the Internet using an iPad Wi-Fi + 3G model and an AT&T 3G data plan.

3G is a family of mobile telecommunications standards allowing simultaneous voice and data services. Apple has chosen to follow the Global System for Mobile Communications (GSM) standard in its telephony products, the iPhone family, and the iPad Wi-Fi + 3G. This standard predominates world mobile telephone systems, which means that iPhones and iPads with 3G capabilities can be used worldwide, although international data roaming is usually quite expensive.

3G bandwidth is generally less than that of Wi-Fi, but 3G is valuable because the data service is available almost anywhere there is a 3G system in place. Wi-Fi is limited to short-range, high-bandwidth connections; 3G is wide-range but lower-bandwidth connections.

What can you do with a 3G connection? A lot. On a 3G-equipped iPad, you're able to browse the Internet with fairly fast response, send photos and even small movies to friends via e-mail, watch YouTube videos, and (as you'll find in Chapter 8) purchase and download apps, music, and books.

The mobility you gain with 3G service comes at a price. You need to sign up for a cellular data plan, which in the United States means that you're contracting with AT&T for that service. AT&T has two plans available—250MB of data during a 30-day period for $14.99 or $25 per month for 2GB data.

If the majority of your iPad use is going to be in an office or home with Wi-Fi service and you intend to use your 3G service only for occasional e-mails on the road, then you'll probably be good with the 250MB plan. For many iPad users, that's not going to be enough. Fortunately, AT&T's plans can change from month to month, so if you find that 250MB is too limiting, you can sign up for the 2GB plan.

To determine what your 3G usage is at any time after you've signed up for a limited monthly plan, go to Settings ➤ Cellular Data ➤ View Account. This information, as well as the reminders that are sent out by carriers when you're nearing a data usage limit, can be very helpful in keeping an eye on how many megabytes you're actually consuming.

Setting Up 3G

There's a very easy way to tell you have a Wi-Fi + 3G iPad in your hands without looking at the box; when you turn it on, the left side of the status bar shows the name of the 3G carrier and the signal strength at your location (Figure 5-8).

Figure 5-8. *The iPad with Wi-Fi + 3G shows the carrier name and signal strength, as well as the network type (3G, EDGE) on the left side of the status bar.*

Setting up your 3G data plan is fast and only requires a credit card. With your iPad turned on, tap Settings ➤ Cellular Data. If 3G isn't turned on, sliding the Cellular Data button to On activates the built-in radio. If no Cellular Data Account has been set up, you're asked to choose a plan and sign up for the service right on your iPad (Figure 5-9).

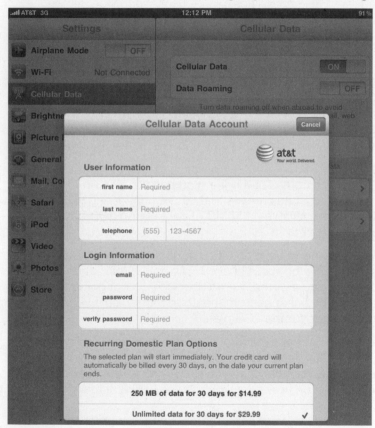

Figure 5-9. *Signing up for a cellular data account on the AT&T Wireless network in the United States.*

Enter your first and last name, as well as a telephone number at which you can be reached. This should also be the phone number that you have given your credit card company as your primary contact number. You need an active e-mail account—it's used as a login—and will need to select a password. Next, tap your choice of data plan. As you're filling out the onscreen form, you can tap the Next button above the keyboard to scroll to different locations on the form.

The next information required is payment and billing information (Figure 5-10). Tap your choice of credit card (Visa, MasterCard, Discover, or American Express in the United States; debit cards are not accepted), and then enter the credit card number, the name as it appears on the card, the expiration date, the three- or four-digit security code, and your billing address. If the address for where you'll be using the service is the same as your billing address, tap the "Service address is same as billing address" button; otherwise, you'll need to fill in the service address separately.

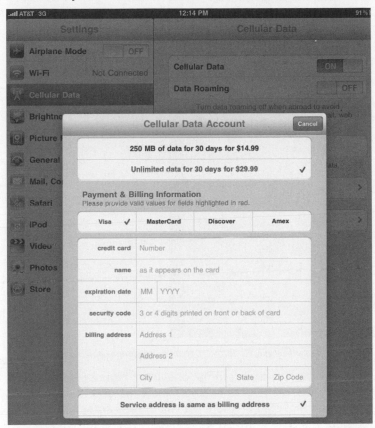

Figure 5-10. *Entering payment and billing information, and selecting the data plan you want to subscribe to*

Moving along through the form, you'll come to the terms of service (Figure 5-11). Read through them if you desire, and then tap the Agree button to move through the process.

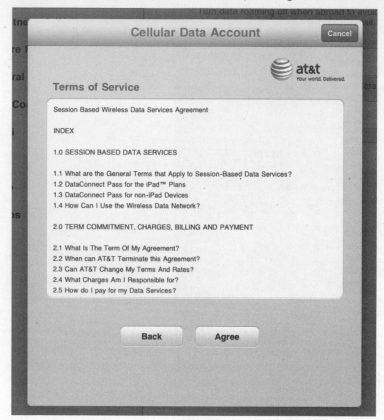

Figure 5-11. *The terms of service explain the month-by-month data plan that you're signing up for with AT&T.*

Next, you have the opportunity to add a one-time international plan (Figure 5-12). As you can see, these plans are very expensive. Make sure that you know the countries you're traveling to are supported by international plans—there's a link on this screen that displays the list of countries. Select the date that you want to start your international plan, and then tap the Done button. If you're not going to be traveling abroad soon, don't tap any of the plans, and just tap Done to continue.

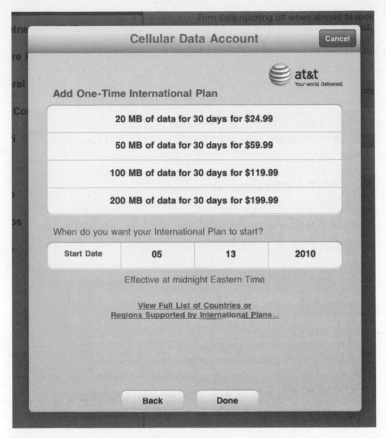

Figure 5-12. *If you'll be traveling soon, you may want to sign up for a 30-day international data plan through AT&T. You can also sign up at a later date.*

After a few minutes, a notification (Figure 5-13) appears on the iPad display telling you the data plan has been activated. That means that you're all set for wandering around town with your iPad, free from the restrictions of needing to be near a Wi-Fi access point (of course, if you're a paying AT&T customer, you get free Wi-Fi at any AT&T hotspot).

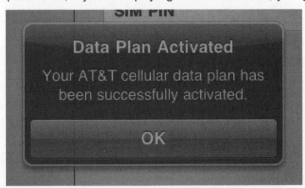

Figure 5-13. *Congratulations! Your iPad is now ready to connect to the world through 3G.*

Data Roaming

If you're using your iPad internationally, it's a very smart idea to know what cellular company or companies your international plan uses and to turn off data roaming. If data roaming is turned on, your device may connect to a cellular carrier that does not have an agreement with AT&T, in which case you'll be charged an even higher rate.

Determining the best international carrier to use in any country is a two-step process. First take a look at the AT&T list of its international roaming partners at http://att.com/ dataconnectglobal (Figure 5-14).

Roam Zone for Discounted Rate Plans

This information applies to discounted rate plans for Laptop Cards (DataConnect Global), PDAs, Smartphones and iPhones.

Country	Carriers	Technology	Frequency
ALBANIA	Vodafone	GSM/GPRS/EDGE	900/1800
ANGUILLA	Cable and Wireless	GSM/GPRS/EDGE	850
	Digicel	GSM/GPRS	900/1900
ANTIGUA and BARBUDA	Cable and Wireless	GSM/GPRS	850
	Digicel	GSM/GPRS	900
ARGENTINA	Telefonica Moviles	GSM/GPRS /EDGE/UMTS	GSM/GPRS/EDGE 1900; UMTS 2100
	Personal	GSM/GPRS /EDGE/UMTS	GSM/GPRS/EDGE 1900; UMTS 2100
ARUBA	Setar	GSM/GPRS/UMTS	GSM/GPRS 900/1900; UMTS 2100
	Digicel	GSM/GPRS/EDGE	900
AUSTRALIA	Hutchison 3G	UMTS Only	2100
	Telstra	GSM/GPRS /EDGE/UMTS	GSM/GPRS/EDGE 900; UMTS 850
	VodaFone	GSM/GPRS/UMTS	GSM/GPRS 900/1800; UMTS 2100

Figure 5-14. *From Albania to Vatican City, AT&T has partners that provide you with discounted data plans.*

This list shows the partner carriers, the technologies used, and the frequencies. For example, if you're traveling to Australia, the list shows three different carriers— Hutchison 3G, Telstra, and VodaFone. To determine the coverage areas and whether you can use an iPad Wi-Fi + 3G on one of those three networks, you need to look at another page: www.gsmworld.com/roaming/gsminfo/index.shtml (Figure 5-15).

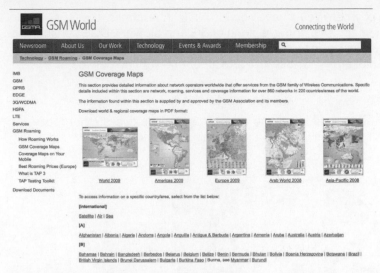

Figure 5-15. *GSM World provides a list of GSM carriers and the standards that it adheres to for operation, as well as maps that show exact coverage areas.*

This web site is run by the GSM Association, the group that sets the standards for GSM-based cellular networks. By looking for the country (Australia) that you're traveling to, you can see that all three of the carriers currently have 3G deployments on the 2100MHz band (Figure 5-16). Why is the band important? The iPad Wi-Fi + 3G operates on 850MHz, 1900MHz, and 2100MHz 3G frequencies, so it's useful to know that the network operates at one of these three frequencies.

Australia

The following networks operate in this country/area:

Hutchison 3G Australia Pty Limited	3G 2100	Live
Network Information | Roaming Partners | Services | Coverage Map		
Singtel Optus Limited (YES OPTUS)	GSM 900/1800	Live
Network Information | Roaming Partners | Services | Coverage Map		
Singtel Optus Limited (YES OPTUS)	3G 900/2100	Live
Network Information | Roaming Partners | Services | Coverage Map	HSPA. MOBILE BROADBAND TODAY	
Telstra Corporation Limited (Telstra MobileNet)	GSM 900/1800	Live
Network Information | Roaming Partners | Services | Coverage Map		
Telstra Corporation Limited (Telstra MobileNet)	3G 850	Live
Network Information | Roaming Partners | Services | Coverage Map		
Telstra Corporation Limited (Telstra MobileNet)	3G 2100	Live
Network Information | Roaming Partners | Services		
Vodafone Pacific Limited	GSM 900/1800	Live
Network Information | Roaming Partners | Services | Coverage Map		
Vodafone Pacific Limited	3G 2100	Live
Network Information | Roaming Partners | Services | Coverage Map		

Figure 5-16. *This chart on the GSM World web site shows that all three of the carriers with discounted roaming plans with AT&T provide 3G services on their networks.*

To get an even better idea of where you'll have service while in Australia, the GSM World web site has downloadable maps that show regions of 3G and slower EDGE service. On Figure 5-17, the light gray areas designate 3G service, while EDGE service is available in the dark gray areas. The white areas? Those indicate locations with no service at all—Australia is a big place.

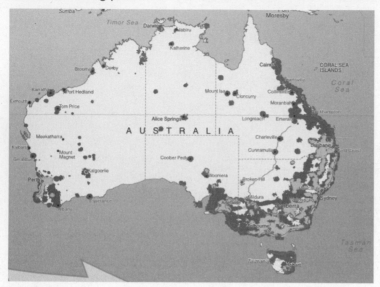

Figure 5-17. *You can find out exactly where your iPad can connect to the world by checking out the service maps on GSM World.*

Summarizing this section, the key things to know when you're taking your iPad Wi-Fi + 3G overseas are to turn off data roaming and to "know before you go."

Changing Account Information or Adding Data

Your iPad is very helpful in letting you know when you're getting close to the 250MB limit on the AT&T $14.99 data plan. It notifies you when you have 20 percent (50MB) left, when you have 10 percent (25MB) remaining, and when your plan has run out of data. You can decide to either stop using data at this point, purchase another 250MB data plan for $14.99, or upgrade to the 2GB plan and pay $25 a month.

To upgrade your data plan, change a credit card, edit your address information, or buy an international data plan, select Settings ➤ Cellular Data. Tap the View Account button, and you'll be able to make any changes instantly on your iPad.

Airplane Mode

When you're flying with an iPad with Wi-Fi + 3G, it's just as if you have a large mobile phone in your possession. Although airlines are much happier with Wi-Fi these days, with many actually providing in-flight Wi-Fi service, you'll still find that 3G and other mobile connections are frowned upon while you're in the air.

Like an iPhone, the iPad with Wi-Fi + 3G has controls for being switched into airplane mode. To turn on airplane mode when the flight attendant makes the announcement that "all cellular phones must be turned off," launch Settings. The first control available at the top of the page (Figure 5-18) is the Airplane Mode switch.

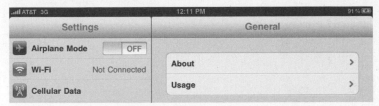

Figure 5-18. *Apple knows how important it is to turn off that 3G radio in your iPad during a flight. That's why Airplane Mode is the first setting available in the Settings app.*

Sliding the Airplane Mode switch to the right so that the switch turns to On and turns off Wi-Fi, 3G, and Bluetooth. If you want to use Wi-Fi during a flight, you can do that by tapping the Wi-Fi Settings button located just below Airplane Mode and then turning on Wi-Fi.

The Alternative to Built-in 3G

One way of getting mobile connectivity without built-in 3G in your iPad is to use a mobile broadband router. These devices are available from a number of cellular carriers and are small boxes that attach to a 3G network and then allow up to five devices near the box to share the 3G connection.

In the United States and Canada, mobile broadband routers are available from Novatel Wireless (brand name MiFi) and Sierra Wireless (brand name Overdrive). These petite boxes are available from Sprint and Verizon, which are oddly enough not carriers associated with the GSM standard used by the iPad.

Sprint's Overdrive 3G/4G Mobile Hotspot (Figure 5-19) is an example of the mobile broadband routers that can be used with your iPad. The interesting thing about the Overdrive is that it works with the Sprint 4G network that is beginning to be rolled out to major cities in the United States. The 4G network is up to 10 times faster than 3G service, meaning that you could conceivably use your iPad at speeds that would be similar to those achieved by a Wi-Fi network.

Several mobile phones (the Palm Pre Plus, for example) can be used as mobile hotspots, so check with your cellular carrier for information about this possibility. In countries other than the United States, some carriers allow *tethering* to an iPhone—that is, using a 3G iPhone as a mobile broadband router.

Figure 5-19. *Want to connect at speeds faster than 3G and share your wireless broadband connection with friends? A wireless broadband router such as the Sprint Overdrive 3G/4G Mobile Hotspot can do that for you. Image courtesy of Sprint.*

Summary

In this chapter, we explained the process of connecting to the Internet both through Wi-Fi and through 3G data connections. You learned some valuable troubleshooting tips for those times that you can't connect to Wi-Fi networks. Here we summarize some of the most important ideas in this chapter:

- Your iPad communicates with the world through Wi-Fi and (if you have an iPad with Wi-Fi + 3G) 3G cellular connections. Without Wi-Fi or 3G, you have no connection to the Internet.

- Security is very important when using Wi-Fi. To achieve the highest levels of wireless security, use WPA2-level encryption.

- Because of the expense, data roaming should be turned off when you're traveling internationally. Instead, use one of AT&T's roaming partners, and sign up for an international data plan.

- Be sure to put your 3G iPad into airplane mode when you're using it on an airplane to comply with federal and international regulations.

Chapter 6

Browsing the Internet with Safari

When Apple introduced the iPhone in 2007, Steve Jobs said it was like having the Web in your pocket. The Safari web browser on the iPhone was revolutionary. It allowed you to literally touch the Web like never before. Take the iPhone Safari experience and magnify it by ten, and you'll have some idea of what browsing the Web is like on the iPad. Web pages on the iPad's screen are large and show you more than ever before in clarity you've never imagined. It's like the iPad turns the Web into an interactive magazinc in the palm of your hands.

In this chapter, you'll discover how to get the most from Safari with all its awesome powers. You'll learn how to navigate web pages, manage bookmarks, and use both portrait and landscape orientations. You'll also discover some great finger-tap shortcuts, bookmarking skills, and the handy Web Clip feature. Read on for all this and more.

Getting Started with Safari

Tap the Safari application icon to launch the program. By default, Apple places it in the bottom left of the Dock. It's marked with a white compass on a blue background (see Figure 6-1). Once tapped, the Safari application opens a new window.

Figure 6-1. *Launch Safari from the Dock on your iPad Home screen.*

Safari's Browser Window

Many elements on the Safari window may look familiar, especially to anyone experienced in using web browsers or Safari on iPhone or iPod touch. Familiar elements include the address bar, the reload button, and the history navigation arrows. Figure 6-2 shows a typical Safari browser window.

Figure 6-2. *The Safari window displays many familiar features, including the address bar and the back, forward, and bookmarks buttons.*

Let's look closer at the top of a Safari page. Atop every Safari window you'll see the navigation bar (see Figure 6-3). The navigation bar contains common buttons and tools found on any modern web browser. From left to right, they are as follows:

Figure 6-3. *The Safari navigation bar*

- *The back button.* This takes you back one page in your browsing history.

- *The forward button.* If you've gone back one page, the forward button will move you one page forward in your history.

NOTE: When the back and forward buttons are grayed out, you haven't yet created a history. The arrows turn from light gray to dark gray once you start browsing, and you can move back and forth through your history to the previous and next pages. Each page maintains its own history. You can't use these buttons to go back to a page you were viewing in another window (see the Pages button discussion next).

- *Pages button.* This button looks like two squares superimposed on one another and allows you to open the page selection browser and select one of your currently open Safari windows. You can open up to nine browser windows at a time. We'll talk more about this button later in the chapter.

- *Bookmarks button.* Tap the book-shaped icon to open your Bookmarks screen. The Bookmarks screen also contains your complete browsing history for Safari.

- *Add Bookmark button.* This plus sign–shaped button adds the current page to your bookmark collection. You'll read more about bookmark creation and management later in this chapter.

- *Address bar.* Use the address bar at the top center of the Safari window to enter a new web address (web addresses are uniform resource locators, also known as a URL).

- *Reload button.* The arrow bent in a semicircle in the address bar field is the Reload button. Tap it to refresh the current screen.

- *Stop button.* As a page loads, Safari replaces the Reload button with a small *X*. If you change your mind after navigating to a page, tap this. It stops the current page from loading any further.

- *Search bar.* Tapping this gives you quick access to Google search.

Navigation Basics

iPad's Safari lets you do all the normal things you expect to do in a browser. You can tap links and buttons. You can enter text into forms and so forth. In addition, Safari offers iPad-specific features you won't find on your home computer: tilting the iPad on its side moves it from landscape to portrait view and back. The following how-tos guide you through Safari's basic features.

Entering URLs

Tap the address bar to open the URL-entry window (see Figure 6-3). The navigation section appears at the top of your screen, and a keyboard opens from below. Between these, the screen dims, and you can still see part of the page you were on (see Figure 6-4).

Figure 6-4. *The Safari window when you are operating in the URL or search fields*

NOTE: If you decide you want to remain on the page you are on, simply tap the dimmed area between the navigation bar and keyboard, and you'll be taken back to the page. Alternatively, you can tap the "hide keyboard" button in the lower-right corner of the keyboard.

You'll also see a bookmarks bar appear below the URL field (see Figure 6-5). These aren't all of your bookmarks but a select few you've decided to add to the Bookmarks Bar folder that's located in your collection of bookmarks. Bookmarks bar bookmarks are generally used for quick access to your most frequently visited web sites. To activate a bookmark in the bookmarks bar, simply tap it, and you'll be taken to its web page.

Figure 6-5. *The bookmarks bar gives you quick access to some of your bookmarks.*

If the current URL field is empty, simply tap it and begin typing. You'll briefly see a contextual menu saying Paste, but don't worry about that. Just start typing, and the contextual menu will disappear (or hit the Paste button if you want to paste a URL that you've copied earlier).

If the current URL field is populated (for example, if you are already on a site and not a blank page), simply tap it. You'll see a small gray *X* appear where the Refresh button normally is (Figure 6-5). Tapping this *X* will clear the contents of the URL field. Additionally, if you'd like to copy the current URL, tap anywhere in the URL field, and you'll get a pop-up menu that says Select, Select All, and Paste. Tap Select All, and then tap Copy in the pop-up that appears.

Don't worry about typing `http://` or even www; Safari is smart enough to know that those are required and will add them automatically. A handy feature on the iPad's keyboard in Safari is the dedicated .com button (see Figure 6-6). This single button makes your fingers do four keystrokes less work. What's even cooler is that when you press and hold the .com button, you'll be presented with a pop-up allowing you to select .edu, .org, and .net.

Figure 6-6. *Safari's keyboard complete with .com, .edu, .org, and .net buttons*

As you type, Safari matches your keystrokes to its existing collection of bookmarks. A pop-up field will appear and display a list of possible matches from both your bookmarks and your history (see Figure 6-7). To select one, just tap it. Safari automatically navigates to the selected URL.

When you are done typing in a URL, tap Go, and Safari navigates to the address you've entered. To return to the browser screen without entering a new URL, tap anywhere between the keyboard and the navigation bar.

TIP: When you see a white *X* in a gray circle in a text entry field, you can tap it to clear the field.

Figure 6-7. *The URL entry window allows you to enter the address that you want Safari to visit.*

Entering Text

Many times you'll have to fill in user names or passwords on a web page to log in, or you may be on a page that asks you to fill in other forms. To edit the contents of any text entry field, simply tap it, and Safari opens a new text entry keyboard.

Although this keyboard is superficially similar to Figure 6-5, it presents a few differences. These differences include Previous and Next buttons atop the keyboard that search for other text fields on your web page (see Figure 6-8). These buttons let you fill out forms without having to go through tedious tap/edit/done cycles. Simply enter text, tap Next, enter more text, and so forth.

Figure 6-8. *The text entry keyboard for web page forms. Notice the Previous, Next, and AutoFill buttons at the top.*

Another difference of the text-entry features in Safari is the AutoFill button. Tapping the AutoFill button will automatically populate the text fields with information from your personal contact card in your address book. It will also enter stored user names and passwords. We'll talk about setting up AutoFill features later in this chapter.

To submit a form after you've entered all the text, tap Go or Search. This is like pressing the Enter or Return key on a regular computer.

Searching

From any Safari window, you'll just be a tap away from web search. As shown in Figure 6-5, a Goggle search field lies just to the right of the URL field. It initially appears light gray, marked with a spyglass. Tap this search field to bring up the keyboard and enter a term you want to search for in Google.

The search field elongates while the URL field shortens, and the Go button on the keyboard switches to a Search button. Type a word or two, and you'll see a pop-up box appear with Google-suggested search terms based on what you've typed (see Figure 6-9). To select one of the Google-suggested terms, simply tap it in the list, or just finish typing what you are looking for and tap Search on the keyboard. Safari will navigate to www.google.com (no matter what page is currently displayed) and search for your queried term.

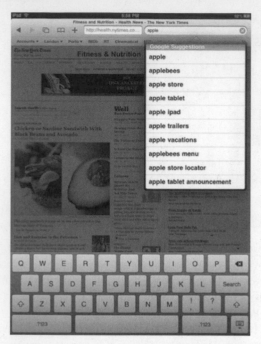

Figure 6-9. *The search field complete with suggested keywords*

If you'd rather use Yahoo! search than Google, you can navigate to Settings ➤ Safari to change your default search engine (we'll go through all of Safari's settings later in this chapter).

Following Links

Hypertext links are used throughout the World Wide Web. Text links are marked with underlines and usually involve a color change from the main text. Image links are subtler, but they can also move you to a new location.

Tap these links to navigate to new web pages or, for certain special links, to open a new e-mail or view a map. When a link leads to an audio or video file that the iPad understands, it will play back that file. Special links include `mailto:` (to create Mail messages), `tel:` (for phone calls, if you have Skype installed on your iPad), and automatic recognition of Google Maps URLs (which will take you to the iPad's Maps app).

> **NOTE:** Supported audio formats include AAC, M4A, M4B, M4P, MP3, WAV, and AIFF. Video formats include h.264 and MPEG-4.

You have other options than simply tapping a link to get to a new page. To preview a link's address, touch and hold the link for a second or two. An address pop-up appears next to the link (see Figure 6-10). Below the link's full address, you'll see three buttons.

Open will take you to the link as if you simply tapped it instead of touching and holding. Open in New Page will take you to the link in a new Safari page. Copy will copy the link so you can later paste it into an e-mail message or URL field. To cancel any of these options and stay on your current page, simply tap your finger anywhere on the screen.

Figure 6-10. *Options when touching and holding a link: Open, Open in New Page, and Copy*

TIP: To detect image links on the screen, tap and hold an image. If it turns gray, it's a link. If it remains at the same brightness, it's just a plain image. When you tap and hold a linked picture, you'll have the same options as you do with a text link. You'll also have one additional one: Save Image. This will save the image to your Photos app on the iPad.

Changing Orientation

One of the iPad's standout features is its flexible orientation support. When you turn your unit on its side, the iPad flips its display to match, as you can see in Figure 6-11. A built-in sensor detects the iPad's tilt and adjusts the display. Tilt back to vertical, and the iPad returns to portrait orientation. It takes just a second for the iPad to detect the orientation change and to update the display. Don't forget you can always lock your screen's orientation by sliding the screen orientation lock button on the side of the iPad.

Figure 6-11. *Safari can display web pages using both portrait and landscape orientation.*

The iPad's landscape view offers a relatively wider display. This is particularly good for side-to-side tasks such as reading book-width text. The wider screen allows you to use bigger fonts and view wider columns without scrolling sideways. The portrait view provides a longer presentation. This is great for reading web content with more narrow columns, like news feeds. You don't have to keep scrolling quite as much as you do in landscape view.

Whether in landscape or portrait view, Safari features work the same, including the same buttons in the same positions. In landscape view, you enter text using a wider, sideways keyboard.

Scrolling, Zooming, and Other Viewing Skills

Safari responds to the complete vocabulary of taps, flicks, and drags discussed in Chapter 2. You can zoom into pictures, squeeze on columns, and more. Here's a quick review of the essential ways to interact with your screen:

- *Drag*: Touch the screen, and drag your finger to reposition web pages. If you think of your iPad as a window onto a web page, dragging allows you to move the window around the web page.

- *Flick*: When dealing with long pages, you can flick the display up and down to scroll rapidly. This is especially helpful when navigating through search engine results and news sites.

- *Double-tap*: Double-tap any column or image to zoom in, autosizing it to the width of your display. Double-tap again to zoom back out. Use this option to instantly zoom into a web page's text. The iPad recognizes how wide the text is and perfectly matches that width.

- *Pinch*: Use pinching to manually zoom in or out. This allows you to make fine zoom adjustments as needed.

- *Tap*: Tap buttons and links to select them. Tapping allows you to move from site to site and to submit forms.

- *Page down*: When zoomed in onto a column, double-tap toward the bottom of the screen while staying within the column. The page recenters around your tap. Make sure not to tap a link!

- *Jump to the top*: Double-tap the very top of the screen (just below the time display) to pop instantly back to the top of the page.

- *Stop a scroll*: After flicking a page to get it to scroll, you can tap the page at any time to stop that movement. Don't forget that you can also manually drag the screen display to reset the part you're viewing.

TIP: Some web pages have text boxes in them, which have their own scrollbars, separate from the scrollbars of the web page. If you come across a web page with a text box while using Safari on the iPad, you can scroll through the text box on the page without scrolling through the entire page. To do this, inside the text box, swipe up or down with two fingers. Only the contents of the text box will scroll, and the main page will stay in place.

Page Management

Safari allows you to open up to nine concurrent browser windows at once. To review your open windows, tap the Pages button in the navigation bar. Safari's page viewer opens, as shown in Figure 6-12.

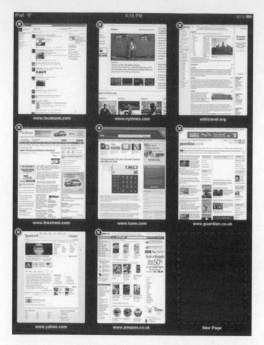

Figure 6-12. *The pages viewer allows you to select which browser window to display.*

This viewer allows you to interactively select a browser window:

■ To select a window, simply tap it. The Safari window springs forward and automatically reloads so it has the most current content on the page.

■ To close a window, tap the Close button—the black circle with an *X* in it at the top-left of each page. The page viewer slides the remaining pages into the gap left by the closed window.

■ To add a new page, tap the dotted, blank New Page. Safari creates a new window and opens the new, blank page for you to work with. You will not see a New Page window if you have nine currently opened pages.

■ The page management tool lets you quickly navigate back and forth between several open Safari windows. If you want, think of the page management window as a replacement for tabs that your desktop browser offers.

Working with Bookmarks

One of the great features of the iPad is that it lets you take your world with you: contacts, calendars, e-mail accounts, and bookmarks. You don't have to reenter URLs for all your favorite pages on the iPad. It loads these bookmarks whenever it syncs, provided you enabled this feature in the iTunes iPad preferences window (see Chapter 2).

Selecting Bookmarks

A bookmarks collection can contain hundreds of individual URLs, which is why people really appreciate the iPad's simple bookmarks browser (see Figure 6-13). When you tap the bookmark button in the navigation bar, a simple bookmarks pop-up appears. It uses the same folder structure that you've set up on your personal computer. You can tap folders to open them and tap the Back button (top-left corner) to return to the parent folder.

Figure 6-13. *Use iPhone Safari's interactive Bookmarks navigation to locate and open your favorite bookmarks.*

Identifying bookmarks is easy. Folders look like folders; each bookmark is marked with a small open book symbol. Tap one of these, and Safari takes you directly to the page in question. If your list of bookmarks is long, simply flick or scroll through the list.

When you are on the first level of your bookmarks, you'll notice a history folder at the top. Tap it, and you'll be taken to all the pages you've visited in Safari since you last cleared the history. To clear the history, tap the Clear History button, and you'll be asked to confirm. Tap the red Clear History button to confirm (Figure 6-14).

You'll also see a folder labeled Bookmarks Bar. Any bookmarks placed in this folder will appear in the bookmarks bar that shows below the bottom of the Safari navigation bar when you are entering in a URL (shown earlier in Figure 6-5).

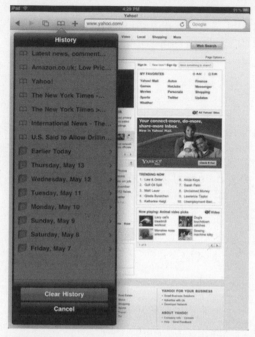

Figure 6-14. *Safari's History folders and the Clear History deletion confirmation*

NOTE: The history of your desktop browser and iPad's Safari browsers do not sync. Any pages you navigate to on your iPad will not show up on your desktop's browsing history, and vice versa.

Editing Bookmarks

As Figure 6-13 shows, an Edit button appears at the top-right of the bookmark's pop-up. Tap this to enter Edit mode (see Figure 6-15).

Figure 6-15. *Safari contains a built-in bookmark management system that allows you to edit and reorder your bookmarks.*

Edit mode allows you to manage your bookmarks on your iPad just as you would on your personal computer:

- *Delete bookmarks*: Tap the red delete circle to the left of a bookmark to delete it. Tap Delete to confirm, or tap elsewhere on the screen to cancel.

- *Reorder bookmarks*: Use the gray grab handles (the three lines on the far right) to move folders and bookmarks into new positions. Grab, drag, and then release.

- *Edit names*: Tap the gray reveal arrow (the sideways V symbol to the right of each name) to open the Edit Bookmark or Edit Folder screen. Use the keyboard to make your changes, and tap the Back button to return to the bookmarks editor.

- *Reparent items*: You can move items from one folder to another by tapping the parent folder field below the name edit field. Select a folder, and then tap the Back button to return to the bookmarks editor. Unfortunately, you don't get the same wild animation you do in Mail when you send an item to a new folder, but at least it works reliably.

- *Add folders*: Tap New Folder to create a folder in the currently displayed bookmarks. The iPad automatically opens the Edit Folder screen. Here, you can edit the name and, if needed, reparent your new folder. Tap Back to return to the editor.

- *Finish*: Return to the top-level Bookmarks list (tap the Back button until you reach it), and then tap Done. This closes the editor and returns to your bookmarks list.

Saving Bookmarks

To save a new bookmark, tap the Add (+) button in the navigation bar of any Safari web page. It's just to the left of the address field. An Add Bookmark pop-up appears, giving you three choices (see Figure 6-16).

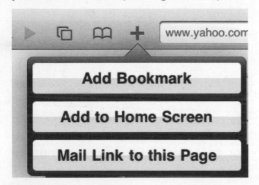

Figure 6-16. *Tap the Add (+) button to see all the bookmarking features.*

- *Add Bookmark*: Tapping this lets you enter a title for the bookmark and then optionally select a folder to save to (see Figure 6-17). Tap the currently displayed folder to view a list of all available folders. The root of the bookmark tree is called Bookmarks. After making your selection, tap Save. Safari adds the new bookmark to your collection. If you want to return to Safari without saving, tap Cancel.

Figure 6-17. *Add Bookmark allows you to rename the bookmark before you save it.*

- *Add to Home Screen*. This is a cool feature. Tapping this adds an icon of the web page to your iPad Home screen. Apple calls these web page icons *Web Clips*. Before you save a Web Clip, you have the option of renaming it. Keep the names short, so you can see the entire name under the Web Clip icon on the Home screen.

> **NOTE:** Some web sites will have an iPad-optimized site icon when you add a Web Clip to your Home screen. Others will just show you a thumbnail of the page in the shape of an iPad icon.

The Web Clips will look just like app icons and allows you to simply tap to open Safari and automatically be taken to the web page. We keep a Home screen on the iPad full of our favorite Web Clips so we can quickly navigate to our most frequently visited sites (see Figure 6-18). We find this much quicker that using the bookmarks feature in Safari.

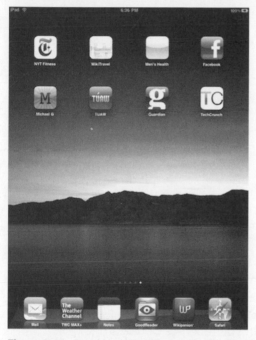

Figure 6-18. *A series of Web Clips on the iPad Home screen. You can see which sites have dedicated Web Clip icons and which ones make iPad use a thumbnail of the web page.*

In iTunes the Web Clips will appear in the virtual iPad screen on the Apps tab (see Chapter 2), but you cannot delete them from within iTunes; you can only rearrange them. To delete a Web Clip icon on the iPad, press and hold it until it jiggles, and tap the X in the upper-left corner.

- *Mail Link to this Page*. Tapping this button opens a new mail message window in Safari and automatically inserts the link into the body of the message.

Safari Settings

Like many apps on the iPad, Safari can be customized to a degree. Customize your Safari settings by navigating to the Settings app on your iPad Home screen and tapping Safari. This screen, shown in Figure 6-19, allows you to control a number of features, mostly security related. Here's a quick rundown of those features and what they mean:

Figure 6-19. *The Safari Settings window is primarily concerned with security features.*

- *Search Engine*: This setting determines which search engine is used for the search field you saw back in Figure 6-3. Choose from Google or Yahoo!

- *AutoFill*: This allows you to turn on AutoFill for use in filling out forms on web pages. In the My Info box, select your address book card to take the AutoFill information from. Here you can also select to turn on Names & Passwords. With this on, Safari will remember login names and passwords to web sites you visit. Tap Clear All to wipe all saved names and passwords from your iPad.

- *Always Show Bookmarks Bar*: Turn this on, and you'll always see the bookmarks bar below Safari's navigation bar and not just when you select the URL field (see Figure 6-5).

- *Fraud Warning*: Turn this preference on, and you'll be presented with a warning before navigating to a potentially fraudulent web sites. Unfortunately, fraudulent sites are rampant on the Internet (like bogus PayPal sites). This feature helps you recognize and avoid those sites.

- *JavaScript*: JavaScript allows web pages to run programs when you visit. Disabling JavaScript means you increase overall surfing safety, but you also lose many cool and worthy web features. Most pages are safe to visit, but some, sadly, are not. To disable JavaScript, switch from ON to OFF.

- *Block Pop-ups*: Many web sites use pop-up windows for advertising. It's an annoying reality of surfing the Web. By default, Safari pop-up blocking is ON. Switch this setting to OFF to allow pop-up window creation.

- *Accept Cookies*: Cookies refer to data stored on your iPad by the web sites you visit. Cookies allow web sites to remember you and to store information about your visit. You can choose to always accept cookies, never accept cookies, or accept cookies only "From visited" web sites.

- *Databases*: You'll see this option only if you've visited a web site that uses database features such as some Google sites, like Gmail. These databases store local information on your iPad for offline browsing.

- *Clear History*: Tap and confirm to empty your page navigation history from your iPad. This keeps your personal browsing habits private to some extent, although other people might still scan though your bookmarks.

CAUTION: Clearing your history does not affect Safari's page history. You can still tap its Back button and see the sites you've visited.

- *Clear Cookies*: Tap and confirm to clear all existing cookies from your iPad.

- *Clear Cache*: Your iPad's browser cache stores data from many of the web sites you visit. It uses this to speed up page loading the next time you visit. As with cookies and history, your cache may reveal personal information that you'd rather not share. Tap Clear Cache and Confirm to clear your cache.

TIP: Clearing your cache may also help correct problem pages that are having trouble loading. By clearing the cache, you remove page items that may be corrupt or only partially downloaded.

- *Developer*. Most people will never have to fuss with this setting. As its title suggests, it's for developers and allows them to turn on a debug console, which helps them when optimizing their web sites for the iPad.

The iPad and Flash Videos

If you've ever watched a video on the Web, chances are the video was encoded using Flash. Ever since Apple unveiled the iPhone to the world, there has been growing tension between Apple and Adobe. The reason is because Apple does not allow Adobe's proprietary Flash plug-in to run on the iPhone—and now the iPad.

Flash, in Apple's estimation, is a slow, buggy, and archaic technology. Steve Jobs himself even posted a letter on Apple's web site effectively telling the world the same thing (www.apple.com/hotnews/thoughts-on-flash/). His letter was the last nail in the coffin for anyone hoping to see Flash on the iPad or iPhone.

What many people misunderstand when they hear "no Flash on the iPad" is that they think the iPad can't play web videos. There's nothing further from the truth. Sure, if a video is encoded in Flash, you can't view it on the iPad (see Figure 6-20), but most videos on the Web (about 75 percent of them, Steve Jobs says) are encoded in Flash, but also in a new, universal web standard called HTML5. HTML5 videos don't require a plug-in to play. HTML5 is also much less power hungry than Flash—an important feature when dealing with mobile devices that consume battery power.

Figure 6-20. *An error message on a site viewed in iPad's Safari saying your need to have Flash installed before being able to view the video. Don't bother clicking the download link; you won't be able to install it.*

The world is moving to HTML5, and Apple chose to support it—and open standards—instead of Adobe's aging and proprietary Flash. Most of YouTube's videos have already been reencoded to support HTML5, and many other major web sites have chosen to drop Flash in favor of the new HTML5 web standard. Apple even has a dedicated page to spotlight the web sites that take advantage of the new HTML5 web standard at www.apple.com/ipad/ready-for-ipad/.

Summary

The iPad turns browsing the Internet from something you did at your desk to something you can do in the comfort of your lap in your living room. In a way, browsing the Internet on the iPad gives web pages a tangibility they've never been capable of before—you can just reach out and touch them. It's very likely that after using Safari on iPad to surf, you'll never want to explore the Web any other way.

Here are a few tips to keep in mind as you move on from this chapter:

- iPads work in more ways than just vertical. Go ahead and flip your iPad on its side. Your Safari pages will adjust.

- Nope, there's no Flash support. There never will be. And you don't need it.

- Web Clips are a great way to access your favorite web sites right from your iPad's Home screen.

- Tap the top of any Safari page (right below the clock in the status bar) to quickly return to the top of the web page.

- Safari's page management tool lets you navigate back and forth between several Safari windows at once. This functions similar to the way tabs function on desktop browsers.

Chapter 7

Touching Your Music and Video

The iPad is a powerful multimedia device that lets you reach out and touch your music and video like never before. Its widescreen playback capabilities offer beautiful, clear images, larger than ever before. Its wireless Internet capabilities allow you to access a huge range of content—from YouTube to embedded video on the Internet to your own personal computer. The iPad is also a magnificent music player. In this chapter, we'll take you through the primary apps that let you enjoy your music and video: Videos, YouTube, Safari, and iPod.

Watching Video on the iPad

Video forms such a basic component of your iPad that you shouldn't think about it as just a single application. Apple provides the base technology used by several built-in apps that support video playback (see Figure 7-1).

Figure 7-1. *Videos, YouTube, and Safari all feature video playback capabilities on the iPad.*

- *Videos*: The Videos application appears on the Home screen of your iPad. The icon looks like a traditional clapperboard, with a black-and-white striped top over a blue base. This application plays back the TV shows, movies, podcasts, iTunes U lessons, and music videos you've synchronized from your home iTunes library.

- *YouTube*: You'll find the YouTube application icon next to the Videos app in Figure 7-1. The icon looks like an old-fashioned TV, complete with a greenish screen and brown dials. YouTube connects to the Internet and allows you to view videos from YouTube.com. You can navigate to www.youtube.com in Safari on the iPad and browse YouTube videos that way, but the iPad's YouTube app wraps www.youtube.com in such a nice and easy-to-navigate package that you'll find it's leaps and bounds better than using YouTube in a web browser.

- *Safari*: Safari, which you read about in depth in Chapter 6, offers a third way to view videos. Like its computer-based equivalents, the Safari app allows you to watch embedded movie files. Safari's icon looks like a light blue compass with a needle pointing to the northeast.

In addition to the three apps that play video that ship with the iPad, there are thousands of other apps that play video. You can discover all these apps in the iTunes Store. Some of our favorites are the BBC News app to view news footage and The Weather Channel app to view weather-related news stories and Doppler video (Figure 7-2).

Figure 7-2. *Myriad apps available on the iPad support video playback, including popular apps like The Weather Channel, BBC News, and The Financial Times.*

> **NOTE:** Apple's iPad officially supports H.264 video, up to 1.5 Mbps, 1024 by 768 pixels, 30 frames per second, and 720p in .m4v, .mp4, and .mov file formats.

For all that the iPad brings to video, it has limits. Your iPad plays H.264 MPEG-4 video, and that's pretty much it. As we talked about in the previous chapter, you cannot use your iPad to view Flash/Shockwave videos or animation. You cannot play AVI videos. You cannot play DivX, Xvid, or any of the other dozens of popular formats. If your video isn't in MPEG-4 H.264 format, your iPad won't understand it.

Video Playback

We've talked about how the iPad is an orientation-agnostic device: you can interact with it in portrait or landscape mode. That's no different for playing video. When you watch a video on the iPad, you can watch it holding the iPad in portrait mode or in landscape mode. Depending on the app you are watching it in, you may see more options for the video being played or indeed for the app itself.

However, most apps display the video interface with all the same elements, meaning once you know how to control video playback in one app, you know how to do it in the rest of them. Here is a quick overview of those controls, which are shown in Figure 7-3.

Figure 7-3. *The iPad's video playback controls allow you to control playback as you watch.*

- *Play/Pause*: Play/Pause appears as either a right-pointing triangle (Play) or a pair of vertical lines (Pause). Tap this button to pause or resume video playback.

- *Rewind*: The Rewind button appears as two triangles pointing left to a line. Tap it to return to the start of the video, or press and hold the button to scan backward.

- *Fast-Forward*: The reverse of Rewind, the Fast-Forward button's triangles point to the right instead of the left. Press and hold this button to scan forward. Tap it to skip to the next video track.

- *Scrubber bar*: The scrubber bar appears at the top of your screen. It is a long line with a small knob that you can drag. (The volume control is the thicker bar at the bottom.) Drag the playhead along the scrubber bar to set the current playback time.

■ *Zoom:* The Zoom button looks like two arrows in a white box pointing away from each other, at the top right of your screen. Either double-tap the screen or tap the Zoom button to switch between full-screen mode and the original aspect ratio. To get back into the original aspect ratio's view, double-tap the screen again, or tap the zoom button again. You'll note that the zoom button changes slightly when viewing a video full-screen: the arrows have turned into a letterbox icon. When viewing in full-screen mode, you use the entire iPad screen, but some video may be clipped from the top or sides of the video. In the original aspect ratio, you may see either letterboxing (black bars above and below) or pillarboxing (black bars to either side), which results from preserving the video's original aspect ratio.

■ *Volume:* The volume control is the large line below the Play/Pause button. Drag the volume control knob to adjust playback volume. Of course, you can always use the dedicated physical volume button on the side of the iPad as well.

■ *Audio tracks and Subtitles:* If alternate audio tracks or subtitles are available in the video you are watching, you'll see an icon that looks like a speech bubble appear in the controls. Tap this icon to select from a pop-up list of audio tracks and subtitles.

■ *Done:* The Done button appears on all video application screens. Tap Done to exit video playback. Press the physical Home button on the iPad's bezel to quit the app and return to your Home screen.

While you're playing a video, the iPad automatically hides your video controls after a second or two. This allows you to watch your video without the distraction of onscreen buttons. Tap the screen to bring back the controls. Tap the screen again to hide them; or leave them untouched for a few seconds, and they once again fade away.

Videos App

To launch the Videos app, tap its blue clapperboard icon. This opens the screen shown in Figure 7-4. As long as you've already synced videos from your iTunes library (see Chapter 2), you'll see them appear here.

Figure 7-4. *The Videos app offers a list of movies, TV shows, podcasts, music videos, and iTunes U lessons you've synchronized to your iPad.*

Playing a Video

As you can see, the Videos interface couldn't be simpler. It displays a series of thumbnail images representing the music videos, TV shows, podcasts, iTunes U lessons, and movies you've synchronized to your iPad (synchronizing these items is discussed in Chapter 2). You can navigate between your various video media categories by tapping the category button that runs along the top of the screen (see Figure 7-5). If you have a lot of videos in a specific category, simply flick your finger to scroll through the list.

Figure 7-5. *Navigate your video categories by tapping the appropriate category button at the top of the screen.*

Tap any video thumbnail, and you'll see the item's icon fly forward as gray panels unfold from behind it like papier-mâché. You'll be presented with the information page that displays the name of the video as well as the year it was made, along with other information that could include the length, dimensions, file size, codecs, and copyright notice.

If you are viewing a video with chapters such as a TV show (each episode in a season is considered a chapter), podcast, or movie, you'll see a list of chapters. If it's a podcast or

TV show, you'll be presented with the episodes you have on your iPad as well as their name, a summary of the episode, their rating, and length (see Figure 7-6).

Figure 7-6. *Information screens for movies and TV shows*

To begin playing the video, tap the circular Play button in the top-right of the screen, or if your video has a list of chapters, tap a chapter from the list. Your screen clears, and the video loads and automatically begins playing. Tap Done to return to the information page.

> **NOTE:** Though any audio Podcasts and iTunes U lessons you've chosen to sync to your iPad show up in the Videos app, tapping them will cause the file to open in the iPod app. When done listening to the audio podcast or lesson, you'll then need to exit the iPod app and return to the Video app.

Deleting Videos

If you want to delete a video from your iPad, simply touch and hold the video thumbnail until a black and white *X* appears in the corner of the video's icon (see Figure 7-7). Tap the *X* to delete. With the exception of a video rented from the iTunes Store, deleting a video from the iPad will not delete it from your computer. You'll be able to sync it again from your iTunes library should you choose to do so.

Figure 7-7. *Tap and hold a video's thumbnail icon, and wait for the X to appear. Tap the X to delete the video.*

Video Settings

You can adjust several settings that affect your video playback. These settings are accessed through the iPad's Settings application (see Figure 7-8).

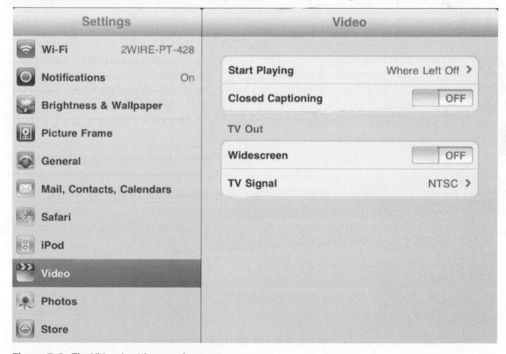

Figure 7-8. *The Videos' settings preferences*

- *Start Playing.* This setting allows you to choose whether to start playing videos from the beginning or where you left off.

- *Closed Captioning.* If your video contains embedded closed captions, you can view them by switching on the Closed Captioning option. Switch the option from OFF to ON.

The iPad's Video app also lets you play content from it through your home television. You'll need to buy some extra cables for this, which we'll tell you about later in the "Video Accessories" section of this chapter, but the Video settings is where you can choose the following options:

- *Widescreen*: Turn this on to force wide-screen videos to be played in wide-screen on your TV. This preserves their original aspect ratio.

- *TV Signal*: Choose either NTSC or PAL. If you are in North America or Japan, you'll most likely have an NTSC TV. In Europe and Australia, it's PAL.

YouTube

Discovering, navigating, and watching YouTube videos on the iPad is an experience that's light years beyond watching them sitting at your desk on your computer. The iPad turns watching YouTube videos into a fantastic leisure experience that you can enjoy from the comfort of your couch.

Unlike the Videos app, the YouTube app requires an Internet connection. As long as you have a Wi-Fi connection, you're all set. Also, to take full advantage of the YouTube app, you'll want to have a YouTube account. You don't *need* one to use the app, but having one makes the app that much more powerful. With a YouTube account, you can view and bookmark your favorite videos; subscribe to YouTube users' videos; see all the videos you've uploaded to YouTube with the tap of a button; and share, rate, and flag videos—all from within the YouTube app. Creating a YouTube account takes only a few minutes and can be done at www.youtube.com/create_account.

To launch the application, tap the YouTube icon, which looks like a retro-styled TV set (shown earlier in Figure 7-1). When launched for the first time, the application displays the Featured screen, as shown in Figure 7-9. This screen showcases videos chosen by YouTube's staff.

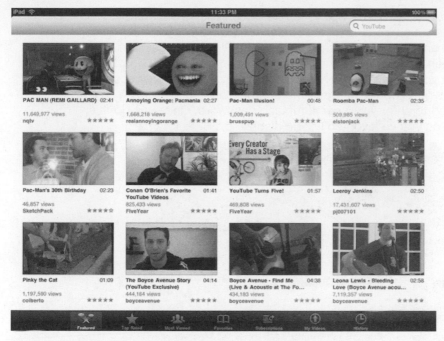

Figure 7-9. *YouTube's Featured screen provides a video showcase.*

Navigating and Finding YouTube Videos

Key elements of the YouTube app include a search field in the upper-right corner of the app and a row of seven buttons at the bottom of the screen. Each button (see Figure 7-10) offers a different way to find YouTube videos.

Figure 7-10. The YouTube navigation bar

- *Featured*: This screen displays videos reviewed and recommended by YouTube staff.

- *Top Rated:* This screen displays videos that have the highest ratings on YouTube. You can choose to show the highest-rated videos for the day, the week, or all-time.

- *Most Viewed*: This screen displays videos that have the most views on YouTube. You can choose to show the most-viewed videos for the day, the week, or all-time.

■ *Favorites*: This screen displays all the videos you've added to your Favorites list on YouTube. This screen will also show you a list of any playlists and their videos when you tap the Playlists tab at the top of the screen. This is one of the features of the YouTube app that requires you to have a YouTube account. To sign in to your account, tap the Sign In button in the top-left corner (see Figure 7-11). You'll be prompted to enter your user name and password. Once you do this, any videos you've favorited will be displayed.

Figure 7-11. *The Sign In button is located in the top-left corner of the Favorites, Subscriptions, and My Videos page. Tap it to log into your YouTube account.*

To remove a bookmarked video, tap the Edit button in the top gray bar. All your bookmarked videos will display an *X* in their top-left corner. Tap the *X* to remove the video from your favorites. When you are finished deleting favorites, tap the blue Done button.

NOTE: Removing a video from your YouTube favorites on the iPad will also remove it from your YouTube account, meaning it will no longer be displayed in your favorites, no matter what device you log into YouTube from.

■ *Subscriptions:* YouTube allows you to subscribe to another YouTube user's videos so you can keep up-to-date with the latest videos they've posted. Any subscriptions you have will show up on this screen. Tap the name of the user to see all their videos displayed to the left of the list. This feature requires you to be logged in to your YouTube account.

■ *My Videos*: This screen displays all the videos you've uploaded to YouTube. This feature requires you to be logged in to your YouTube account.

■ *History:* This screen displays the videos you have viewed on your iPad. The history does not reflect the videos you've viewed on your computer while logged into your YouTube account. To clear your history, tap the Clear button in the top-left corner.

You can also use the search field, found in the upper-right corner of any of these screens, to search YouTube's library of videos.

Viewing YouTube Videos

So, you've found a video you want to watch. Now what? This is one of the situations where the next step depends on whether you're holding the iPad in landscape or portrait mode. If you tap the video thumbnail in portrait mode, the video's information screen will appear, and the video will automatically begin playing in the information screen. If you tap the video thumbnail in landscape mode, the video will begin playing full-screen, and you'll need to tap the Done button to view the video's information screen.

Video information screens provide detailed information for each video. Depending on which orientation you are holding your iPad in—landscape or portrait—you'll see that information laid out slightly differently, but either orientation gives you the same information. Figure 7-12 shows the same info screen in both landscape and portrait modes.

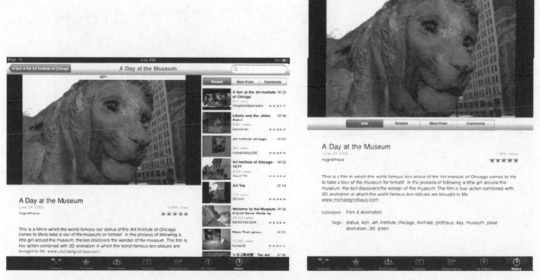

Figure 7-12. *A YouTube video's information screen offers information about the video in both landscape and portrait modes.*

On the video information screen you'll find the name of the video, its rating (in stars, from zero to five), the number of times the video has been viewed, its run time, and more. You'll also see tabs labeled Related, More From, and Comments.

- *Related*: Tap this tab to see videos related to the one you're watching.

- *More From*: Tap this tab to see more videos from the YouTube user who uploaded the video you are currently watching. From this tab you can also tap a Subscribe button to subscribe to the user's video feed. The user's YouTube name and videos will show up on the Subscriptions page.

- *Comment*: Tap this tab to read comments left by other YouTube users about the video you are watching. You can also tap the "Add a comment" field to write your own comment. You must be logged into your YouTube account to write a comment.

Managing Videos: Rating, Sharing, and So On

You can do more with videos in the YouTube app than just sort and view them. While in a video's information screen, you can bookmark, share, rate, and flag the video.

As you see in Figure 7-13, tapping the video image brings up opaque bars at the top and bottom of the video. The bar at the bottom allows you to play/pause the video, scrub backward or forward with the slider, and switch to full-screen mode by tapping the double-arrow expand button. The bar at the top allows you to select several options for managing the video. All options require a YouTube account.

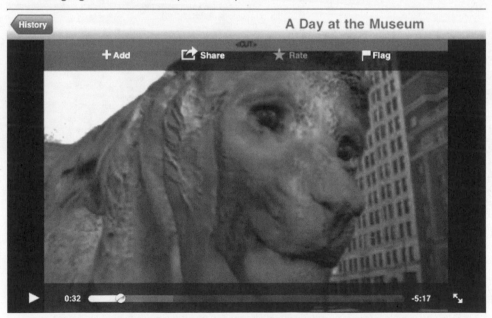

Figure 7-13. *Tap a video in the video information screen to open its managing options.*

NOTE: You must be viewing the video in the video's information screen to rate, share, and so on. The managing video toolbar does not show up when you are playing a video in full-screen mode. The only exception is bookmarking. In full-screen mode, a bookmark icon will appear next to the volume slider at the bottom of the screen. Tap it to add the video to your favorites.

- *+Add*: Tap this to bookmark the video to your favorites. If you have more than one Favorites list, you'll be able to select the list you'd like to add the video to. The video will immediately appear under the Favorites button in the YouTube app. This requires a YouTube account.

- *Share*: Tap this to send a link to the video in an e-mail message. Without taking you out of the YouTube app, an e-mail compose window will pop up with the name of the video in the subject field and a link to it in the body of the message. Just enter the e-mail of the person you want to send it to, and you're done! You can also add your own text to the body of the e-mail like any other e-mail. This requires a YouTube account.

- *Rate*: Tapping this will display a rating pop-up that allows you to rate the video between one and five stars. This requires a YouTube account.

- *Flag*: Tapping this button will display a red Flag as Inappropriate button. Tap that to send a notification to YouTube. They will review the video and pull it from the site, if they deem it necessary. This requires a YouTube account. Don't go crazy with flagging videos just because you don't like the content. If you falsely flag too many videos, you could have your YouTube account suspended.

NOTE: The Rate and Flag buttons will be grayed out if you've already rated or flagged the video.

YouTube Tips

Here are some tips for using the YouTube application:

- Use the Clear button at the top-right corner of the History screen to erase your YouTube viewing history. People don't have to know you've been watching that skateboarding dog.

- Don't overlook the Related Videos list. Scroll down on the video information screen to find related videos that you may want to view. YouTube is pretty clever about adding listings that you may actually want to see.

■   While navigating videos on the Featured, Top Rated, and Most Viewed pages, scroll all the way down, and you'll see a gray video icon with the words "Load More…" on it. Tap this to load more videos on the selected page.

Watching Videos on the Web with Safari

Video on the iPad isn't limited to special-purpose applications. You can also watch MPEG-4 movie files with the iPad's Safari application. Chapter 6 introduced Safari. Here you'll see how you can connect to video on the World Wide Web and watch it in your Safari browser.

Many web sites besides YouTube feature embedded video. For example, go to virtually any news site, and you're sure to find embedded video. As we mentioned in Chapter 6, the iPad, and thus Safari, does not support Flash playback, which limits the iPad's ability to display every single web video (see Figure 6-20 to see what happens when a Flash video is displayed on a web site in iPad's Safari). However, many web sites serve HTML-5 and MPEG-4 videos, and these are fully iPad-compliant.

For example, the web site TED (www.ted.com) where you can watch videos of some of today's greatest minds talk about science, education, technology, and art is fully iPad-compatible. Figure 7-14 shows this site's video of author Elizabeth Gilbert talking about creativity playing back in the iPad's Safari web browser.

Figure 7-14. *Many videos on the Web can be played natively in the Safari web browser.*

Simply tap an embedded video to begin playing it. Depending on the speed of your Internet connection, it may take a few seconds before the video begins playing. You can watch the video in-page or full-screen. To navigate between the two views, tap the video, and a navigation bar appears along the bottom of it. It displays the Play/Pause button, the navigation scrubber, and the familiar full-screen double-arrow button. Tap the double arrows to enter full-screen view. To exit full-screen view and return to the web page, tap the Done button on the video playback screen.

Video Accessories

As far as video goes, if you are going to be watching a lot of them, there are several iPad accessories you should consider purchasing:

- *Stands*: Several companies make them, and they range in price from $5 to $100. Whatever stand you choose, make sure it holds the iPad in landscape mode, because that gives you maximum screen real estate to watch your videos. Some cases also double as an iPad stand. Apple's iPad case ($39) folds into a stand.

- *iPad Dock Connector to VGA Adapter* ($29): The VGA end of the adapter can be connected to external monitors, some TVs, and PC projectors. You'll need this, or the cables listed next to connect your iPad to your home television.

- *Apple Component AV Cable* ($49) and *Composite AV Cable* ($49): These also work with the iPad, providing two more methods of linking external monitors and projectors to the device.

Don't worry if you don't know the difference between VGA, Composite, and Component. All three are types of physical video connectors that link devices to TVs.

- *VGA* is a 15-pin connector that you can still find on the back of many PCs. It supports resolutions up to 2048×1536.

- *Composite* is a video connector that channels three video source signals through a single connection. It's the oldest of the three technologies, but it still supports a resolution of up to 720×576i.

- *Component* is a video connector that takes three video source signals and outputs them through three different connections. It's basically a Composite cable with three heads, but Component offers a much better resolution, up to 1920×1080p (otherwise known as *full HD*).

Many modern TVs support all three connections. Check your TV's manual to see which yours supports.

Listening to Music on the iPad

When Apple introduced the iPad, many people on the Internet (who had never used one) started complaining that it was nothing more than a big iPod touch. Matter of fact, there's a popular parody video that shows joggers carrying an iPad instead of an iPod on their morning run. By now you've discovered that the iPad is much more than just a big iPod touch, but it also *does* play music like an iPod (just don't go jogging with it; or, if you do, get a Bluetooth headset and throw the iPad in a backpack, so you don't look silly running with something the size of a laptop screen in your hands).

Unlike previous generations, when it comes to the iPad, the iPod is not a device—it's an application. Once you get past the slightly confusing name switch, you'll discover that the iPad's iPod app brings all the functionality and ease of use you expect from an iPod, but it delivers that functionality in a distinctive iPad package.

If you are used to listening to music on an iPod, iPod touch, or iPhone, you may expect the iPad to have the same kind of interface for its music player. In actuality, the iPad's music player interface shares a closer resemblance to iTunes on your computer than to any previous iPod interface. This is great news, because if you are used to using iTunes on a Mac or a Windows computer, you'll be instantly familiar with the basic layout of the iPad's music player app.

> **NOTE:** Do not confuse the iPod and iTunes applications on your iPad. iPod is used to play back your music tracks. iTunes connects you to the mobile iTunes Wi-Fi Music Store and is not a general music player.

Navigating the Music Library and Playlists

Tap the iPod icon on your iPad's Home screen to launch the app. The iPod icon is orange with a white iPod classic on it. The first thing you'll notice about the iPod app (see Figure 7-15) is that, as mentioned earlier, it shares a similar layout to iTunes. Not only can you listen to music in the app, but you can also easily create and edit playlists like you would on your desktop. Before we get into that, let's start by exploring the iPod interface.

Figure 7-15. *The iPod app on the iPad closely resembles iTunes on your computer.*

The iPod window is composed of five key elements:

- *The play bar*: This runs along the top of the app and contains the volume slider; the Play/Pause, Forward, and Rewind buttons; and the search field.

- *The library source list*: Here you'll see your music separated into different categories (see Figure 7-16). Tap any category to see its contents.

  - *Music*: Contains all the music on your iPad

  - *Podcasts*: Contains your audio and video podcasts

  - *Audiobooks*: Contains your audiobooks

  - *iTunes U*: Contains your iTunes U lectures and classes

  - *Genius Mixes*: Contains any genius mixes you've chosen to sync from iTunes

  - *Purchased*: Contains all the music and music videos you've bought through the iTunes Music Store

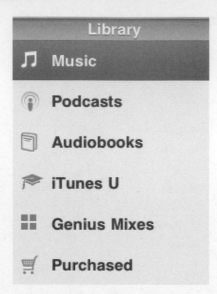

Figure 7-16. *Source list categories include Music, Podcasts, Audiobooks, iTunes U, Genius Mixes, and Purchased.*

NOTE: Though any video podcasts, iTunes U lessons, and music videos you've chosen to sync to your iPad show up in the iPod app, tapping them will cause the file to open in the Videos app. When done viewing the video, you'll then need to exit the Videos app and return to the iPod app.

Below these five categories you may see a number of different playlists. Playlists come in three types (see Figure 7-17):

- *Regular playlist*: An icon with four lines and a music note symbolizes this kind of playlist. A regular playlist contains any music you've manually added to the list. It does not update itself and changes only when you add or remove a song.

- *Smart playlist*: A cogwheel proceeding the name symbolizes this kind of playlist. A smart playlist is one in which you set a specific set of rules that songs must contain. Any songs that match the rules will show in the playlist.

- *Genius playlist*: An icon that looks like an atom surrounded by electrons symbolizes this kind of playlist. A Genius playlist is a playlist that iTunes or the iPod app automatically generates based on a single song in your library. The playlist will be populated with songs that go great with the song you've selected to originate the playlist from.

See the "Creating Playlists" section later in this chapter to find out how to create playlists on the iPad.

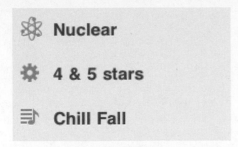

Figure 7-17. *Types of playlists include (from top to bottom) Genius, smart, and regular.*

- *The songs list:* This is the main body of the iPod app. It shows all the songs in any selected category or playlist. Navigate the list by scrolling up or down with your finger. If the list is long, you'll see an alphabet control on the right side of the screen, as shown in Figure 7-15. Tap a letter, or slide your finger down the alphabet to move to the section you want to view.

- *The create and sort bar:* This is the bar that runs along the bottom of the app (see Figure 7-18). From this bar you'll be able to create new playlists and genius playlists, as well as sort music from the songs list by song, artist, album, genre, or composer.

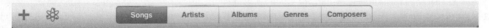

Figure 7-18. *The create and sort bar*

- *Cover art:* A song's cover art (the cover of the album the song is from) is displayed in the lower-left corner of the iPod app's screen, right below the library source list (see Figure 7-15). Tap the cover to enter the Now Playing window.

> **NOTE:** Only playlists and the Music and Purchased categories in the Library source list can be sorted by song, artist, album, genre, or Composer. Podcasts, audiobooks, iTunes U, and Genius mixes do not feature sorting options.

Playing Audio from the Music Library and Playlists

Whether you are in your main music library or a standard, smart, or Genius playlist, to start playing a song, simply tap it. Figure 7-19 shows the iPod app's Now Playing screen. You arrive at this screen whenever you start playing a song.

Figure 7-19. *The iPod app's Now Playing screen provides an interactive screen that controls playback for the currently playing item. From this screen, you can adjust the volume, pause and resume playback, and loop the current track.*

You'll also notice that a Play indicator has appeared in the iPad's status bar (see Figure 7-20). The right-pointing Play indicator at the top-right of the screen (just left of the battery status) appears universally when you're playing back music. This tells you at a glance that music is playing. You'll find this especially helpful when you've removed your earbuds and placed the iPad on a table. It alerts you that your battery is gleefully emptying itself as your iPad plays music that no one is hearing.

Figure 7-20. *The Play indicator is next to the battery status in the iPad's status bar.*

Now Playing Screen

The Now Playing screen (see Figure 7-19) is divided into three sections.

Title Bar

The title bar (see Figure 7-21) is the black bar at the top of the Now Playing screen and contains the following items.

Figure 7-21. *The title bar on the Now Playing screen*

- *Volume slider*. Drag along the slider to adjust the volume here. You can also use the iPad's physical button to adjust the volume. If you've attached an external speaker or remote control, you can use its switches to control the playback volume as well.

- *Artist, song, and album*. These items appear at the top middle of the screen and are for information only. Tapping them does nothing.

- *Rewind*. The Rewind button looks like a line followed by two left-pointing triangles.

  - Tap to move back to the beginning of the currently playing song.

  - Double-tap to move to the previous song in the album or playlist. If you are already at the start of the song, a single tap moves you back; if you're already at the first song, this works as if you had pressed the Back button—you return to the most recent album or playlist screen.

  - Touch and hold to rewind through the current song. You'll hear very short snippets as you move backward through the song. This feature proves especially handy while listening to audiobooks.

- *Play/Pause*. Play looks like a right-pointing triangle. Pause looks like a pair of upright lines. Tap this button to toggle between playback and pause modes.

- *Forward*. The Forward button looks like the Rewind button in a mirror. The line is to the right, and both triangles point right instead of left.

  - Tap once to move to the next song in the album or playlist. If you're at the last song, tapping Forward moves you back to the album or playlist.

  - Touch and hold to fast-forward through your song.

Below the title bar, you'll find a thin bar that contains the loop button, the scrubber bar, and the shuffle button (see Figure 7-21).

- *Loop control*. This control, which looks like a pair of arrows pointing to each other in a circle, appears when you tap album art.

  - Tap once to loop the currently playing album or playlist. After the last song plays, the first song starts again.

- Tap a second time to loop just the current song. The number 1 appears on the loop, telling you that the loop applies to just this song.

- Tap once more to disable looping.

- A blue loop (both the regular loop and the loop with the number 1) indicates that looping is enabled. A white loop means looping is switched off.

- *Scrubber bar*. The scrubber bar appears to the right of the loop control. Tap the album cover to make this control appear; tap again to hide it.

  - The number at the left of the bar shows the elapsed playback time. The number at the right shows the remaining playback time.

  - Drag the playhead to set the point at which your song plays back. You can do so while the song is playing, so you can hear which point you've reached.

  - Look just below the scrubber bar to see which album or playlist track is playing back. In Figure 6-5, this is track 1 of 1.

- *Shuffle*. The shuffle control looks like two arrows making a wavy *X*. It appears to the right of the scrubber bar and, like the loop and scrubber controls, appears only after you tap the album cover.

  - When the shuffle control is off (white), album and playlist songs play back in order.

  - When the shuffle control is selected (blue), the iPod randomly orders songs for shuffled playback.

NOTE: If you are using Apple's iPhone earphones with a remote and mic to listen to music on your iPad, all the buttons and click features of the iPhone's earbuds work just fine (despite Apple not listing the earbuds as an official iPad accessory). Click to play/pause a song. Double-click to skip to the next song. Triple-click to return to the previous song. Tap the + or – button on the earphone control to increase or decrease the volume. The microphone on the iPhone earbuds also work fine with the iPad. The Apple Earphones with Remote and Mic cost $29 at the Apple Store.

Album Cover

Below the scrubber bar, you'll notice the song's album art taking up a majority of the display (see Figure 7-19).

- *Album art*: When you've downloaded album art, the cover image appears just below the top bar and occupies most of your screen. (When the iPad cannot find album art, it instead displays the same light gray music note on a white background).

- *Song count*: This is a little pill-shaped button that shows you the number of the song in the playlist and how many songs are in it in total.

- *Lyrics*: If the song has lyrics embedded in the music file, the lyrics will be displayed over the album art. You can make them go away by tapping them once. Tap the album art again to bring them back.

Bottom Bar

At the bottom of the Now playing screen you'll see a thick black bar containing (see Figure 7-22) the following:

- *Back button*: Tap the Back button at the lower-left corner (the arrow pointing left) to return to the most recent album or playlist screen. Tapping the back button does not stop playback. Your song continues to play as you browse through your categories or tap the Home button to do other things on your iPad.

- *Genius button*: This button looks like an atom with electrons swirling around it and lies in the center of the bottom bar. Tapping this will create a Genius playlist based on the song that is currently playing. When you navigate back to the music library, you'll see a playlist labeled "Genius" along with several other options. We'll discuss those options in just a bit.

- *Album View button*: This button looks like a three-item bulleted list and appears at the right of the bottom bar. Tap this to switch between your Now Playing screen and its Album view.

Figure 7-22. *The bar at the bottom of the Now Playing screen allows you to create a Genius playlist and enter Album view.*

Album View

Album view is a powerful and fun way to navigate your music. You can access Album view in two ways, both from the Now Playing window. As a matter of fact, Album view is part of the Now Playing window. When you access it, you'll see the bars at the top and bottom of the Now Playing window stay the same (see Figure 7-23).

- Double-tap the album art area to reveal Album view. The cover art will flip around, and you'll be presented with the full list of songs from that album.

- Tap the Album View button in the thick bottom bar of the Now Playing window. The cover art of the current song will flip around, and you'll be presented with the full list of songs from that album.

Figure 7-23. *The Album view shows a list of tracks and durations for the current album or playlist.*

To leave Album view, tap the small thumbnail of the album art in the bottom-right corner of the screen (where the Album View button used to be). The list of the albums songs will flip back around and display the cover art again. Alternatively, tap the Back button at the bottom left of the screen, and you'll be taken back to the main iPod app screen. Your music will keep playing.

Why use Album view? Pretend you are listening to a playlist and a song comes on you haven't heard in a while. It's a great song, and you want to check out what other songs are on the album. Album view lets you do this without leaving the playlist. Simply access it by using either of the methods mentioned earlier, and you'll be presented with a screen that shows a track list of all the songs from that album along with their names and durations. Scroll up and down the track list to see all the items on the current playlist or album. Tap any item to start playback.

Album view also allows you to rate your songs. Use the star control that appears below the scrubber bar to rate the current song, from zero to five stars. Drag your finger along the stars to set your rating. These ratings sync back to your computer. Rating your music is a good thing to do because it lets you keep track of songs you really like. You can create smart playlists to contain all of your five-star songs, enabling you to access them all in one place instantly. Also, if you use the iTunes DJ feature in the desktop version of iTunes, higher-rated songs will be played more often. iTunes DJ is an iTunes feature that picks songs from your library and creates an endless playback of music. It's great when you are having a party. iTunes DJ is not a feature of the iPod app on the iPad.

> **TIP:** When there's empty space on the track list in Album view—for example, when you have only one or two tracks— double-tap the empty areas to return to the Now Playing screen. Alternatively, double-tap either side of the rating stars display.

Creating Playlists

We talked about the kinds of playlists earlier in this chapter. Any playlists you've chosen to sync from iTunes will automatically appear in your iPod app. But you aren't limited to creating playlists on your computer. You can create playlists and Genius playlists right from your iPad.

Creating a Playlist

To create a standard playlist, tap the + button in the lower-left of the iPod screen (see Figure 7-18). A pop-up will appear asking you to name the playlist. Choose a name, and tap OK.

A list of all the songs on your iPad will slide up the screen. Select the songs you want by tapping the blue + button next to it. When you select a song, it will appear grayed out. You also have the Add All Songs option at the top of your list of songs. Adding all the songs in your library defeats the purpose of a playlist, however.

While adding songs to a playlist, you have several options to navigate your library to find the songs you want. At the bottom of the Add to Playlist screen, you'll see the five category views of the iPod app: Songs, Artists, Albums, Genres, and Composers. Select any of these to sort through your song library, and then click the appropriate song to add it to the playlist.

You also have the option of navigating through your iPod app's library source list to find items to add to your playlist. To do this, tap the Source button in the upper-left corner of the screen, and you'll be presented with a drop-down list of the sources and existing playlists in your library (see Figure 7-24). You can combine audiobooks, songs, and podcasts in the same playlist. Tap the blue Done button when you are finished adding songs.

Figure 7-24. *Adding songs to a playlist. You can search through your entire library for songs or choose a source or playlist from your library.*

Editing a Playlist

When you are finished adding songs to your new playlist and have tapped the blue Done button in the upper-right corner, you'll be taken to the playlist edit screen (see Figure 7-25).

Figure 7-25. *The playlist edit screen*

You can also access the playlist edit screen from any existing playlist by tapping the gray Edit button in the top-right corner of any playlist. The playlist edit screen allows you to do a few things:

- *Add Songs*: Tap the Add Songs button to be presented with the Add to Playlist screen again, and follow the previous steps until you've added the items you want; then press the blue Done button again.

- *Delete songs*: Tap the white and red minus (–) button to remove a selected song. Tap the red Delete button that appears to the right of the song to confirm deletion. Removing a song from a playlist will not delete it from your music library on your iPad or on your computer.

- *Rearrange songs*: Tap and hold the grip bars to the right of a song, and drag to rearrange it in the playlist.

- *Delete playlist*: If you decide you no longer want the playlist, tap the white and red minus (–) button next to the name of the playlist in the source list to delete the playlist. Tap the red Delete button that appears to the right of the playlist's name to confirm deletion. Deleting a playlist will not delete the songs it contains from your music library on your iPad or on your computer.

NOTE: You can only edit standard playlists. If you have synced a smart playlist (the kind with the icon of a machine's cogwheel next to it) from iTunes on your computer, you won't be able to edit it.

Creating a Genius Playlist

Genius is a feature in iTunes that finds songs in your music library that go together. It does this by matching rhythm, beat, artists, genres, and Internet data. A Genius playlist is a list of songs that result when you choose to run the Genius feature on a song you are listening to.

Genius playlists can be created in iTunes on your computer or on the iPad. However, to enable the Genius feature, you need to turn it on through iTunes on your computer first. To do this, launch iTunes on your computer, go to the Store menu, and select Turn on Genius. You'll need to log in with an iTunes Store account (see Chapter 8 for creating an iTunes account) to access the Genius features. Enter your user name and password, agree to the terms and conditions, and sit back as Apple analyzes your music library.

You can create Genius playlists in two ways:

- Tap the Genius icon at the bottom of the main iPod screen (see Figure 7-18). The icon looks like an atom surrounded by electrons. If no song is playing, you'll be presented with a list of songs like you were when you created a playlist. Tap a song to base the Genius playlist on.

- From the Now Playing window, tap the Genius icon in the center of the bottom bar (see Figure 7-22).

A new playlist named Genius will appear in your music library's source list (see Figure 7-26). In its list of songs, you can scroll through to see what Genius has picked out. You then have three options via three buttons at the top of the song list:

- *New*. Tap New if you don't like the Genius Playlist compilation. You'll then be presented with a list of your songs to choose a new song from.

- *Refresh*. Tap Refresh if you want to keep the Genius playlist based on the original song you chose but want to get other songs that go well with the original one.

- *Save*. Tap Save once you are satisfied with the Genius playlist. After tapping Save, the Genius playlist labeled Genius will disappear, and it will be replaced by a Genius playlist that is named after the title of the song you chose to create the playlist.

Figure 7-26. *The Genius playlist creation screen*

Editing a Genius Playlist

You have only two options when editing a Genius playlist. Both appear as buttons above the song list when the Genius playlist is selected (see Figure 7-27).

Figure 7-27. *The Genius playlist edit screen*

- *Refresh*: Tapping Refresh will populate the Genius playlist with new songs that go well with the original one. The songs that were previously on the playlist will be removed from it (but they'll still remain in the main music library).

- *Delete*: Tapping Delete will prompt the white and red minus (–) button to appear next to the name of the Genius playlist in the source list. Tap the minus button. If you choose to cancel the deletion, tap the blue Done button above the song list. If you want to continue with the deletion, tap the red Delete button that appears to the right of the Genius playlist's name to confirm deletion. A pop-up will appear warning you that deleting the Genius playlist will delete it from your computer's iTunes library the next time you sync. Tap Delete to delete.

> **NOTE:** Once a Genius playlist is synced back to iTunes on your computer, you will not be able to delete it on your iPad. Your only option will be Refresh. If you want to delete the Genius playlist, you must do so through iTunes on your computer.

Playing Genius Mixes

Another way to explore the music on your iPad is by playing a Genius mix. A Genius mix is similar to a Genius playlist, but you have no control over what songs appear on it, and the songs change each time you play it.

iTunes will automatically create Genius mixes when you turn on the Genius feature. A Genius mix is based on genre and format, not an individual song like a Genius playlist is. You can have any number of different mixes—it all depends on the types of songs you have in your iTunes library. Examples of Genius Mixes are Punk Mix, Pop Mix, Classical Crossover Mix, Folk Mix, Soundtrack Mix...the list goes on and on.

To play a Genius mix, tap Genius Mix in the source list. You'll be presented with a series of Genius mixes represented by squares formed of four album covers representing a sample of songs in the mix. To begin playing the mix, tap it (see Figure 7-28). The mix's four-covers icon will transform into the album cover of the currently playing song in the mix.

Figure 7-28. *Genius mixes on the iPad can include the four in this figure, along with many others.*

Your navigation options are limited while in a mix. You can't see a list of the songs in the mix and can only move through the songs by using the Forward and Backward buttons.

Playing Podcasts, Audiobooks, and iTunes U Lessons

If you've synced podcasts, audiobooks, and iTunes U lesions to your iPad, their categories will show up in the iPod app source list (see Figure 7-29). To view the items available in each category, simply tap the category name. Unlike with music, there is no way to sort podcasts, audiobooks, and iTunes U lessons in the items list.

Figure 7-29. *The Podcast and iTunes U screens*

For podcasts and iTunes U, tap the series or class, and then select the episode or lesson to begin playing it. To play an audiobook, tap your chosen audiobook in the list.

When you select a podcast, audiobook, or iTunes U lesson, the Now Playing screen will appear. This screen is similar to the Now Playing screen for music, but it has some subtle differences (see Figure 7-30).

Now Playing Screen

As you can see, the Now Playing screen is laid out in the same way that it is for music playback (see Figure 7-30). There are some new features, however:

- *E-mail:* Tap the letter icon next to the scrubber bar to compose an e-mail with a link to the currently playing podcast in it. This button appears only when listening to a podcast.

- *Audio speed button:* Tap the 1X icon once, and it becomes a 2X icon. This doubles the speed of the audio playback. Tap the 2X icon, and it becomes a 1/2X icon. This plays the audio back at half the normal speed, which is helpful if the dialogue is being spoken too fast for you to follow. Tap the 1/2X icon, and it turns into a 1X icon, returning the rate of audio playback to normal speed.

- *30 seconds button.* This button appears in the bottom center of the screen. The number 30 with a double-headed arrow wrapped around it counterclockwise denotes it. Tap this button to jump back 30 seconds in the podcast or audiobook. This is a nice feature so you don't have to mess with rewinding with the scrubber bar, which can quickly take you back much farther than you intended to go. If you got distracted and missed what was just said, a quick tap of the 30-second rewind button will quickly get you caught up.

- *Album View.* Album view in a podcast, audiobook, or iTunes U class shows you a list of all the episodes, chapters, or lessons in each one, respectively.

Figure 7-30. *The Now Playing screen when listening to a podcast*

Additional Song Controls

The iPod app offers a series of sorting options (see Figure 7-18) when you are viewing music in your library. We've mentioned these sorting option earlier, but let's look at them briefly here:

- *Songs*: Displays songs in a list.

- *Artists*: Displays an alphabetical listing of all the artists in your library. Tap an artist to see all their albums and the songs under each album. Tap any song to play.

- *Albums*: Displays an alphabetical thumbnail list of all the albums in your library (see Figure 7-31). Tap an album cover, and it springs forward and flips around to reveal a miniaturized Album view. Tap a song to begin playing.

- *Genres*: Displays an alphabetical thumbnail list of all the genres of songs in your library. Tap a genre cover, and it springs forward and flips around to reveal a miniaturized Album view. The songs displayed can be from many different artists. Tap a song to begin playing.

- *Composer*: Displays an alphabetical listing of all the composers in your library. Tap a composer's name to see all their albums and the songs under each album. Tap any song to play.

Figure 7-31. *Album sort view in the iPod app*

Searching

The iPod app has powerful search features that enable you to find a song quickly. Tap the search field in the top-right corner of the iPod screen. A keyboard appears. Simply type in your search keyword, and a list of results automatically begins to populate (see Figure 7-32).

Figure 7-32. *The iPod app's search function*

You can navigate through the search results by song, artist, album, composer, podcast, or audiobook by tapping their respective buttons above the keyboard. You can also scroll through the results with your finger. Doing so hides the keyboard so you can see a longer list of results. To get the keyboard back, tap the search field again. To play a song, simply tap it. Your search results list will remain until you navigate to a category or playlist in the source list or tap the *X* button in the search field.

TIP: You can also search for songs without opening the iPod app. Use the iPad's Spotlight feature to the left of the Home screen to search for a song; then tap it to begin playing.

Display Music Playback Controls When in Another App

We've already mentioned how your music, podcasts, and audiobooks will keep playing even when you leave the iPod app. The good news is that you don't need to go back into the iPod app to change tracks. Simply press the iPad's physical Home button twice in quick succession to bring up the iPod playback control (see Figure 7-33). From this small pop-up, you'll be able to navigate through songs and adjust the volume. To close the pop-up, click Close. To be taking immediately to the iPod app, click iPod.

Figure 7-33. *The iPod control pop-up window*

You can even access these controls when your iPad is locked. Simply press the iPad's Home button twice, and the iPod navigation bar will appear at the top of the display (see Figure 7-34).

Figure 7-34. *iPod controls on the iPad's lock screen*

iPod App Settings

Surprisingly, for a feature-rich application like iPod, the iPad provides just a few settings for its music player. You'll find these in Settings ➤ iPod (see Figure 7-35), and they work as follows:

- *Sound Check*: Say you're listening to a song that was recorded way too low. So, you crank up the volume during playback. Then when the next song starts playing back, *boom!*—there go your eardrums. Sound Check prevents this problem. When you enable Sound Check, all your songs play back at approximately the same sound level.

TIP: You can also use Sound Check in iTunes. Choose Edit ➤ Preferences ➤ Playback ➤ Sound Check (Windows) or iTunes ➤ Preferences ➤ Playback Sound Check (Mac).

- *EQ*: The iPad offers a number of equalizer settings that help emphasize the way different kinds of music play back. Choose from Acoustic, Dance, Spoken Word, and many other presets. To disable the equalizer, choose Off.

- *Volume Limit*: Face it, personal music players bring your audio up close and very personal—so up close, in fact, that your hearing may be in peril. Though not a dedicated music player, the iPad is no different. We strongly recommend you take advantage of the iPad's built-in volume limit to protect your ears. Tap Volume Limit, and adjust the maximum volume using the slider. All the way to the left is mute—sure, you'll protect your ears, but you won't be able to hear anything. All the way to the right is the normal, unlimited maximum volume. If you're super paranoid or, more usually, if children have access to your iPad, tap Lock Volume Limit to open a screen that allows you to set a volume limit passcode. No one may override your volume settings without the correct passcode.

- *Lyrics & Podcast Info*: This setting allows or disables the ability to view lyrics and podcast information on currently playing audio. You will see this information when viewing a song in the Now Playing window.

TIP: If your songs don't have lyrics embedded in them, you can add them yourself. In iTunes, select a song, and then press Command-I (Mac) or Control-I (Windows). On the song's Get Info screen, navigate to the Lyrics tab. You can paste any lyrics for the song you have in the lyrics field. There are also a number of apps that search your iTunes songs and automatically add lyric information. Try Get Lyrical (www.shullian.com) on the Mac and LyricTunes (www.lyrictunes.com) on the Windows computer.

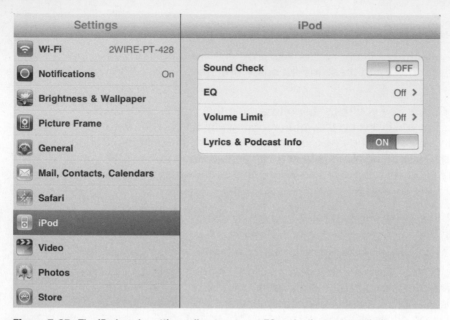

Figure 7-35. *The iPod app's settings allow you to set EQ and adjust volume limits.*

Summary

In this chapter, you learned how to watch videos through the YouTube and Videos apps, as well as in the Safari web browser. You also learned how to browse and play back your music and podcasts using the iPod application.

Here are a few points you should take away and consider:

- Video playback is consistent across applications. If you can handle video in YouTube, you'll know how to use it in Safari. The changes between the screens are minor and easy to follow.

- Set up a free YouTube account to enjoy the YouTube app even more. You'll be able to bookmark your favorite videos, subscribe to video feeds, and rate and share your favorite clips.

- There are three types of playlists: standard, smart, and Genius. The iPod app lets you create and edit two of those kinds: standard, which lets you manually add songs to it, and Genius, which automatically generates a list of songs based on a single song in your music library.

- Save your ears. Adjust your playback volume using the built-in volume controls and limiters. You can find out more about the increasing occurrence of noise-induced hearing loss at www.cdhh.org/resources.php.

- Don't forget about double-tapping the Home button to pull up music controls, regardless of your current application.

Chapter 8

Shopping for Apps, Books, Music, and More

You might think of your iPad as an Internet-connected computer, but it's much more than that. It's also a software store, a bookstore, a music store, and a place to buy videos and movies. Why drive to that increasingly deserted neighborhood video store to rent a movie or wait for a Netflix DVD to show up in the mail when you can rent a movie on your iPad and watch it immediately?

The iPad builds upon Apple's history of building electronic storefronts that make it easy to purchase digital content. This started with the iTunes Music Store on April 28, 2003, resulting in Apple becoming the number-one seller of music in the United States just five years later. Now known as the iTunes Store, Apple's digital store accounts for 70 percent of all worldwide digital music sales.

Through the iTunes Store, you have access to more than 11 million songs available worldwide. Your iPad, if it is using the U.S. iTunes Store, provides access to more than 1 million podcasts; 40,000 music videos; 3,000 TV shows; 20,000 audiobooks; 2,500 movies; and close to 200,000 iPhone and iPad apps.

Starting with the launch of the iPad on April 3, 2010, Apple opened the virtual doors of a new store, the iBookstore. Although it doesn't yet have the selection of Amazon's Kindle Bookstore, a large number of classic and new titles are available.

In this chapter, we'll take you on a virtual shopping spree buying apps, music, movies, videos and TV shows, and books, all while sitting with your iPad in front of you.

The App Store

The App Store opened its doors on July 11, 2008, and as of the printing of this book, more than 4 billion apps have been sold. Most of those apps were written for the iPhone and iPod touch but can run on an iPad unchanged. Many apps have been written especially to take advantage of the larger screen and faster processor of the iPad, and some apps run on both platforms but have improved capabilities that appear only when viewed on the iPad.

When you activated your iPad in Chapter 1, you were asked either to enter an existing Apple ID (iTunes or MobileMe account) or to sign up for one. By doing this, Apple set up both the payment and authorization mechanism that is used by all of the on-device stores. That means you're ready to make purchases in any of the Apple stores directly from your iPad.

When you launch the App Store on your iPad, you're greeted with a screen that looks like Figure 8-1.

Figure 8-1. *The iPad App Store*

By default, the App Store initially shows you featured apps. How can you tell? There are four icons at the bottom of the App Store page: Featured, Top Charts, Categories, and Updates.

Featured Apps

At the top of the store you'll see three buttons: New, What's Hot, and Release Date. Each one of these buttons displays a slightly different view of the inventory of the App Store. Start by looking at the New view.

At the top of the page is a CoverFlow listing of apps "In the Spotlight." These apps have been highlighted by the App Store staff as being either unique or best-selling. To navigate through In the Spotlight, simply flick a finger left or right on the screen to see each of the apps in turn. When you see an app that you'd like more details about, just tap it, and a detailed app description appears (Figure 8-2).

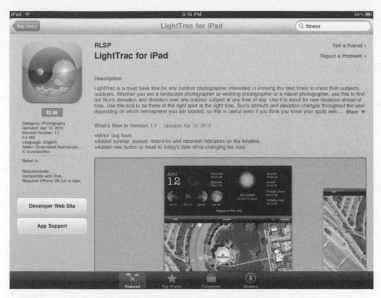

Figure 8-2. *Detailed description of an app in the App Store*

The app description screen displays a large version of the icon that appears on your iPad screen, as well as the price, the category that the app is in, information about the latest release, compatibility, and customer ratings. Want to tell a friend about the app that you found? Tap the Tell a Friend link, and the App Store creates an e-mail that you can send to your buddy.

NOTE: If you have purchased an app and have problems with it, tap the Report a Problem link, and you can let both Apple and the developer know about the issue. To report a problem, choose the appropriate type of problem (a bug, something offensive in the app, or something else), fill in the Comments section, and then tap the Report button to send the information.

The description of an app shows a maximum of about five lines of information on the iPad screen. To read more, tap the More link to expand the description (Figure 8-3).

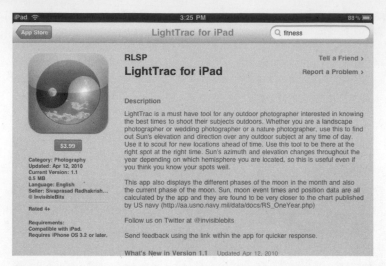

Figure 8-3. *Tapping the More link expands the description of an app. Compare this description with the five-line description shown in Figure 8-2.*

Buttons on the left side of the screen provide direct links to the developer's web site and support page. The images displayed on the screen scroll, so to see all of them, just drag the visible picture to the left.

We recommend reading the customer ratings and reviews at the bottom of the app description page, although they can sometimes be misleading. We find that the reviews often point out common issues that other users may be having with the app, so you can decide whether to purchase the app now or wait for a revision. When you buy an app, you can also rate it and leave a review for others to read.

When you've decided to purchase an app, all you need to do is tap the price. The price turns to a green Install App button, which you then tap. A dialog box appears on your iPad screen asking you to enter your iTunes password and then tap OK. Once you've done that, the app is downloaded and installed onto your iPad. You'll receive an e-mail receipt from Apple outlining your purchase within a few days.

> **WARNING:** When you tap OK and the download begins, the App Store closes, and the home screen of your iPad appears. Don't be alarmed; this is normal. This also happens when you're updating apps.

Let's go back to the App Store for a few minutes and talk about the other areas on the New screen. Below the In the Spotlight section is a New and Noteworthy section of apps (Figure 8-4). Apple's staff chooses this crop of apps from new entries to the App Store, and they're often unique and fun. To scroll through the New and Noteworthy apps, tap the white arrows on the left and right sides.

Figure 8-4. *New and Noteworthy apps are singled out for extra attention in the App Store for interesting functionality, fun game play, or tremendous value.*

Next on the screen is usually a small group of icons, pointing to an App of the Week, groups of similar apps (apps for kids or music creation apps, for example), or apps that deserve special attention.

Continuing down the App Store screen, there's a selection of staff favorites (Figure 8-5). These may not necessarily be new apps, but they've captured the hearts of the App Store staff, and they'd like for you to know about them. As with the New and Noteworthy apps, you can browse through the selection by tapping the white left or right arrows.

Figure 8-5. *Staff favorites, Quick Links, and the common App Store buttons are found at the bottom of the App Store screen.*

At the bottom of the App Store is a set of Quick Links. If your account currently has an unspent balance, that amount is listed. By tapping that balance, you can view or change any of your iTunes account information. If you don't have a balance, that information is available by tapping the Account button at the very bottom of the App Store screen.

See that Redeem button in Figure 8-6? That's a fun way to buy apps on someone else's dime. You may be lucky enough to get a "promo code" from a developer. That's a code that can be redeemed for a free copy of an app. When you tap Redeem, a dialog box appears into which you can enter that code, an iTunes Gift Card code, or a gift certificate code number. Enter the code and tap Redeem, and then enter your iTunes password. If you've entered a promo code for a specific app, that app is downloaded and installed. If you've entered a gift card or certificate code, then your iTunes account is credited for the value of the card or certificate.

Figure 8-6. *Redeeming promo codes, gift cards, and gift certificates is a nice way to buy many apps.*

The last button on the bottom of the App Store screen is for Support. Tapping this button directs you to the iTunes support web page (`www.apple.com/support/itunes`) in the Safari web browser.

The answers to many common questions are found on the iTunes support page, so be sure to browse through the information before requesting further help. If you don't see an answer for your questions about iTunes, the App Store, the iBookstore, or purchases of music or videos, there's a button for sending an e-mail to the iTunes Store support team. In most cases, you'll receive a response with 24 hours.

The What's Hot screen displays a similar layout to New, except with a listing of What's Hot apps in place of New and Noteworthy and the Newsstand taking the place of Staff Favorites. The Newsstand is of interest because it's where you can find electronic editions of magazines and newspapers.

Finally, the Release Date button on Featured provides a scrolling look at the last 6,000 or so apps that have been released in reverse chronological order. For each day, the apps are listed alphabetically. First you'll see apps released today listed in alphabetic order, then apps for yesterday also listed in alpha order, and so on.

> **NOTE:** The descriptions of the virtual stores on the iPad are based on how they appeared during the writing of this book. Apple frequently changes the design of the stores, so specific details described in this chapter may be different by the time you read this.

Top Charts

Whenever we want to see what's popular on the iPad, we start up the App Store and immediately tap the Top Charts button at the bottom of the screen. A list of the Top Paid iPad Apps and Top Free iPad Apps is displayed (Figure 8-7). Scrolling further down the screen, there's a list of top-grossing iPad apps.

Figure 8-7. *The Top Charts screen in the App Store displays the top paid and free iPad apps.*

Apple defines Top Paid and Top Free iPad Apps by the number of downloads of each app, while the lower list is calculated on the total revenue generated by apps. That means that if a high-priced app sells well in the App Store, it's going to top the Top Grossing iPad Apps list.

Categories

Sometimes you don't want to browse through hundreds or thousands of iPad apps, and you'd much rather just see all apps that pertain to a specific category. The Categories button at the bottom of the App Store displays a set of buttons that lead to app listings by category (Figure 8-8).

Figure 8-8. *Looking for a specific type of app? The category listing groups apps with similar functionality.*

This is a great way to find the top entries in a particular category of app. For example, let's assume that you're looking for an iPad app to help you balance your checkbook and home budget. The most likely category for an app of this type would be Finance.

A quick tap on the Finance button displays a familiar-looking screen (Figure 8-9) with a number of apps displayed in CoverFlow along the top and a list of new or recently updated iPad apps in the Finance category at the bottom.

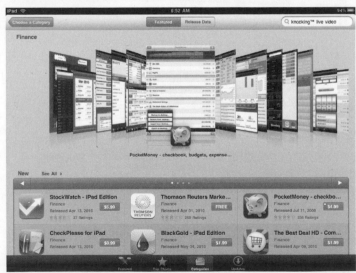

Figure 8-9. *Viewing the new and recently updated apps in the Finance category of the App Store*

By using categories, you've reduced the number of apps to look through to a manageable number. It's a great way to make the best use of your App Store shopping time.

Searching

What if browsing through the App Store just isn't leading you to the one product you're looking for? If that's the case, then it's time to do a search.

The search box is in the upper-right corner of the App Store screen. To search for a keyword, type it into the search box, and then press the Search button on the iPad's virtual keyboard. You'll notice that as you're typing your keyword, the App Store app provides a list of suggestions (Figure 8-10).

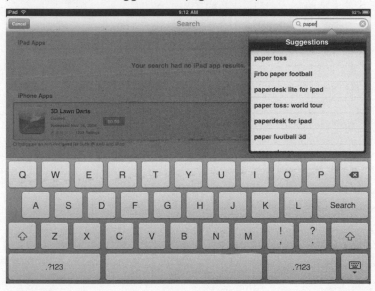

Figure 8-10. *As you type a word into the App Store search box, suggested apps are listed.*

Searching can be very useful when you know part of the name of an app but can't remember the exact spelling. For instance, one of us was trying to find a note-taking app for the iPad recently. We knew that it was called either DeskPaper or PaperDesk but couldn't remember for sure. Typing **paper** into the search box brought up a number of suggestions, and sure enough, PaperDesk for iPad was listed. We tapped the suggestion, which took us right to the description of the app.

Updates

One great thing about buying all your iPad apps electronically is that whenever a new version of the software is published, the App Store automatically notifies you. The Updates button is the last button on the bottom of the App Store screen and is probably one of the most important for keeping your apps up-to-date.

If some of the apps on your iPad have been updated, you'll be notified through the App Store icon. A small red notification circle appears on the icon displaying the number of apps that have updates waiting to be installed (Figure 8-11).

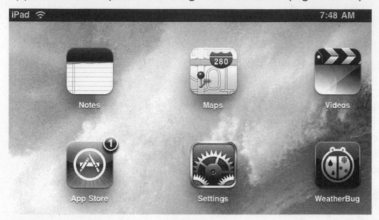

Figure 8-11. *When you have an app update available for download and installation, a notification circle will appear on the App Store icon on your iPad home screen.*

That same number appears on the Updates button in the App Store. To install the updates, open the App Store, and tap Updates. A listing of all the available updates occupies the screen, and there's an Update All button in the upper-right corner of the screen (Figure 8-12). Tap that button to begin the download and installation of the app updates.

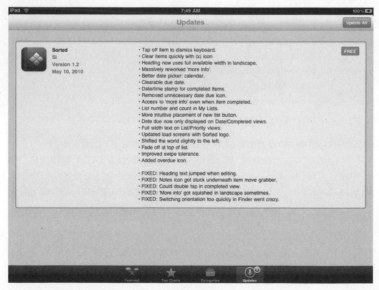

Figure 8-12. *When there are app updates available, tapping the Update All button downloads and installs all of them.*

You'll be prompted to enter your iTunes password in order to validate your request. Once that's been done, the application updates download and install. If the application update is more than 20MB in size and you're using an iPad with Wi-Fi + 3G, then a warning appears noting that you must be connected to the much faster Wi-Fi network before downloading the update. Any smaller updates are downloaded and installed immediately, even over the 3G network.

At the time of publication, app updates are free. However, there has been some discussion of allowing developers to charge for major version updates of their apps to provide for funding of continued development.

The iTunes Store

The App Store is the place to shop if you're looking for games or other software, but what if you want to buy music, movies, or TV shows? That's the purpose of the iTunes app on your iPad (Figure 8-13).

Figure 8-13. *The iTunes Store. Just tap the iTunes app icon on your iPad to enter.*

The first thing you may notice is the similarity in the design of the iTunes Store and that of the App Store. The iTunes Store came first and was refined over many years, so Apple took the same concept and applied it to the App Store and the new iBookstore. The iTunes store has one nice feature the App Store doesn't: 30-second previews. To preview any song, video, or movie in the store, tap it.

Both stores have a set of buttons across the top and bottom of the screen. For the App Store, those buttons were New, What's Hot, and Release Date. In the iTunes Store, the buttons are replaced with Featured, Top Charts, and Genius.

Along the bottom of the screen are buttons for all the different types of media that you can download from iTunes. The media types consist of Music (single tracks or albums by musical artists), Movies, TV Shows (single episodes or full seasons), Podcasts, Audiobooks, and iTunes U.

The top and bottom buttons work in tandem to show you what's hot in all the different media. I'll explain how they work similarly for music, movies, and TV shows.

Featured

Tapping the Featured button at the top of the iTunes Store when Music is selected at the bottom of the screen displays the now-familiar New and Noteworthy list. This time, of course, we're not talking about apps; instead, we're talking about music. Both singles and full albums can be found in New and Noteworthy.

Further down the screen will be buttons linking to special singles and albums, music videos, and items available for pre-order, followed by a section containing content that varies. For example, this section featured "Great Albums for $7.99" when we were writing this paragraph. The section changes depending on what the iTunes Store staff decides to sell at any point in time, so expect this section title to change often.

At the bottom of the Featured screen is the familiar Quick Links section described in the App Store part of this chapter. The links are different, including links for music videos, for items that are free on iTunes, and for pre-ordering new albums. Finally, the Account, Redeem, and Support buttons once again reside at the bottom of the page, providing much the same functionality that they do in the App Store.

Now, when you tap the Movies button, things change a bit. For example, New and Noteworthy changes to New to Rent or Own. We'll elaborate on movie rentals shortly, but for the time being, it's sufficient to understand that you can either buy or rent movies from the iTunes Store.

Below that is a changing section, similar to that found in the music section of the store. It's often seasonal; this chapter was written around Mother's Day, so the section featured 24 "Memorable Movie Moms." The Quick Links and various buttons take their usual place at the bottom of the page.

By now, you'd expect the TV Shows button to display something similar to what you saw for Music and Movies, and you'd be correct. New and Noteworthy appears again, along with the traditional Quick Links and buttons near the bottom of the page. The same is also true for Podcasts, Audiobooks, and iTunes U.

If you're not familiar with iTunes U, it's an innovative section of the iTunes Store that provides educational podcasts and videos from universities around the globe. Yes, you can learn linear algebra, explore concepts in sedimentology and stratigraphy, or follow the history of Rome from Augustus to Constantine, and you can do it all from the comfort of your own home and your iPad.

Genres and Categories

At the top of the iTunes screen on the left side, you'll see a button that changes from Genres to Categories, depending on whether you're viewing music, TV shows, movies (Genres), or podcasts or audiobooks (Categories).

In either case, tapping this button displays a list of types of media. For example, podcast categories include arts, business, comedy, and education, to name a few. Music genres include alternative, blues, children's music, and more. Like categories in the App Store, genres and categories in the iTunes store make it much easier to find what you're looking for.

Movie Rentals

At any time, you can choose to rent a movie from the iTunes Store and view it on your iPad. Rentals differ from purchases in that they have a limited lifetime on your device. When you tap the Rent button, the clock starts. You have 30 days to start watching the movie, so you can preload your iPad with movies before going on a trip. Once you have started watching the movie, you have 24 hours in which to complete your viewing. Want to watch the *Star Trek* movie ten times during that 24-hour period? No problem.

Once that 24-hour period of obsessive rewatching of the rental is complete or you've reached the end of 30 days without watching the movie, the movie disappears from your library. You can only watch the movies you've rented from your iPad on your iPad, so they can't be transferred to another computer or iPhone. Movies that are purchased on your computer can be transferred to your iPad or iPhone.

If you have one of the optional video-out cables that I discussed in Chapter 1, you can pipe the video that's playing on your iPad into a TV with a component or composite video input. The Apple Component AV Cable or Apple Composite AV Cable ($49.00 each) are perfect for watching video from the little screen (iPad) on the big screen.

When you rent a movie directly from your iPad, consider your network speed. Wi-Fi connections are generally much faster than 3G, so you'll be able to start watching the film sooner when it's downloaded over Wi-Fi.

Season Passes

For ongoing TV series, Apple has created the concept of Season Passes. These allow you to download every episode of a TV season. Current episodes that have previously aired are downloaded to your iPad immediately, while future episodes download after their initial TV airdate the next time you sign into iTunes.

Season Passes are a boon to series fans who don't want to miss an episode of their favorite show, and they make it easy to keep a copy of the show for posterity. As with movies, TV series can be purchased in either high or standard definition.

HD vs. Standard Definition

Many movie titles offer the choice of high definition (HD) or standard-definition downloads (Figure 8-14). HDTV fans might be disappointed to find that they're not going to be able to watch your videos in true HD on your iPad. What do we mean by that? The 1024 × 768 pixel iPad display doesn't match the aspect ratio—the ratio of width to height of a display—of either the common 1080i (1920 pixels wide by 1080 pixels high) or 720p (1280 pixels wide by 720 high) HDTV formats. The iPad display also lacks the exact aspect ratios found in many movies, commonly 16:9 or 2.35:1.

Figure 8-14. *High-definition video on the iPad lets you see every wrinkle and hair on actor Hugh Laurie's (House) face. This image shows letterboxing (the black stripes at the top and bottom of the screen).*

That's not to say that you can't display these high-definition video or movies on the iPad—you can, but they'll be letterboxed. That means black bars surrounding the top and bottom of the video screen. The 720p HD–formatted movies are also downscaled to the width of the iPad screen. On the plus side, video and movies look wonderful on the iPad's display regardless of letterboxing. Part of this is because of Apple's adherence to the H.264 compression scheme, which is able to compress digital video to relatively small sizes without compromising quality.

Standard-definition movies from iTunes are in a format called 720xN Anamorphic. Files are upscaled to fit the width of the iPad screen, resulting in movies that aren't as sharp as those that are HD formatted.

Another major difference between HD and standard-definition iPad movies is the size of the movie file. As an example, *Star Trek* is 1.82GB in size in standard definition and 3.95GB in HD (Figure 8-15). Owners of 16GB iPads might want to stick to standard-definition movies or download only a few movies at a time.

Figure 8-15. *This detailed description of* Star Trek *displays the Buy and Rent buttons, as well as the buttons for selecting HD or standard definition. The description displays the size of the file as well, which is important if your iPad is low on storage.*

The rental and purchase prices for movies increase as you go from standard to high definition. An HD movie purchase often costs about $5 more than its SD counterpart, while rentals are usually about $1 more for HD.

Top Charts

Looking at Top Charts while browsing music in iTunes displays two lists: Top Songs and Top Albums. Moving downward on the Top Charts page displays Top Music Videos for your purchasing pleasure.

For movies, Top Charts displays two columns: Top Movie Rentals and Top Movie Sales. In the TV Shows category, Top Charts shows a list of Top TV Episodes and Top TV Seasons. For podcasts, the iTunes Store splits Top Charts into Top Audio Podcasts and Top Video Podcasts.

In the audiobooks category, there's simply a listing of the top 12 audiobooks, and in iTunes U, the Top iTunes U Collections shows you what is popular in the academic world.

Genius

When you're looking at music, movies, or TV shows, there's another button at the top of the page: Genius (Figure 8-16).

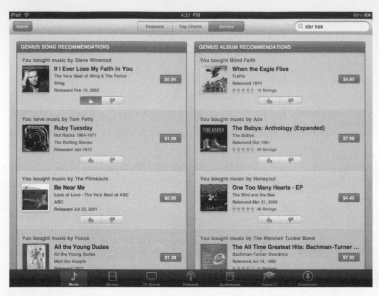

Figure 8-16. *The iTunes Genius is like having your own personal shopper to recommend music or movies. Of course, you'll have to start by telling your personal shopper what you like.*

Have you ever wanted to have your own consultant who could check out what music you like or the movies and TV shows you watch and then suggest new albums to listen to or videos to watch? That's exactly what the iTunes Genius function does for you.

Based on media that you have purchased through iTunes or have moved from your computer to your iPad, the Genius recommends different albums, TV shows, or movies that you may like. You can improve the accuracy of Genius recommendations by occasionally looking at them and voting with a "thumbs up" or "thumbs down."

Accuracy of Genius picks improves with frequency of purchases and rentals. Based on one movie purchase and one rental, the movie Genius did a remarkable job of picking out comedies that we might be interested in, but it also threw in some movies we'd never watch. In the TV area, we had purchased the entire first season of *Star Trek: The Original Series*. That made the Genius think that we would like *Star Trek: Deep Space Nine*, which we loathed. Once again, voting for or against recommended movies is a great idea for improving how well your Genius picks match your true preferences.

The iBookstore

What? You haven't spent enough money yet? You can take care of that quickly with the new addition to Apple's digital stores, the iBookstore. Created for the iPad, the iBookstore will also be available for other platforms in the future.

There's a reason why Apple chose to debut the iBookstore on the iPad. The iPad's book-sized backlit LED screen makes it perfect for reading books in just about any lighting condition. The battery life on the iPad is wonderful, so unless you're planning on doing a marathon reading of *War and Peace*, there should be no need to plug in your device while you're reading.

To take advantage of the iBookstore, you'll need to install the free Apple iBooks app onto your iPad. Probably the easiest way to do that is to tap the App Store icon and then type **iBooks** into the search box. The app should appear at the top of the list of suggestions, and tapping iBooks will display a handful of apps. Look for the free iBooks app, install it by tapping the Free button, and then tap the Install App button. Your iPad downloads the application and installs it.

> **NOTE:** Case doesn't matter when searching in the stores. You can type a search word or phrase in lowercase, uppercase, or mixed-case letters, and you'll get the same results.

Once you've installed the iBooks app on your iPad, launch it. Unlike the App Store and the iTunes Store, iBooks doesn't start in the iBookstore. Instead, you'll see your book library, a beautiful wooden bookshelf with book covers artfully displayed (Figure 8-17). There will probably be only one book on your bookshelf when you first start iBooks; Apple includes a copy of the illustrated *Winnie-the-Pooh* by A. A. Milne with the iBooks app. We'll talk more about iBooks in the next chapter; here we're just concerned with the iBookstore and how to buy books.

Figure 8-17. *Your iBooks library displays your books in a familiar place—on a bookshelf.*

> **EASTER EGG ALERT!** An Easter egg is a little treasure hidden in a computer program. To see an example of an Easter egg in iBooks, use your finger to drag down the bookshelves. You should find something very familiar hidden above the top row of books.

In the upper-left corner of the bookshelf is a Store button. That button is your gateway to the iBookstore. Tapping it loads the iBookstore (Figure 8-18), which looks surprisingly similar to the App and iTunes Stores. It works the same, too; tap the price to see a Buy Book button, and then tap that button to sign into iTunes, pay for the book, and download it.

Figure 8-18. *Inside the iBookstore. It's very similar to the App and iTunes Stores in both looks and in operation.*

Apple made the iBookstore similar to a bricks-and-mortar bookstore in that you can browse books. If you're not sure about a book, check for the Get Sample button that downloads a sizable chunk of the text for you to read. It's like leafing through a book at the bookstore.

To return to your bookshelf, tap the Library button. The Categories button provides a way to narrow down your search to a certain type of book. You know how real bookstores have signs pointing out Mysteries and Thrillers in one area and Cookbooks in another? The iBookstore categories provide the same function as those signs (Figure 8-19).

Figure 8-19. *Categories are like the departments found in real bookstores. They contain books that are similar by type of content.*

In keeping with the general layout of the iTunes and App Stores, buttons across the bottom of the iBookstore include Featured, NYTimes, Top Charts, and Purchases.

Featured

As you'd expect, the Featured button displays lists of New & Notable titles and icons that lead to collections of books about a specific topic or books that the iBookstore team deems must-reads, and then another list of books that changes regularly. As we were writing this, for instance, the list was "Bestselling Bios Under $10," and it featured two books that we ended up buying.

Near the bottom of the iBookstore Featured page, you'll find the familiar Quick Links box, which in this case features not only a link to your account information but also links to book specials (Figure 8-20). If you're a fan of Oprah's Book Club, one tap of the special link in the Quick Links box displays a list of most of the books that have been recommended by Oprah Winfrey. Build Your Library displays a collection of new best-sellers and classics that make a good addition to any library, while Free Books generates a list of classic public-domain titles from authors such as Jane Austen, Henry James, Oscar Wilde, Charles Dickens, and William Shakespeare. They're free downloads and make wonderful additions to any library.

Figure 8-20. *Fans of Oprah's Book Club will be happy to know that there's a Quick Link available to view all the books that have been chosen for the club over the years.*

At the very bottom of the page you'll find the familiar Account, Redeem, and Support buttons, which perform the same functions that they do in the App and iTunes Stores.

NYTimes

The New York Times Best Seller list is considered to be *the* list of best-selling books in the United States. Published weekly in the *New York Times Book Review* magazine, the best-seller list has been published continuously since 1942.

It's fitting that Apple chose to pick the authority on published books to provide an automatically updated list of fiction and nonfiction best-sellers for the iBookstore. Tapping the NYTimes button at the bottom of the iBookstore brings up the lists, which show the top ten books in each category (Figure 8-21). To see more of the Fiction and Non-Fiction Best Seller lists, there's a Show More button at the bottom of the page that will add another ten books to the list each time it is tapped.

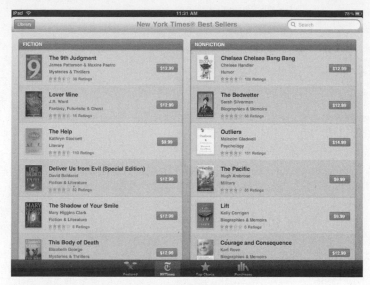

Figure 8-21. *The New York Times Best Sellers list*

Top Charts

The Top Charts button provides a function that is very similar to the same button in the App Store. In other words, it displays lists of the top paid and free books. The Top Paid Books list is often different from the New York Times Best Seller list, because it is compiled from the sales of books available in the iBookstore.

The Top Free Books aren't likely to change very often, although renewed interest in a classic book may move a certain title up or down the list.

Purchases

The Purchases screen displays any book that you have bought in the iBookstore. As you'll find out in Chapter 9, you may eventually want to delete some of the books in your personal iBooks library. If you ever want to read those books again, or at least add them back to the library for future reference, Purchases shows a Redownload button next to the title (Figure 8-22) that you can use to reload a previously purchased book.

Figure 8-22. *If you've deleted a book from your library and want to add it back, you can do that from the Purchases screen in the iBookstore. Tapping Redownload reinstalls the book to its rightful place on your bookshelf.*

When you tap the Redownload button, the iBookstore prompts you for your iTunes password in order to validate your request. Upon entering the password and tapping OK, the book downloads and appears in your iBooks library with a "New" banner on it.

Summary

The iPad makes keeping up with your favorite TV shows, finding new music and applications, and watching your favorite movies as easy as tapping a button. Through the App Store, you have access to a large and expanding selection of software written to take advantage of the features of the iPad. The iTunes Store brings a wide variety of audio and visual entertainment to your iPad, while the iBookstore is sure to give traditional paper books a run for their money.

The following are the key points of this chapter:

- The App Store, iTunes Store, and iBookstore all require an iTunes account for billing and validation purposes. Although you can set up the account on your iPad, it's usually much easier to accomplish this feat on your home computer.

- All the stores require an Internet connection over Wi-Fi or 3G.

- The free apps that are portals to the digital App and iTunes Stores come preloaded on every iPad. The iBookstore is accessible through iBooks, which is a free download from the App Store.

- Do you need a hand in picking out movies to watch, music to listen to, or TV shows to follow? The iTunes Genius provides recommendations that get better the more you use iTunes to buy or rent media.

- Be sure to consider the amount of storage in your iPad when purchasing or renting videos and movies from iTunes, because HD content consumes much more space than standard definition.

- Take advantage of the free previews of music and books in the iTunes Store and iBookstore as a way to "try before you buy."

Chapter 9

Using iBooks

Not only is your iPad a wonderful device for playing games, surfing the Web, and watching videos, it's also a powerful e-book reader with a library of more than 30,000 free books at your fingertips as well as thousands more paid books, including many *New York Times* best-sellers. But iBooks doesn't stop there! You can add your PDFs to iBooks, so you can carry them with you on the iPad. This allows you to access all your PDFs from the same library as your books – a great feature for those of you who regularly work with or receive PDF files.

In this chapter, you'll discover how to navigate your iBooks bookshelf and the books themselves. You'll also learn about bookmarking favorite passages from books, creating notes, and even having a book read to you. Finally, we'll take you through all the PDF features of iBooks. Let's get started.

iBooks App

As you discovered in Chapter 8, the iBooks application does not ship on the iPad. To use it, you must download it first for free from the iTunes Store. Once you have done this, the iBooks icon will appear on your iPad's Home screen (see Figure 9-1).

Figure 9-1. *iBooks icon*

Tap the icon to launch the iBooks app. When you do, you'll be presented with your iBooks bookshelf (see Figure 9-2). The bookshelf will be populated with any e-books you have added to your books library in iTunes (more on that in a moment). You'll also see at least one e-book on your bookshelf: *Winnie-the-Pooh* by A. A. Milne. Apple gives everyone this book for free so they can become accustomed to navigating books on the iPad.

Figure 9-2. *The iBooks bookshelf in landscape and portrait views*

Syncing Books

Before you can sync books, you need to first get some to sync. We talked about syncing books to your iTunes library in Chapter 2, but we'll touch on it again here. There are a few ways for you to obtain books to sync to your iPad.

iBookstore

In the upper-left corner of your bookshelf, you'll see a Store button (see Figure 9-3). Tap this button, and your bookshelf will flip around like it's a secret passageway. On the backside of the bookshelf, you'll be presented with the iBookstore. In the previous chapter, you learned how to buy books and download free Project Gutenberg books from the iBookstore. Any book you download from the store will appear on your bookshelf and automatically sync with your computer when you connect your iPad. For a complete walk-through of buying books in the iBookstore, see the previous chapter.

ePub Books

A second way to get books on your bookshelf is to download ePub-formatted books from other web sites and then drag them into your books library in your iTunes source list on your computer. Any ePub books you've added to your iTunes library will be automatically synced the next time you connect your iPad to your computer.

What Is ePub?

ePub is a universal e-book file format. Any device capable of opening and displaying ePub files can display the book no matter where you bought the e-book. In other words, you don't need to buy your books from the iBookstore only. Several sites sell e-books in the ePub format that are compatible with the iPad. ePubbooks (www.epubbooks.com/buy-epub-books) has an excellent list of sites that offer ePub books for sale and for free download. Once you've downloaded an ePub book, simply drag it to your iTunes library, and the book will sync to your iPad on the next connection.

> **NOTE:** Amazon's Kindle bookstore is another popular place to buy e-books. However, Kindle books don't use the ePub format. If you buy an e-book from the Kindle store, you'll need to download Amazon's free Kindle book reader app for the iPad to read those books. You will not be able to read a Kindle book in the iBooks app. Barnes & Noble's BN eReader for iPad is another way to buy e-books on the iPad, but the BN eReader app supports the standard ePub format so you can move books back and forth between various ePub readers.

Navigating Your Bookshelf

OK, you have a bunch of books downloaded and synced. Before you start reading them, let's get a little better acquainted with navigating all your books on your bookshelf.

Figure 9-3. *From the title bar of the iBooks bookshelf, you can access the iBookstore, navigate between your bookshelf and PDFs, and acess view and edit modes.*

The title bar in the iBooks bookshelf features four buttons:

- *Store*: As mentioned, tapping this will take you to the iBookstore.

- *Books*: When you tap *Books*, you'll be present with your bookshelf. This contains all the ebooks you have in the iBooks app.

- *PDFs*: Tapping *PDFs* will take you to your PDF bookshelf. We'll talk more about the PDF features of iBooks in the second half of this chapter.

- *Icon View*: This is the default view of your bookshelf. The button with four white squares shows you all your books' covers in large, easy-to-see thumbnails.

- *List View*: This is the button next to the Icon View button. It has three white lines in it. Tap it to display a list view of your iBooks bookshelf (see Figure 9-4).

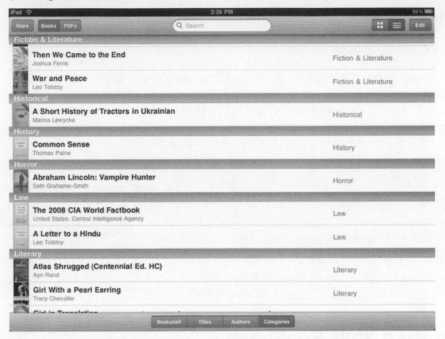

Figure 9-4. *List view with sorting options by bookshelf, title, author, and category*

When you tap the List View button, you'll notice the genre of the book is displayed next to the book's name. You'll also notice that at the bottom of the screen you have four ways to sort your lists:

- *Bookshelf*: Displays your books in the order that they appear in icon view.

- *Titles*: Displays your books in alphabetical order by title.

- *Authors*: Displays your books in alphabetical order by name of author.

- *Categories*: Displays your books in genre groups. Books are arranged alphabetically in each grouping.

List view also displays a search field in the title bar. Tap the search field to open the keyboard and type in your search keywords. You can search through your books library by words in titles or the author's name. Tap a book in the search results to open it.

- *Edit*: The edit button is in the top-right corner of the bookshelf. Tapping this button will cause you to enter edit mode. Edit mode allows you to rearrange the order of books or delete books from your library completely.

- *Rearranging books*: In icon view in edit mode, simply tap and hold a book's cover and drag it to a new position on your bookshelf. This is no different from the way you arrange apps on your iPad's Home screen. In list view in edit mode, you can only rearrange books in the Bookshelf sorting category. Tap and hold the grip bars on the right of the book's genre and drag to your preferred position.

- *Deleting books*: In icon view when you tap edit, you'll see black and white *X*s appear on the left corner of a book's cover. Tap the *X* to open a deletion confirmation window. Tap Delete to remove the book from your iPad. In list view in edit mode, you can delete books from any of the four sort views. Simply tap the white minus (–) button in the red circle, and then tap the Delete button that appears at the opposite end of the screen to confirm the deletion.

> **NOTE:** Deleting a book from the iPad will not delete it from your iTunes library on your computer. You will be able to resync the book any time you want.

You may notice that some of your books have a blue or red ribbon in their cover's right corner. The red ribbons say Sample, and they signify the book on your bookshelf is a sample you've downloaded from the iBookstore. Samples will stay on your iPad until you delete them or buy the full book, but they will not sync back to your iTunes books library.

Blue ribbons say New, and they signify that you have not begun reading the book yet. The New ribbon will appear until you've turned at least one page inside the book (Figure 9-5).

Figure 9-5. *Books with the New and Sample ribbons next to a previously read book*

Reading Books

The bookshelf displays your books in a gorgeous and easy-to-find layout, but books are meant to be read, not looked at. Let's get started!

To read a book, simply tap its cover. The book will fly forward and open. If it's the first time you've opened the book, you'll be on the first page. If you have opened the book before, it will open on the page you left off on.

While reading a book, you can choose between landscape or portrait orientation. As you can see in Figure 9-6, landscape mode shows you two pages side by side, and portrait mode shows you one page. You can navigate between the two modes by simply rotating your iPad.

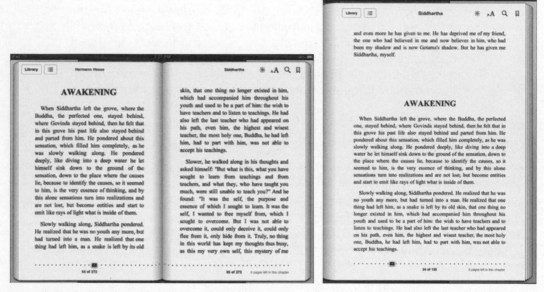

Figure 9-6. *Reading a book in landscape and portrait modes*

At the top of any book's page, no matter what orientation you are in, you'll notice a menu that contains a series of buttons (see Figure 9-7). We will get to using all these features momentarily, but we'll familiarize you with the menu first.

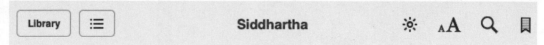

Figure 9-7. *A book's menu buttons*

- *Library*. Tapping this effectively closes the book and takes you back to your bookshelf. The next time you open this book, you'll be taken to the page you were on when you left it.

- *Table of Contents/Bookmarks*: This button is signified by three dots, each with a line after them. Tap this button to be taken to the book's Table of Contents and Bookmarks page.

- *Brightness*: This is the button that looks like the sun and changes the screen brightness while inside the iBooks app only.

- *Font*: This button, symbolized by a small and big *A*, allows you to change the font of the book's text as well as the font size. This is helpful for those people who need larger text while reading, such as older people or anyone with sight difficulties. You can also change the background of the book's page to a sepia tone.

- *Search*: The magnifying glass button allows you to search through a book's text.

- *Bookmark*: Tap the bookmark ribbon to lay down a red bookmark in the upper right corner.

- *Page scrubber*: This is the series of dots that run along the bottom of a book's page (see Figure 9-9). Tap and hold the square button that sits on the dots; then drag it left or right to quickly navigate through the book's pages.

While reading, you can tap the center of a book's page to show/hide the menu bar and page scrubber. You'll be left with only the title of the book and name of the author (in landscape view) at the top of the page and the page number at the bottom.

Turning Pages

You have three ways to move through a book's pages:

- Tap and hold the side of a page; then drag your finger across, and the page will curl on the screen (see Figure 9-8). When you lift your finger, the page turn will be complete.

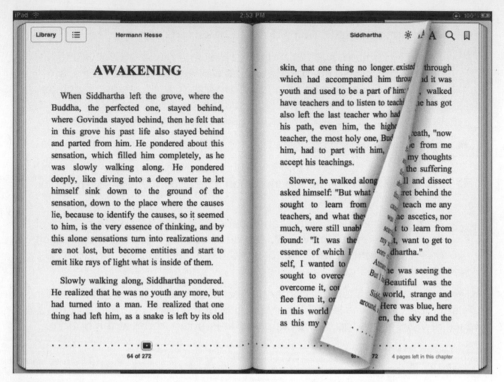

Figure 9-8. *You get cool eye candy when turning a page.*

- Tap the right or left side of the screen to move forward or backward. This accomplishes the same function as the previous one, but with less interactive eye candy.

- Tap and hold the scrubber bar at the bottom of a page (see Figure 9-9); then slide your finger in either direction. The name of the chapter and the page number will appear above the scrubber as you slide. When you've found the right page, remove your finger from the scrubber, and the page will flip, taking you to the page you've selected. The scrubber lets you go to a specific page number quickly without having to flip through all the pages of the book.

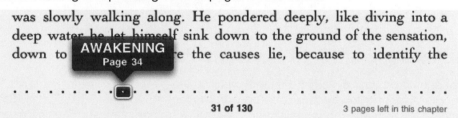

Figure 9-9. *The page scrubber shows the page number and chapter title.*

> **NOTE:** Many people read in bed. Reading an iPad in bed is fine, but because of its built-in accelerometer that detects orientation, you may find the screen rotating back and forth depending on the angle you are holding it at. To lock the iBooks app into one page view while reading in bed, switch the orientation lock on the side of the iPad to "on."

Adjusting Brightness

Depending on your eyes, you may find it easier to read text with a brighter or darker screen. To adjust the iPad's screen brightness while reading a book, tap the Brightness button (the one that looks like a sun) in the menu bar. A drop-down menu will appear with a slider in it (see Figure 9-10).

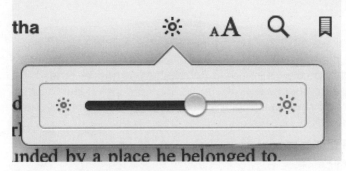

Figure 9-10. *The brightness slider*

Slide to the left to reduce brightness and to the right to increase it. When adjusting the brightness in the iBooks app, the entire screen will brighten or dim according to your slider settings, but once you leave the iBooks app, the screen brightness will return to the settings you have specified in the iPad's Settings application. This is a great feature because you can instantly switch between brightness levels when you enter or exit the iBooks app without having to reconfigure them each time.

To change your iPad's overall brightness levels, go into Settings on the iPad's Home screen, and choose Brightness & Wallpaper. Adjust the slider there to set your preferred brightness.

Adjusting Font, Font Size, and Page Color

Depending on your eyesight, you may want to adjust the font size of the text. Tap the double-*A* font button to be presented with the font menu (see Figure 9-11). Tap the small *A* to decrease the font size and the large *A* to increase it. Increasing or decreasing the font size will result with fewer or more words on a page, respectively.

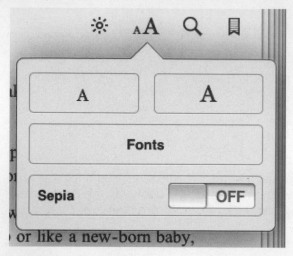

Figure 9-11. *The font panel*

Below the font size controls, you'll see a button that says Fonts. Tap this to select from six font types (see Figure 9-12). Different font types can affect the number of words you see on the screen slightly. Why change the font? Some people have an easier time reading different fonts, especially serif or sans serif fonts. A sans-serif font is like the font of the text of this book; there are no little lines hanging off the letters. A serif font is one like Times New Roman.

Below Fonts, you'll see the Sepia button. Tap to toggle on or off. When ON, the entire book will take on a yellow-brown tone, similar to how pages in an old paper book start to turn color after a while. Some people find reading from a sepia screen easier on the eyes since you aren't staring at a bright white background.

Figure 9-12. *The fonts you can choose from*

Searching Text

You can search for any word or text in the book you are reading by simply tapping the magnifying glass icon. A search field will pop up along with the keyboard. Type any search term you want, and you'll be presented with a list of results, displayed by order of page number (see Figure 9-13). Tap any result to be taken instantly to that page. On the page, your search term will have a brownish yellow bubble over it.

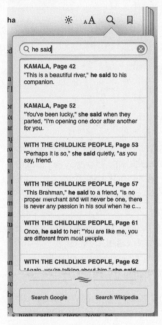

Figure 9-13. *The search panel lets you perform in-text searches as well as quickly link to Google and Wikipedia searches on the Web.*

You can also perform a Google or Wikipedia search for your word or phrase. Below the search results, you'll see a Search Google button and a Search Wikipedia button. Tap either to leave the iBooks app. You'll be taking to Safari where the Google search results or Wikipedia entry page will be presented.

Bookmarking a Page

Tapping the bookmark icon will cause a red bookmark to be laid down at the top of the page (see Figure 9-14). Laying down a bookmark adds a shortcut of the page to the Table of Contents/Bookmarks page so you can quickly access the bookmarked page later. Bookmarking in iBooks isn't really like using a bookmark in a physical book. In the iBooks app, the bookmarking feature is more akin to dog-earing a page on a real book, since you aren't limited to one bookmark. You can bookmark as many pages as you want. To unbookmark a page, tap the red bookmark ribbon.

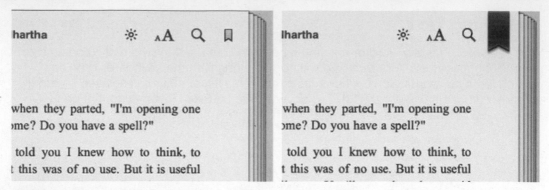

Figure 9-14. *Tap the bookmark button (left) to lay down a bookmark (right).*

Interacting with Text

Your interaction with the book's text isn't limited to search. What we'll show you next is one of the reasons why e-books are superior to traditional paper books. However, paper books still have a leg up on e-books in many ways. See an article about the two formats here: www.tuaw.com/2010/05/08/a-tale-of-two-mediums-despite-the-ipad-traditional-books-aren/. Paper books have the advantage over e-books that they are relatively cheap (especially if you buy them used), and you don't need to be afraid to take them to a park or a beach. Sand or dirt isn't going to affect the usability of a paperback like it will an electronic device like the iPad. Also, while reading in public, paper books are a much lower theft target than Apple's latest gadget wonder.

While on any page, press and hold your finger to the screen, and a spyglass will pop up on the page. To move it around, simply drag your finger. Below the spyglass, a single word will be highlighted in blue. When you've found the word you want, remove your finger from the screen. The spyglass will disappear, and the word will be highlighted with grab bars on either side. Drag the grab bars to select more than one word, such as a sentence or entire paragraph.

With your selection confirmed, you'll be presented with five text-selection tools from the black pop-up menu that appears (see Figure 9-15):

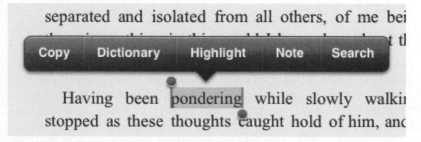

Figure 9-15. *The text selection tools*

■   *Copy.* Select to copy the text so you can paste it into another application or the search field.

■   *Dictionary.* This is our favorite feature of the iBooks app because it shows you one of the primary advantages—and ease-of-use features—that e-books have over traditional paper books. When reading a paperback book, if you don't know a word, you need to put the book down and grab a dictionary. On the iPad, if you don't know a word in a book, you can simply select it and tap the Dictionary button. A window will pop up on page with the definition of the word (see Figure 9-16). You can then tap elsewhere on the page to close the dictionary window and get back to reading the book. Simple.

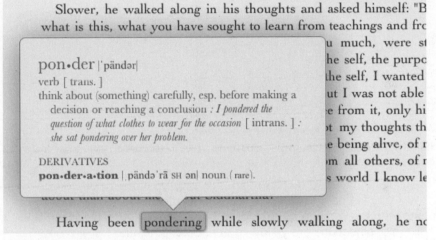

Figure 9-16. *The dictionary panel*

■   *Highlight.* Tapping highlight will mark the text as if it's been highlighted by a highlighter (see Figure 9-17). Apple has outdone itself here, because the highlighting actually looks the same as it does on physical paper.

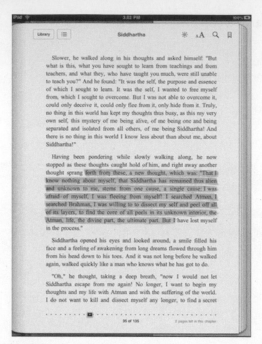

Figure 9-17. *Highlighted text. When you highlight text, it automatically gets added to the bookmarks page.*

If you tap the colored highlight, another pop-up menu appears that allows you to change the color of the highlation, create a note to go along with the highlighted text, or remove the highlation (see Figure 9-18). Color selections are yellow, green, blue, pink, and purple. Any newly selected text you choose to highlight will be highlighted the color of your last choosing. Any text you highlight will show up in a list on the bookmarks page (which we'll get to in a moment).

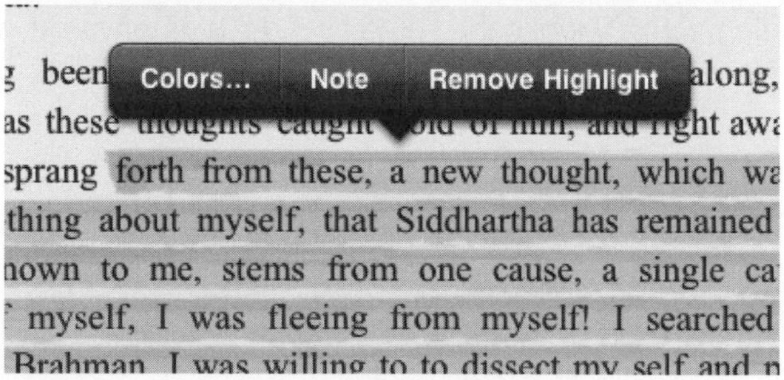

Figure 9-18. *Options for highlighted text.*

■ Note: Tapping Note will automatically highlight the selected text, then cause a Post-It not to fly forward on the screen and the on-screen keyboard to appear (see Figure 9-19). You can type as much as you want in the note and scroll up and down using your finger. The color of the note will be based on the color you chose for your highlation. Tap anywhere on the screen to close the note. You'll see a small not icon appear on the side of the page with with date you wrote the on (see Figure 9-19). Tap the note's icon to edit the note. Tap the text's highlation and select *Remove Note* to delete the note.

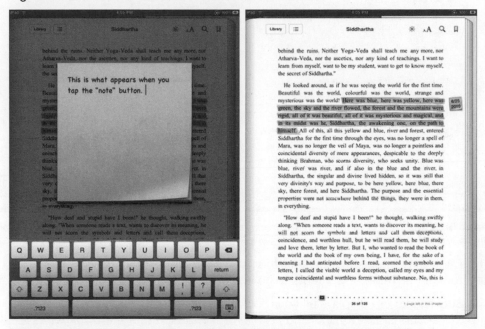

Figure 9-19. *Creating a note and the note icon in the margin of the page after creation..*

■ *Search*. Tapping Search will open the magnifying glass search window in the upper-right corner of the page. The text you selected will be automatically filled in as the search query.

Accessing the Table of Contents, Bookmarks, and Notes

Tap the Table of Contents/Bookmarks button (the botton that has three dots followed by three lines – see Figure 9-7) at the top of your page to be instantly taken to the Table of Contents and Bookmarks page (see Figure 9-20).

The Table of Contents and Bookmarks page is, unsurprisingly, divided into a Table of Contents and Bookmarks section; each has their own tab.

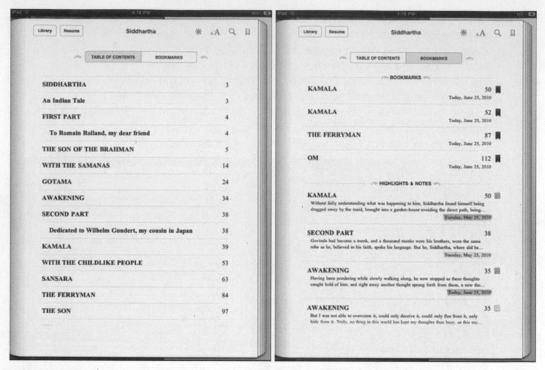

Figure 9-20. *The Table of Contents and Bookmarks page. Switch between the two by tapping the appropriate tab. Return to your last position in the book by tapping the Resume button.*

The Table of Contents tab displays the book's table of contents as a scrollable list. Tap any item in the Table of Contents to be instantly taken to it.

The Bookmarks tab displays all your bookmarks, highlights and notes. They are divided into two sections: *Bookmarks* and *Highlights & Notes*. Under the *Bookmarks* heading, you'll see a list of chapter names or numbers that hold the bookmark, as well as the page number of the bookmark and the date you bookmarked the page. A red ribbon representing the bookmark lies next to the bookmark's page number. Tap any bookmark to jump to the bookmarked page.

Under the *Higlights & Notes* heading you'll see a list of all the higlations and notes you've created. For each highlight and note, you'll see the beginning of the first sentence that the highlight or note appears in, as well as the chapter name or number and also the page number and the date you marked the page. The date is highlighted in the color that you choose to highlight the text in. This is a nice feature if you use different colors for different bookmark classifications, such as quotes from the antagonist in blue and from the protagonist in pink.

Remember than whenever you create a note, a highlation is automatically created. You can distinguish between a highlight and a note easily. Any note has a tiny Post-It note icon in the right hand margin. To be instantly taken to any highlight or note, tap it in the list. To read a note you created without leaving the Table of Contents page, tap the note icon in the margin. The note will spring forwards on the screen (see Figure 9-21). You can then tap the note to bring up the onscreen keyboard to edit it. Tap the area outside of the not to close the note.

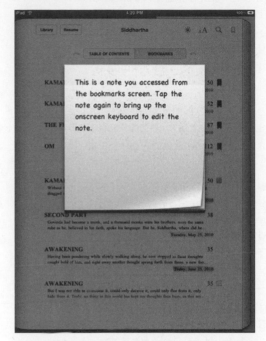

Figure 9-21. *Reading a note on the Bookmarks page..*

To exit the Table of Contents/Bookmarks page, tap the *Library* button to return to your bookshelf, or the *Resume* button to return to your last position in the book.

Having a Book Read to You

Not only can you read books on the iPad, but you can have the iPad read books to you. Using iPad's VoiceOver screen reader technology, you can make the iPad read any text to you, including the text of an entire novel. We talked about VoiceOver in Chapter 2, but we'll touch on how to activate it for iBook reading.

1. Turn VoiceOver on. Go your iPad's Home screen and tap Settings; then choose General ➤ Accessibility ➤ VoiceOver. Tap Triple-click Home ➤ Toggle VoiceOver.

2. Return to your book in iBooks. Triple-click the Home button, and a pop-up will appear. Tap Turn VoiceOver On.

3. Now you have two options. To have everything read to you from the top of the page, use two-fingers held together and flick up. Everything from the top of the screen down will be read. To have everything read to you from your current position in the text, use two fingers held together and flick down. Everything from the position where you flicked will be read. When VoiceOver reaches the bottom of the page, it will automatically turn it for you and continue reading.

4. To stop VoiceOver reading, tap anywhere on the screen with one finger. It would also be a good idea to triple-click the Home button and select Turn VoiceOver Off now, unless you want to continue using VoiceOver gestures.

Now, you might be wondering why you would have VoiceOver's mechanical voice read you a book when you can just buy an audiobook and sync it to the iPad. The simple answer is because not all books are in audiobook format. It should also be noted that iBooks VoiceOver ability isn't a feature intended to appeal to a large number of readers but an accessibility option to help those who are hard of sight read their favorite books.

Syncing PDFs

PDF support was a big feature request when people started playing around with iBooks. Apple listened to them and added it with the introduction of iBooks 1.1. Don't worry about whether or not you have the latest iBooks app. If you've updated or downloaded the app recently, you've got the latest version – which supports PDF viewing. If you aren't sure, open the App Store application on the iPad to check if any updates are available for your apps.

You have two ways of syncing PDFs to iBooks on your iPad: using iTunes or using the iPad's Mail app. To sync PDFs via iTunes, simply drag any PDFs you want to sync into your iTunes library. They will automatically be added to the Books section of your iTune library. The next time you sync your iPad to iTunes, your PDFs will sync as well.

You can also add PDFs to iBooks through the iPad's Mail app. To do this, open Mail and select an email that has a PDF attachment. Tap the attachment in the body of the email to see it previewed full screen. While previewing it full screen, you'll see an *Open In...* button in the upper right hand corner. Tap this button and select iBooks from the drop down list (see Figure 9-22). Mail will close and the PDF will automatically open in iBooks and be added to your PDF bookshelf. When you sync your iPad with iTunes, any PDFs you have added to iBooks in this manner will be added to your iTunes books library.

Figure 9-22. *Opening a PDF in iBooks using Mail.*

Navigating the PDF Bookshelf

To see all your PDFs that iBooks cointains, open iBooks and tap the PDF button in the iBooks menu bar (see Figure 9-3). Doing so will take you to your PDF bookshelf. As you can see from Figure 9-23, the PDF bookshelf is similar to the regular bookshelf. The PDF bookshelf will be populated with any PDFs you have added to iBooks.

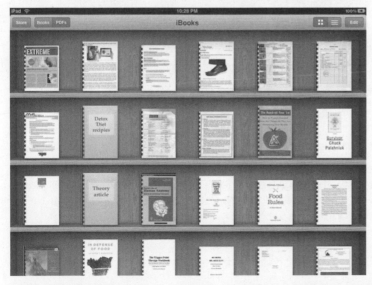

Figure 9-23. *The PDF bookshelf is identical to the regular bookshelf. If you know how to navigate one, you know how to navigate the other.*

Just like with the regular bookshelf, you can choose to view your PDFs as icons or in a list. In list view you will find you can sort your PDFs by titles, authors, catagories, or bookshelf (the way they are arranged in icon view). List view also presents you with a search field so you can search your PDFs by name or author. The PDF bookshelf works just like the regular bookshelf in editing and deleting items as well. Simply tap the *Edit* button to rearrange or delete PDFs.

Navigating and Reading PDFs

To read a PDF, simply tap its cover. The PDF will fly forward and open. If it's the first time you've opened the PDF, you'll be on the first page. If you have opened the PDF before, it will open on the page you left off on.

You can view PDFs in portrait or landscape modes (see Figure 9-24) but unlike with books, viewing a PDF in landscape mode does not show you two side-by-side pages. It's baffling why Apple didn't add this feature (at the time of this writing), but most likely it will be added sometime in the future.

Figure 9-24. *Vieing PDFs in landscape and portrait modess.*

At the top of any PDF's page, no matter what orientation you are in, you'll notice a menu that contains a series of buttons with the name of the PDF document in the center (see Figure 9-25). These buttons will already be familiar to you because they are similar to the ones you see while reading an ebook.

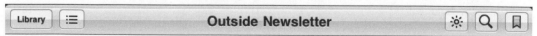

Figure 9-25. *A PDF's menu buttons*

- *Library:* Tapping this closes the PDF and takes you back to your PDF bookshelf. The next time you open the PDF, you'll be taken to the page you were on when you left it.

- *Contact Sheet:* This button is signified by three dots, each with a line after them. Tap this button to be presented with a contact sheet – a series of thumbnails of all the pages in a PDF.

- *Brightness:* This is the button that looks like the sun and changes the screen brightness while inside the iBooks app only.

- *Search:* The magnifying glass button allows you to search through a PDF's text. It also has quicklinks to search Google and Wikipedia for your selected search term.

- *Bookmark:* Tap the bookmark ribbon to bookmark the current page you are on. Remember that iBooks uses bookmarks differently than traditional bookmarks are used in a paper book. To bookmark a page in iBooks means you have effectively "dog-eared" the page. You can have multiple bookmarks in the same document. To remove a bookmark, tap the bookmark icon again.

- *Page scrubber:* This is the series of page icons that run along the bottom of a PDF's page (see Figure 9-26). Drag your finger across the thumbnails to quickly navigate through the PDF's pages. You'll see the page number of the page currently selected float overhead. You can also just tap any thumbnail to jump right to that page.

Figure 9-26. *The page scrubber at the bottom of a PDF.*

While reading, you can tap the center of a book's page to show/hide the menu bar and page scrubber. While on a page, you can double tap it to zoom in or, for more control, you can use a pinch gesture to zoom in or out. To navigate the pages of a PDF, simply swipe your finger to the left or right to move forward or backwards one page. You can also tap the margins of a page to move forwards or backwards, or you can use the page scrubber at the bottom of the page. Alternately, you can scroll through large thumbnails representing all the pages in the PDF document by using the contact sheet.

Using the Contact Sheet

As you can now see, you already know how to use the PDF menu bar because it is so similar to an e-book's menu bar. The only feature that is slightly different is the Table of Contents button, which has been replaced with a contact sheet button (though both icons are identical – three dots, each followed by a line).

Figure 9-27. *The contact sheet lets you see all the PDF's pages as large thumbnails.*

Tap the contact sheet button and you'll see all the pages in the PDF document presented to you in large thumbnails which you can then scroll through with the swipe of you finger (see Figure 9-27). This is useful when you are dealing with a very large document with lots of diagrams or images. It allows you to quickly search the PDF by eye. When you find the desired page, tap it and you'll be instantly taken to that page in the document.

You'll also notice that some contact sheets might have a little red bookmark in their upper-right corner. This means you've bookmarked that page by tapping the bookmark button in the PDF menu bar (see Figure 9-25). To see only your bookmarked pages, tap the bookmark button in the upper-right corner of the contact sheet menu (see Figure 9-28). Any page without a bookmark will be hidden from view.

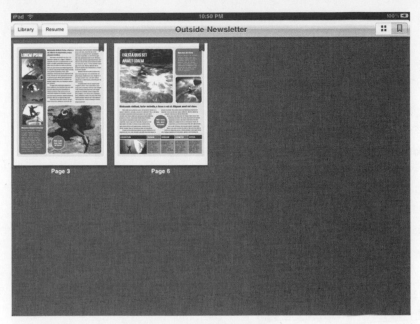

Figure 9-28. *The contact sheet bookmarked pages view.*

To leave the contact sheet you can tap the *Library* button to return to your PDF bookshelf, the *Resume* button to return to the page you were on when you navigated to the contact sheet, or you can tap any page to be taken to that page.

> **TIP:** On a Mac, if you can print it, you can PDF it. Simply choose what you want to turn into a PDF, then from the *File* menu of the application you are in (Word or Firefox, etc.) choose *Print.* You'll see a PDF button in the lower left corner of the Print dialogue box. Click it and select *Save as PDF...* from the dropdown menu. Name the PDF, click *Save*, then drag it to your iTunes library. On your next sync, your new PDF will appear in iBooks. If you own a PC, there are several options to turning documents into PDFs. Google "print to PDF" to find the right solution for you.

Settings

There are a few external settings for the iBooks app. Navigate to Settings from the iPad's Home screen, and select iBooks from the Apps header on the left side. You'll see three settings (see Figure 9-29):

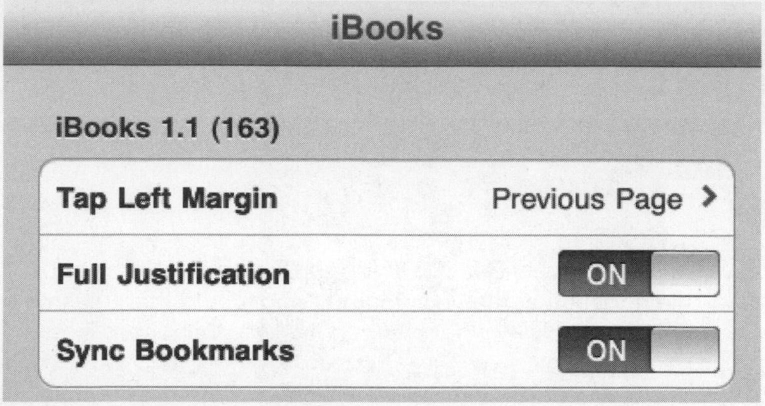

iBooks

iBooks 1.1 (163)

Tap Left Margin	Previous Page >
Full Justification	ON
Sync Bookmarks	ON

Figure 9-29. *The iBooks app settings.*

■ *Tap Left Margin*. You can set this to *Previous Page* or *Next Page*. If you set it to *Next Page*, tapping the left margin of a book will advance you to the next page in a book instead of taking you back one page. This setting might be nice while reading a book on the iPad at odd angles, like in bed. With *Next Page* selected, the only way to go back one page in your book is by using the page scrubber bar at the bottom of the page.

■ *Full Justification*. When this set to *ON*, the text on a book's page will fill the width of the page evenly. When full justification is set to OFF, the text on the right side of the page will be raggid (see Figure 9-30).

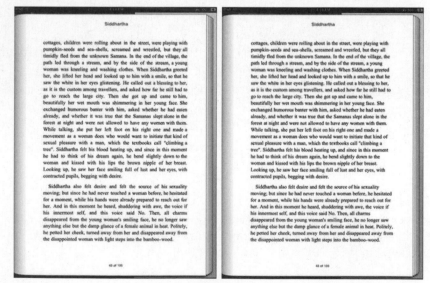

Figure 9-30. *The same page with full justification on (left) and full justification off (right).*

■ *Sync Bookmarks*: When set to *ON*, this will sync a book's bookmarks, highlights, and notes between devices. This is nice if you are using iBooks on an iPad and iPhone. When you create a note or bookmark in the book on one device, it will appear on the other.

Summary

In addition to doing so many other things, the iPad is also a breakthrough e-book and PDF reader. iBooks, the all-in-one application that lets you buy books and read, search, and mark them up, is an elegant yet powerful tool for discovering new titles and taking your entire book library with you. Here are a few key tips for you to carry away with you:

■ You aren't limited to buying books from the iBookstore. Many web sites sell books in the ePub format that you can download and sync to the iPad. A great place to start is www.gutenberg.org. Also, Googling *free e-books* will return a host of results of sites that let you download e-books for free.

■ iBooks has a powerful dictionary-lookup feature that gives you the definition of a word on the book's page.

■ iBooks bookshelf has many views and a search function to help you navigate your books library.

■ Use the iPad's physical orientation-lock button to freeze your iBooks screen in place, avoiding any unwanted screen rotation while reclining on a couch or reading in bed.

■ No audiobook? No problem. You can use the iPad's built-in VoiceOver technology to read any book out loud to you.

■ Choose different colors for your notes and highlighting. Maybe use blue for passages you like and green for something you want to reference later. See all your bookmarks, notes, and highlights in one easy place (the Bookmarks page, of course!), and tap any one to instantly jump to it in the book.

■ iBooks isn't limited to reading ebooks. It's also a PDF reader. Now you can organize, view, and easily navigate all your PDFs – even while on the go!

Chapter 10

Leveraging Your Desk Set

Back in the days before iPads and iPhones, we used what was commonly referred to as a *desk set*. That set varied from year to year but usually consisted of a notebook in which we'd keep meeting notes and reminders, a Day-Timer planner where we'd write our appointments, and an address book into which we laboriously wrote all of our contact names, addresses, and phone numbers.

In the 1990s, many Mac owners were proud owners of a series of Apple Newton MessagePads. These were referred to as *personal digital assistants* (PDAs), and they were the first electronic organizers to synchronize notes, calendars, to-do lists, and contacts to equivalent applications on a desktop computer. Alas, the Newton MessagePad was quite a bit ahead of its time and rather expensive, and Apple dropped the device in 1998.

The PalmPilot took the place of the Newton, followed by several handheld devices running Microsoft operating systems, which were followed by the first series of smartphones. All of these devices had their special capabilities and quirks, and they all had some sort of note-taking facility, a calendar, and an address book.

In 2007, the first iPhones appeared on the market, making life good again for Apple fans and introducing the world to a new form of handheld computing. The iPhone has always had three apps—Notes, Calendar, and Contacts—to perform common desk-set tasks. Now with the introduction of the iPad, the three apps have made the move to another platform.

Notes, Calendar, and Contacts really shine on the iPad thanks to the larger-than-iPhone screen. In this chapter, we'll show you how to make the most of these built-in apps and how they synchronize to other devices. Since Apple's MobileMe service can synchronize your desk-set apps to their counterparts on other computers and devices, we'll also describe how to sign up for and enable the service.

Notes

On the iPhone, Notes is roughly the equivalent of a small pocket notepad. You probably wouldn't want to attempt to take a long set of notes with the app. Even though the note can be scrolled, there isn't a lot of available room. Typing would most likely be done with one finger, slowing down your text entry and making errors more likely.

The Notes app on the iPad is a totally different animal. It's more like a legal pad (Figure 10-1), both in looks and in how it can be used. In landscape orientation, Notes looks like a leather-bound portfolio, with a small, white, paperlike index list on the left side and a legal pad at the right (complete with margin lines as well as the remnants of torn-off pages at the top).

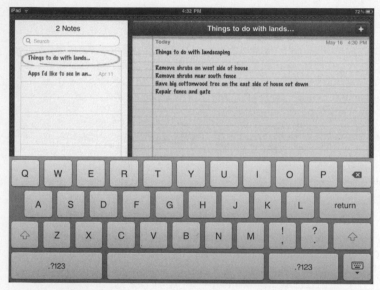

Figure 10-1. *Your iPad's legal pad, the Notes app. The list on the left side displays all the notes you've written.*

Flipping the iPad into portrait orientation (Figure 10-2), Notes appears to be just a normal legal pad. We personally find the landscape orientation easier to use for data entry in Notes, since we get an almost full-sized keyboard to touch type on.

When you're using Notes in portrait mode, the index list disappears from the left side of the portfolio, and a Notes button appears at the top of the note pad. To display the index list, just tap the Notes button.

Figure 10-2. *The Notes app in portrait orientation really looks like a legal pad, complete with yellow paper.*

When Notes is being used in landscape mode, touching a note on the white index list highlights it with a red-penciled oval and displays the full note on the legal pad. At the top of each page, whether you're using Notes in landscape or portrait orientation, is the date and time when the note was created, as well as how many days ago it was written. If it was just written, the notebook will display "Today" at the top; if it was written yesterday, it will display "Yesterday." After that, the number changes to the number of days ago that the note was written.

On the bottom of each page are four icons (Figure 10-3). Tapping the left and right arrow icons flips between pages in the notebook. Tapping the envelope icon creates a new e-mail containing the text of the note page, while tapping the trash can icon displays the Delete Note button you see in Figure 10-3.

Figure 10-3. *The Notes app icons at the bottom of each page are (from left to right) used to go to the previous note, send the note in an e-mail, delete the note, or move to the next note.*

Adding and Deleting Notes

To create a new notebook page, tap the plus sign (+) in the upper-right corner of the notebook. The first line of text typed on the note page is the title of your note and is repeated both on the index list and at the top of the note pad. To search for a word or phrase in any of the notes, type it into the Search box at the top of the index list. The list magically shrinks to show only those notes containing the search word or phrase (Figure 10-4).

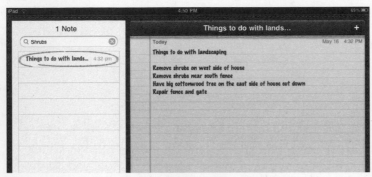

Figure 10-4. *Typing letters or words into the search field narrows the index list to only the notes containing the search criterion.*

You can delete notes in two ways. First, tapping the trash can icon at the bottom of each note displays a Delete Note button. Tap that button to complete the deletion.

The second way to delete a note is to swipe your finger either left or right over the title of the note in the index list. This is easier to do in landscape mode, since the index list is always in view on the left side of the Notes window. In portrait orientation, tapping the Notes button at the top of the notebook displays the index list; then you can swipe to delete a note.

Syncing Notes

If you're writing notes on your iPad, you may want to use them on your Mac or Windows computer. There are a couple of ways to go about moving them to a personal computer—either e-mail them to yourself using the e-mail button we described earlier or use Notes syncing.

To set up Notes syncing, launch iTunes on your computer, and then connect your iPad to the computer using the USB cable, as described in Chapter 2. When the name of your iPad appears in the Devices list on the left side of the iTunes window on your computer, click it, and then click the Info tab. Scroll down the window a bit, and you'll see the cryptic Other heading (Figures 10-5 and 10-6). Under that heading is the check box you're looking for.

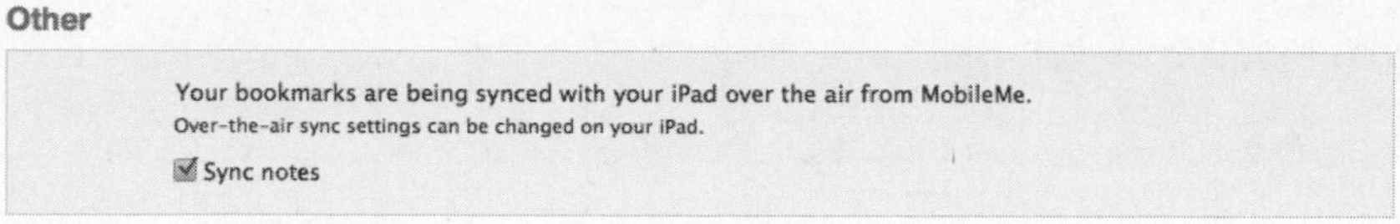

Other

Figure 10-5. *The Other section under Info in iTunes contains a check box for syncing notes from the iPad to your Mac.*

Other

Figure 10-6. *You can find the check box for syncing notes with Outlook under Other in iTunes for Windows.*

To sync notes to your computer from your iPad, select that box, and then click the Sync button on the bottom-right side of the iTunes window.

So, now you've synced all of those notes to your computer—where are they? Oddly enough, there is no similar app on the Mac, so notes end up in Mail. Launch Mail on your Mac, and then take a look at the sidebar on the left side of the Mail window (Figure 10-7).

See the Reminders heading? There is a small replica of the Notes icon from the iPad below that. Click that icon, and you'll see two more notepads—one that says "On My Mac" and another that says "MobileMe." Click the On My Mac icon, and the notes you've created are there.

On your Windows computer, Notes are synced to Microsoft Outlook 2003, 2007, or 2010 (Figure 10-8). To view your synced notes in Outlook, click the Notes button.

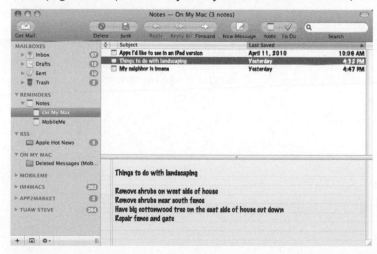

Figure 10-7. *The text you create in Notes on your iPad syncs to Mail on your Mac.*

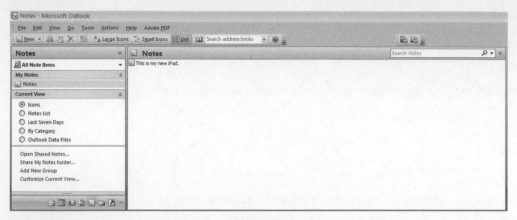

Figure 10-8. *The text you create in Notes on your iPad syncs to Microsoft Outlook 2003 or 2007 on your Windows computer.*

These notes are fully synced, so if you choose to make a change to one of them or create a new one on your Mac or Windows computer, the changes or new file is moved to the iPad the next time you sync. Likewise, any changes, additions, or deletions you make on the iPad are reflected on your computer.

So, what's that MobileMe icon all about? If you happen to have an Apple MobileMe account, then you'll actually be able to synchronize your notes on all sorts of devices and in various places when iOS 4.0 is released for iPad in 2010. Right now, the only way to sync your notes between your computer and iPad is through that hardwired USB connection.

Calendar

Like many people who enjoy the layout of the Day-Timer planner, we were thrilled to see how Apple changed the plain-Jane iPhone Calendar app to a thing of beauty on the iPad. In landscape orientation (Figure 10-9), Calendar looks remarkably like that old Day-Timer.

Figure 10-9. *The iPad Calendar app in Day view looks like a traditional paper appointment book.*

There are four Calendar views, each of which provides a slightly different view of your calendar information. To switch between them, tap Day, Week, Month, or List at the top of the calendar.

The view shown in Figure 10-9 is the Day view, which displays an hour-by-hour listing of what's going to happen during the current day. See that pinhead with the line across from it at about 2 p.m.? That indicates the current time so you can see at a glance how much time you have until your next appointment.

On the left side of the Calendar app in Day view, there's a handy month calendar and a list of all the appointments scheduled that day. To turn to the next page in this virtual appointment book, tap the right arrow at the bottom of the page. Moving to the previous page just requires tapping the left arrow. You can also drag a finger back and forth on the days of the current month, which are listed between those two arrows, to navigate to a particular date.

If all of this moving around in Calendar causes you to get lost, there's a Today button in the lower-left corner of the app to quickly jump to the current day. Before we talk about adding or searching for Calendar events, let's take a look at the rest of the available Calendar views.

The Week view (Figure 10-10) is helpful in mapping out what tasks need to be accomplished during a specific week. Any items listed at the top of the calendar are all-day events, while colored boxes denote the time and duration of your meetings. The days of the week are listed across the top, with the hours of the day on the left side. To scroll earlier or later in the day (the calendar shows only 12 hours of each day at a time), use your finger to scroll up or down.

Figure 10-10. *Using the Calendar app's Week view to capture a week at a glance*

The Week view lists ten one-week periods at the bottom of the page, and you can tap any one of those weeks or slide a finger left or right to look at previous or future weeks. The Month view (Figure 10-11) provides the look of those "Month at a Glance"–style calendars that have been sold for years as desk pads. Here, every appointment during the month is designated by a small dot on a particular day. To get details about an appointment, just tap the dot, and a pop-up arrow appears with the time of the appointment and an edit button.

Figure 10-11. *You can look at an entire month's worth of appointments in the Calendar app's Month view. Tap an appointment to open a pop-up arrow for details or to edit the event.*

The area at the bottom of the page changes to a list of the months of a year for jumping to a specific month with the tap of a finger. There are also buttons to navigate to the previous and next years. The last view is the List view (Figure 10-12), which lists upcoming appointments on a scrollable list on the left side of the page, along with a close-up view of a current event on the right side.

Figure 10-12. *The List view in the iPad Calendar app displays a list of upcoming appointments (left) and details of any appointment you tap (right).*

Tapping any of the appointments in the list on the left displays the details of that event on the right side. Any alerts that were set are listed, as well as notes that are associated with the event. If someone else sent the appointment to you and you accepted it, the detailed view will also show who sent the original appointment and list anyone else who has accepted the event invitation.

Adding Calendar Events

From any of the views listed earlier, tapping the plus sign (+) icon in the lower-right corner of the calendar reveals an Add Event dialog box and the standard iPad virtual keyboard. To enter event information, tap any one of the fields and begin typing on the keyboard. Tapping Start & End, which is used to enter the beginning and ending of an event, displays a date and time picker (Figure 10-13). Use your finger to roll the start date and time up or down, and then do the same with the ending time of the event. If an event is going to last all day (for example, an all-day meeting or a birthday), then slide the All-day button to On.

Figure 10-13. *Whenever you're adding events to a calendar, the date and time picker is used to select the starting and ending dates and times.*

If you want to make the event repeat at regular intervals, just tap the Repeat field. You'll be given the choice (Figure 10-14) of repeating the event every day, week, two weeks, month, or year. A daily repeating event would be useful in reminding yourself to take important medication, while an annual repeating event could save your marriage by reminding you of an impending anniversary.

Figure 10-14. *Any event can be set up to repeat at distinct time intervals that you set.*

Any event can have up to two alerts. Alerts on the iPad are both audible and visual; there is no choice between the two types of alerts as there is on the Mac. Tapping the Alert or Second Alert field displays a list of times before an event at which an alert can go off. Those times vary from five minutes to two days before, or you can have your iPad alert you on the date of the event.

What happens when the alert goes off? A small visual alert appears on the screen (Figure 10-15), with a Close button that dismisses the alert with a tap and a View Event button that takes you to the calendar to see the details. If you have the sound turned up on your iPad, you'll also hear an alert tone ring.

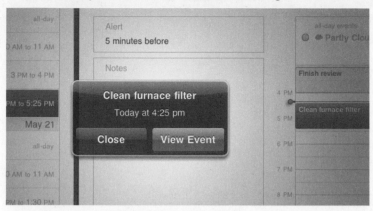

Figure 10-15. *Your iPad alerts you of impending appointments with an alert tone and a visual reminder.*

There are also fields for entering the location of an event or notes about it. When you're done entering the event information, tap the Done button, and the event appears on the calendar.

Syncing Calendar

As with the Notes app, much of the power of Calendar on the iPad becomes apparent when you synchronize to Microsoft Outlook 2003, 2007, or 2010 on your Windows computer, or to iCal on your Mac. The method of setting up synchronization is similar to how you set up Notes.

Connect your iPad to your Windows computer or Mac using the Dock Connector to USB cable, and then launch iTunes if it doesn't start by itself. In iTunes on your computer, click the icon designating your iPad under Devices in the sidebar on the left side of the window. Next, click the Info tab, and scroll down until you see the words *Sync iCal Calendars* (Mac; Figure 10-16) or *Sync Calendars* (Windows; Figure 10-17).

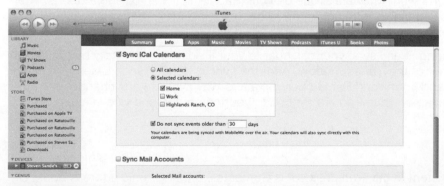

Figure 10-16. *Setting up Calendar syncing in iTunes. Note that this iPad is already syncing through Apple's MobileMe service.*

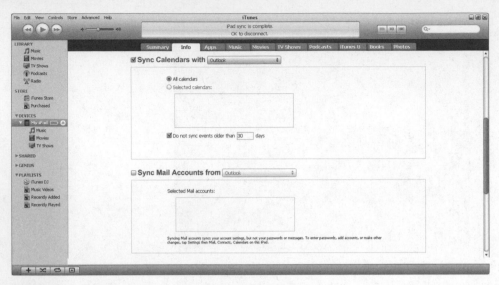

Figure 10-17. *Setting up Calendar syncing in iTunes on Windows*

To set up synchronization of iCal and the Calendar app on your iPad, select the Sync Calendars or Sync iCal Calendars box. Below the check box are radio buttons for syncing all calendars on your Mac or Windows computer to the iPad or just selected calendars. You might want to select certain calendars for syncing if you have many calendars on your computer and really don't need to view or edit all of those on your iPad.

In Figure 10-16, you can see three calendars on a Mac—one for Home, one for Work, and a third one called Highlands Ranch (it is created by a Mac application called WeatherCal from Bare Bones Software and displays weather forecasts on a calendar). To sync only the Home calendar to the iPad, select the Selected Calendars radio button, and then select only the Home calendar box.

You can choose to sync only future and recent events by selecting the "Do not sync events older than 30 days" box. That's very useful if you have many events on your calendar and don't want to waste space on your iPad filling it with calendar debris. The number of days is editable, so if you'd like to only sync events back two weeks and into the future, you can change the number 30 to 14.

To apply the changes and sync your calendar to your iPad, click the Apply button in the lower-right corner of the iTunes window. After the sync is done, launch Calendar on your iPad; then applaud your work! Remember, it's a two-way sync, so any changes or additions you make on your iPad are synced to your computer, and vice versa.

Contacts

The third component of the iPad desk set is Contacts, your electronic address book. On the left side of the address book is a scrolling list of names, while the details of a specific person or company appear on the right side (Figure 10-18).

Figure 10-18. *Contacts is your personal address book, synchronized to your Mac or Windows computer and to other devices if you want.*

Compared with Calendar, the Contacts app is very simple. Instead of multiple ways to display the information, there's only one view. That's not to say that Contacts isn't useful; in fact, the address list is used by Mail and many other iPad apps to enable sharing of information with other people.

Adding a Contact

To add a contact, tap the plus sign (+) icon on the bottom of the left page. A blank page in the contacts book appears (Figure 10-19) with helpful labels to tell you what information needs to be entered into each field. To start entering information into any field, tap it, and the iPad's virtual keyboard appears.

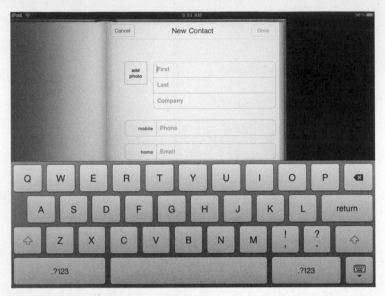

Figure 10-19. *Starting with this blank page, your contact information can be simple or complex.*

Apple did a great job with the Contacts edit fields. Entering a phone number as a string of numbers produces a nicely formatted number with dashes and parentheses in all the proper places for your country. Adding a state or province code in the address area locks the caps key so that all the letters in the code are capitalized. It's little details like this that make the iPad such a joy to use.

You can even add a photo to each Contacts entry by tapping the "add photo" box. This displays a list of photo albums stored on your iPad, which you can browse until you find a photo of the person you're entering information about. Tap their photo, and you can move and scale the image with the common iPad gestures until the photo looks just right. Finally, tap the Use button, and their photo is inserted into the page.

Once you're done entering information about a person or company, tap the Done button in the upper-right corner of the Contacts app to see the finished page in your virtual address book.

Should you need to add or change information at any time, tap the Edit button to reveal the edit fields for Contacts. There's also a Share button at the bottom of each Contacts entry that creates an e-mail containing a .vcf (vCard file format) file that can be opened by most address book applications.

To delete a contact, tap the Edit button, and then scroll to the bottom of the contact information. There's a large red Delete Contact button there. Tap it, and a small dialog box appears asking whether you want to delete the contact or cancel the deletion. When you tap Delete, the contact is removed from your iPad contacts list.

Groups and Searching

At the top of the left page in Contacts is a small red ribbon bookmark with the word *Groups* on it. Tapping that red ribbon lists all the groups that you have created...but not on your iPad. You cannot create groups of contacts on your iPad. That task has to be done on your Mac or Windows computer.

Why use groups? It's a great way to make it easier to find certain people who you know are in a specific group or to list everyone in a certain group. In other words, instead of searching 2,000 contacts for a person you know is a member of a particular group, you can narrow it down to the people in that group.

Speaking of searching, you can use the Search field at the top of the Contacts left page to look for specific people or companies. Tap in the Search field, and start typing, and Contacts provides a list of people or companies that fit the search criteria. As an example, searching for *Steve* produces a list of people with that first name who are included in the contacts list (Figure 10-20).

Figure 10-20. *The Search field is helpful when you need to find someone quickly in a large number of contacts.*

Syncing Contacts

Remember how you set up syncing of Calendar and Notes earlier in this chapter? That's how you're going to set up syncing of Contacts as well. The companion applications on a Windows computer can be Microsoft Outlook 2003, 2007, or 2010; Windows Address Book (Windows XP), or Windows Contacts (Windows Vista and Windows 7). On the Mac, contact synchronization can be set up with Address Book and Microsoft Entourage 2004 or 2008. Which application should you use? If you use Outlook on your Windows computer, then sync with the Outlook contacts list. If you use web mail or an application other than Outlook for mail, contacts, and calendar, then use either Windows

Address Book or Windows Contact depending on which is available in the version of the Windows operating system you're using.

Connect your iPad to your Mac using the Dock Connector to USB cable, and then launch iTunes if it doesn't start by itself. In iTunes on your computer, click the icon designating your iPad under Devices in the sidebar on the left side of the window. Next, click the Info tab and scroll down until you see the words *Sync Address Book Contacts* (Mac; Figure 10-21) or *Sync Contacts* (Windows; Figure 10-22).

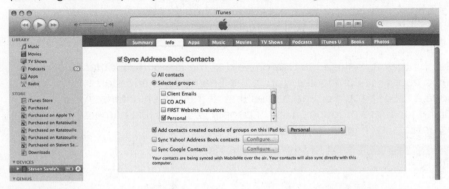

Figure 10-21. *To sync Contacts with your Mac, select the Sync Address Book Contacts box. Note that this iPad is already syncing through MobileMe.*

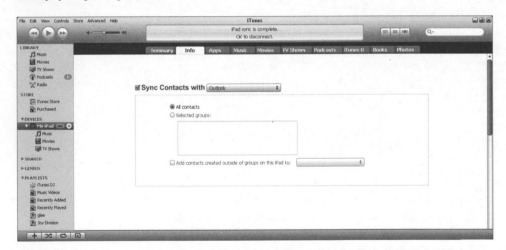

Figure 10-22. *To sync Contacts with your Windows computer, select the Sync Contacts in iTunes box.*

As with syncing calendars, you have the choice of either syncing all your contacts to the iPad or just selected groups. There are several other check boxes to consider when setting up address book syncing.

First, you may want to add contacts that you create on your iPad to a specific group. That's what the "Add contacts created outside of groups on this iPad to" check box is for. Select the box, and then select a group. Any new contacts created on the iPad are automatically added to that group.

Apple also built in synchronization with other address books. The next two check boxes are used to set up synchronization with Yahoo! Address Book or Google Contacts. Checking either of the boxes displays a legal agreement allowing iTunes to synchronize with Yahoo! or Google. You can either agree or disagree with the statement, but realize that you won't be able to sync with these services without clicking the Agree button.

Once you've agreed to allow the sharing of information with Google or Yahoo!, a configuration screen appears requesting your user ID and password for that service. Entering that information and then clicking Apply in the lower-right corner of iTunes ensures that your Contacts information is synced between your iPad, your computer's address book or Contacts application, and either Yahoo! Address Book or Google Contacts.

MobileMe Synchronization

All the sync setup you've just done assumes one thing—that you don't have a subscription to Apple's MobileMe service. MobileMe provides more than just synchronization of data between Macs, Windows computers, iPhones, iPads, and the Web. It also provides you with a me.com e-mail address, online storage of data through iDisk, online photo galleries, and a way to find your iPad if you lose it. What's truly magical is that all of this happens over your iPad's Wi-Fi or 3G connection, so there's no need to constantly connect your device to your Mac or Windows computer through the Dock Connector to USB cable.

MobileMe is available from Apple for an annual subscription fee of $99 (www.apple.com/mobileme), although subscriptions are often available at a discount from Amazon.com. If you've purchased a subscription from one of these sources, you can enable the services on your Mac by selecting System Preferences ➤ MobileMe and signing in with your member name and password (Figure 10-23). Those who aren't members can sign up for a 60-day free trial of MobileMe through the same System Preferences pane. Windows computer owners can sign up for MobileMe or the same free trial by pointing their web browser to www.apple.com/mobileme.

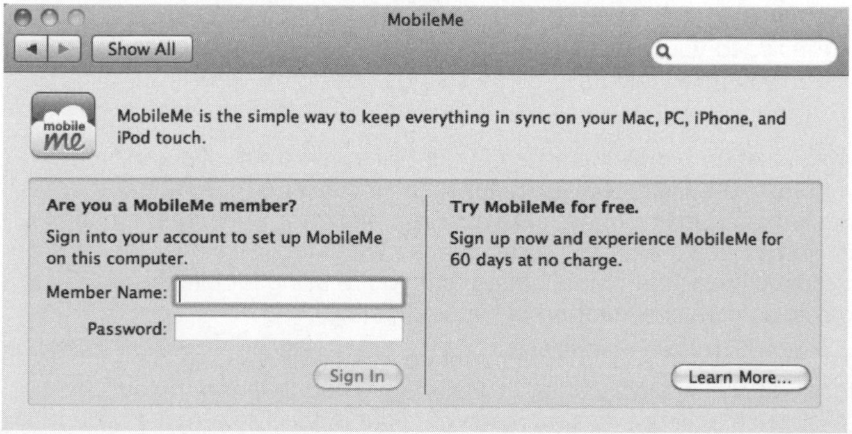

Figure 10-23. *Not only is MobileMe a great way to do over-the-air synchronization of your iPad, iPhone, and Mac, but it also provides features to let you find your iPad if you lose it and do a remote wipe of your data.*

Once you've logged into your MobileMe account from the MobileMe system preferences panel, you can set up synchronization from your Mac by clicking the Sync button and ensuring that the Synchronize with MobileMe box is selected (Figure 10-24).

Figure 10-24. *Syncing with MobileMe provides two-way updates to Calendar and Contacts wirelessly.*

Below the check box is a list of things that MobileMe can synchronize between different devices signed into the same MobileMe account. Primary to those items are your three desk-set apps—Calendars, Notes, and Contacts—but Mail accounts and Safari web browser bookmarks can also be synced between your Mac, iPad, and iPhone or iPod touch.

We recommend setting up automatic synchronization so that any time a change is made to iCal or Address Book or a note is added to Mail on your Mac, those changes are immediately synchronized to your iPad. Remember that the synchronization is two-way, so making changes on your iPad results in those changes being made on your other devices as well.

You'll notice that if you set up MobileMe sync of your Calendar, Contacts, and Notes information, those items are deselected on the Info tab in iTunes. A message at the bottom of the Sync Address Book Contacts, Sync iCal Calendars, and Other areas of the iTunes Info tab notes that your data is being synced with MobileMe over the air. You can choose to sync directly and with MobileMe, but if you're using MobileMe, we recommend using that as your sole method of syncing data.

For Windows users, the best and easiest way to set up MobileMe syncing is on the iPad. On your iPad, select Settings ➤ Mail, Contacts, Calendars, and then tap the button designating your MobileMe account. It is marked with your MobileMe e-mail account name. In the dialog box that appears (Figure 10-25), you'll see buttons to turn on syncing of Contacts and Calendar. Sliding those buttons to On enables the synchronization of Calendar and Contacts between the iPad and MobileMe. Synchronizing MobileMe with your Windows computer is beyond the scope of this book, but you can find out more at www.apple.com/mobileme/setup/pc.html.

We'll tell you how to set up MobileMe on your iPad in the next chapter.

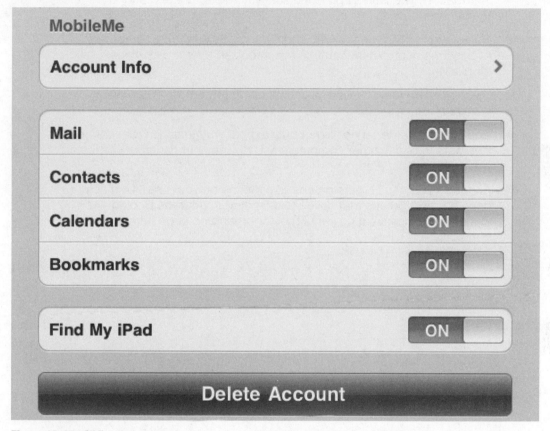

Figure 10-25. *Sliding the relevant buttons to On enables the synchronization of Calendar and Contacts between the iPad and MobileMe.*

Summary

Some of the most useful apps on your iPad consist of Calendar, Notes, and Contacts—the desk set of your device. In this chapter, you learned how to use your iPad as a digital notepad, Day-Timer, and address book, as well as how to sync that information to your Mac or Windows computer. These are several important topics to remember from this chapter:

■ The desk-set application(s) on your computer (iCal and Address Book on your Mac, Outlook on your Windows computer) can sync with similar apps on your iPad. Calendar is a powerful desk calendar on the iPad, while Contacts gives you access to all your address book information. The Notes app is a quick way to capture text and move it to your computer.

■ Notes sync to Mail on the Mac and Outlook on Windows computers. At this time, Notes data can't be synchronized over the air using MobileMe.

■ There are four ways to view your calendar information—Day, Week, Month, and List views.

■ Apple's MobileMe service is not only a great way to sync Calendar and Contacts info with other computers and devices but can also provide a way to find a lost iPad.

■ Although you can't create groups of contacts on your iPad, Contacts does support groups that have been created in Address Book or Outlook. Groups are a powerful tool for organizing large numbers of contacts.

Chapter 11

Setting Up and Using Mail

Ask most people what they'll be using their new iPad for, and a good number of them will reply "e-mail." The iPad uses the Mail app to compose, send, and receive e-mail. Many iPad apps use Mail as a conduit for sharing documents or files with others, so Mail is a good app to know.

In this chapter, we'll show you how to set up e-mail accounts on your iPad, give you tips on composing and organizing mail, and demonstrate how Mail works with other iPad apps to help you share information with others.

Setting Up Your Mail Accounts

The iPad Mail app is instantly recognizable, with an icon that looks like a blue sky behind a white paper envelope. Many users place it in the Dock at the bottom of the iPad screen so that Mail is easily accessible from any one of the panes of the Home screen.

In Chapter 10, we talked about how to synchronize your calendar, contacts, and notes between your iPad and computer. If you already have multiple e-mail accounts set up on your Mac or Windows computer, there's no reason to reenter all of the information to set them up on your iPad. You can use the same process used in Chapter 10 to sync Mail accounts to your iPad for a quick method of setting up Mail, or you can set up the accounts on the iPad—it's your choice.

Syncing Mail Accounts

The fastest way to set up all of your e-mail accounts on your iPad is to use Mail syncing in iTunes on your Mac or Windows computer. Connect your iPad to your Windows computer or Mac using the Dock Connector to USB cable, and then launch iTunes on your computer if it doesn't start by itself. In iTunes, click the icon designating your iPad under Devices in the sidebar on the left side of the window. Next, click the Info tab and scroll down until you see the words Sync Mail Accounts (Figure 11-1).

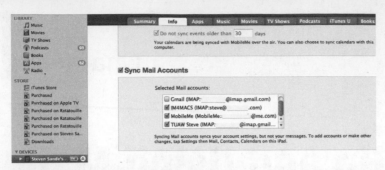

Figure 11-1. *Already have multiple e-mail accounts set up on your Mac or Windows computer? Sync those mail accounts to your iPad for fast and reliable setup.*

To enable mail account syncing between your computer and iPad, select the Sync Mail Accounts check box, select the mail accounts that you want to set up on your iPad, and then click the Apply button at the bottom-right corner of the iTunes window.

One important thing to remember about syncing Mail accounts is that this synchronizes only your account settings, not the messages. For Post Office Protocol 3 (POP3) mail accounts configured to download e-mail to your computer or device and remove it from the mail server, this means that if you receive e-mail on your iPad, you'll never see it on your computer. If the mail account isn't set up to remove the message from your mail server, you'll have a copy on both the iPad and the computer, and removing it from one machine won't remove it from the other.

Apple's MobileMe mail and some other Internet Message Access Protocol (IMAP) mail systems retain a copy of a message on your Internet service provider's server until you delete it. What that means is that you will see the message on multiple devices, and they'll all have the same status. Unopened messages will be that way on all devices, and read messages show up as read on all devices.

Microsoft's Exchange Server is widely used in business, so it's important to know that Mail provides excellent support for this e-mail standard. Exchange provides push mail capabilities (discussed later in this chapter) for almost instantaneous receipt of incoming mail. iPad fully supports both Exchange Server 2003 and Exchange 2007 synchronization and will support Exchange 2010 as well.

Although setting up Exchange accounts on the iPad is no more difficult than configuring other types of e-mail, it's comforting to know that most organizations that use Exchange can also provide technical support to iPad-toting clients if you run into problems.

If you're interested in using Exchange for your iPad e-mail hosting but don't have the technical expertise available to configure and maintain Exchange Server, there are many Exchange hosting services available worldwide. An Internet search of *Exchange Server* displays many companies that host Exchange for you.

Setting Up Mail Accounts on the iPad

If you have only one or two e-mail accounts and you don't want to synchronize account information between your iPad and your computer, you can set up mail accounts directly on the iPad.

Before you start setting up the accounts, make sure that you have the following information on hand:

- *Name of your e-mail service provider.* Common providers include Apple's own MobileMe service, Google's Gmail, Yahoo! Mail, AOL, or Internet service providers such as Comcast and Time Warner.

- *Your e-mail address.* All e-mail addresses are set up in the common myname@domain.tld format, where myname is a name or pseudonym for an individual or company, domain is the domain name being used by an organization, and tld is the "top-level domain" for the domain (.com, .gov, .edu, and so on).

- *Your e-mail password.* This is the most critical piece of information for setting up an e-mail account, but surprisingly few people remember what their password is! You may want to either contact your Internet service provider or IT department directly to get the password if you don't remember it or have the password reset to something more memorable.

- *Server information.* Some accounts will be set up automatically by Mail. In other words, it will know whether your server is an Exchange server, POP server, or IMAP server, and it will adjust settings accordingly. However, it's a very good idea to get this information before you start and keep it for your records.

   The information to gather includes server addresses (your e-mail provider may refer to this as a server URL) for both your incoming e-mail server (usually prefaced with POP or IMAP) and your outgoing (usually SMTP) server. The e-mail provider may also require that your mail be channeled through specific Internet Protocol ports for security reasons, so requesting port information prior to setup can save headaches later. Exchange setup also requires a domain name, which can be as simple as a word—HOST—or as complicated as host.admin.mycompany.com.

In the following example, we'll show how to set up a Gmail account. Although the individual types of e-mail accounts vary in the amount of information required for setup, they all work in a very similar manner. Follow along as we set up a Gmail account on an iPad:

1. To start with, make sure that your iPad is connected to the Internet through a Wi-Fi or 3G connection.

2. In Settings   Mail, Contacts, Calendars, look for Accounts; then tap Add Account.

3. Choose the proper account type from the list that appears (Figure 11-2). Here, of course, we'd tap Gmail. If you don't see your e-mail service provider listed here, tap Other.

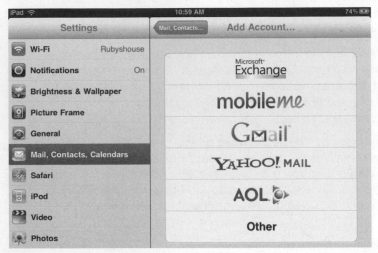

Figure 11-2. *If you're using any of these major e-mail service providers, Mail does most of the setup work for you.*

4. Now it's time to start entering information into the setup window (Figure 11-3). Enter the name that you would like recipients to see. For example, if your name is John Appleseed, you can enter that, John, Mr. Appleseed, or the Apple Tree Guy, and recipients will see your choice as the person who sent them e-mail.

Figure 11-3. *Setting up a new e-mail account is easy in Mail, especially using an e-mail service provider like MobileMe, Gmail, or any of the others listed earlier.*

5. Enter the e-mail address. For this e-mail account, the address is takingyouripadtothemax@gmail.com.

6. Now type in the e-mail account password. As with all password fields on the iPad, the password is hidden by a series of dots almost as quickly as you type it in.

7. Finally, you can create a description of the account. In this case, we've named it Book Email. It's important to have a description of each e-mail account, especially if you have many accounts. These short, descriptive names show up in the list of accounts in Mail on your iPad.

8. Tap the Save button. At this point, your iPad goes through a validation process to make sure that there is an account with that e-mail address, that the password is correct, and that the settings have been properly made for that account. If everything checks out properly, you'll see your list of e-mail accounts in Settings, with the new account added at the bottom of the list.

If something wasn't entered properly, the iPad notifies you of the error. In most cases, the e-mail address or the password was mistyped. Mail does an excellent job of making e-mail setup easy to do on the iPad, so in most situations you'll be done with setup in a few minutes. But what if you need to change settings at a later date?

There's a button for each e-mail account that is listed under Settings Mail, Contacts, Calendars on the iPad (Figure 11-4). A tap of that button displays more detail about the account.

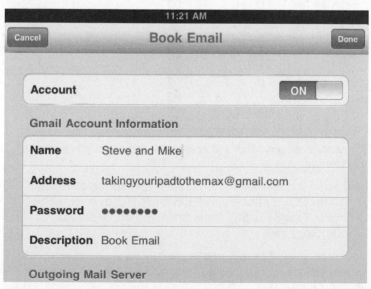

Figure 11-4. *Detailed account information including the name that is displayed to recipients, the name of the account in Mail, and the full e-mail address are listed for each account.*

If you're in a low-bandwidth situation and want to turn off e-mail accounts, simply open the detailed settings for each account, and slide the Account button to Off. Mail no longer checks the e-mail server for that account, and the account shows up as Inactive. To reverse the process, just slide the Account button to On.

Occasionally you may be asked by your Internet service provider or IT department to change some settings for the e-mail servers, or you run into issues sending, receiving, or configuring Mail. We recommend using Apple's handy cheat sheet, available from http://support.apple.com/kb/HT1277, to get the proper e-mail account settings from your e-mail providers and document them.

Under Outgoing Mail Server for a specific e-mail account, it's possible to edit the settings. The SMTP button indicates the Simple Mail Transport Protocol server that is being used as the primary server for an e-mail account, and tapping the primary server name displays the settings for the server (Figure 11-5). If the settings are grayed out like in Figure 11-5, then they are correct and cannot be edited. If they are editable, you can use your cheat sheet to change the settings to their proper values.

Figure 11-5. *If the Outgoing Mail Server settings are grayed out as they are in this figure, then your settings are correct for the server and should not be changed.*

For security reasons, most mail servers now use authentication and specific server ports. Standard ports include 110 for POP3 servers and 995 for POP3 over TLS/SSL, 143 for IMAP and 993 for POP3 over TLS/SSL, 587 for submission of password information, and 25 for SMTP (outgoing) mail.

Authentication means that Mail must submit a user name (usually your e-mail address) and a password to the mail server before being allowed to download mail to your iPad. There are four common types of authentication: MD5 Challenge Response, NTLM, HTTP MD5 Digest, and Password. As always, check with your mail provider for this information if your password is not accepted properly.

Other Mail Settings

Many more settings (Figure 11-6) exist in Settings   Mail, Contacts, Calendars that can be changed to suit your personal preferences. Most of these settings never need to be touched, but it's comforting to know that you can change them if necessary.

Figure 11-6. *Mail settings can be changed to make reading and sending e-mail more enjoyable and productive.*

Fetch New Data

The first button to note is Fetch New Data. For MobileMe and other e-mail accounts that support this service, you can choose to use push. With push enabled, new e-mails immediately transfer to your device when the e-mail server receives them. Although this is a great way to get mail as quickly as possible, it also requires more communications between the iPad and e-mail server. That can reduce battery life, but even more importantly, it increases the amount of bandwidth used by your device. Although this isn't an issue if you're on a Wi-Fi network, 3G network data plans are costly.

The alternative to push, and the method that is used most often for e-mail accounts, is *fetch*, otherwise known as *pull*. With this method, your iPad checks for new mail on the server only when you tell it to or at preset intervals. You can set the schedule to have e-mail accounts check for mail every 15 minutes, 30 minutes, 60 minutes, or manually. Manually means that the account doesn't check for mail until you open the inbox in the Mail app or tap the Refresh button that is found at the bottom of most mailboxes.

For most purposes, we recommend leaving push notification turned on for MobileMe accounts and any other e-mail accounts, such as Exchange, that can provide push notification. For other accounts, it's your choice depending on whether you want to have new mail waiting for you when you open your inbox or want the iPad to fetch it at the time you actually open the inbox.

The Advanced button provides the configuration in place for each e-mail account on your iPad. Each account has a separate button that lists the name of the account and displays Push, Fetch, or Manual depending on how the account is configured.

Show

The next section of the settings page is more about the look and feel of the Mail application. The first button, Show, provides a choice of how many recent messages you'll see in your inbox at any time. The default value is 50 messages, but you can also select 25, 75, 100, or 200 messages. If you don't receive a lot of e-mail, setting the value to 25 messages is fine. When you receive a ton of e-mail or don't check your inbox for a while, you can always pull more messages down from the server by tapping the Load More Messages link at the bottom of your inbox.

Preview

Each message in a Mail inbox can include a short preview of the contents. The Preview button allows you to set the length of the preview from none (no preview) to five lines. The default setting is two lines of the message, which is usually sufficient to see whether the message is important.

Minimum Font Size

If you wear bifocals or otherwise have issues with reading e-mail, you're going to love the next setting. Minimum Font Size lets you change the size of text in Mail from Small to Giant, with three other sizes in between.

Show To/CC Label

When Show To/CC Label button is enabled (set to On), a small label appears next to every message in an inbox indicating whether the message was sent directly to you or whether you were cc'd (carbon copied) on an e-mail sent to another person.

Ask Before Deleting

On occasion, you may accidentally delete an e-mail. Enabling Ask Before Deleting forces you to validate that you do indeed want a mail message to be deleted. iPad owners who frequently have to perform mass deletions of e-mails should probably disable this setting to avoid getting bogged down in validations.

Load Remote Images

When you're on a slow Internet connection, receiving e-mails with lots of images can be a recipe for frustration because it takes a while for those images to load. What do we mean by a slow Internet connection? When you're in a location with a weak 3G signal, the radio in the Wi-Fi + 3G iPad reverts to much slower cellular networks like EDGE or GPRS. Even a Wi-Fi network can be connected to a slow Internet connection. As an example, many cruise ships provide Wi-Fi networks onboard yet are reliant on one very slow satellite connection over which all shipboard Internet traffic must pass. Load

Remote Images enables and disables the capability of Mail to load those images. You can still view the images by manually downloading them with a tap.

Always Bcc Myself

Do you want a copy of every e-mail you send to be sent to yourself as well? Setting Always Bcc Myself to On automatically sends a blind carbon copy (bcc) to your inbox. What does *blind carbon copy* mean? It just means that the recipients of the e-mail don't know that you're also getting a copy of it. When you want to send copies of e-mails to co-workers but don't want the original recipient to know that you're sending those copies, bcc is very useful.

Signature

If you'd like every e-mail sent from your iPad to have a special signature, you can customize it by tapping the Signature button. Unlike most Mac or Windows e-mail programs, Mail on iPad doesn't let you have a signature for every mail account. Instead, you create a generic signature that is used by every account. The default signature says "Sent from my iPad," and you can change it to add your name, web site address, or anything else you want.

Default Account

Finally, there's a Default Account setting. When you're in Mail, you can select which e-mail account you want to send a message from. When you send messages from other applications on your iPad, they'll always be sent from the default account. Tap the Default Account button to view a list of the accounts on your iPad, and then select the default account.

Viewing and Managing Your Incoming Mail

Now that Mail is set up on your iPad, you're probably starting to receive e-mail messages. Your first indicator of a new e-mail message is the New Mail sound. Although it's nice to have an audible indication that you're getting mail, it can get a little obnoxious if you receive a lot of mail every day. To turn off the New Mail sound, visit Settings ➤ General ➤ Sounds; then slide the switch to Off.

There's also a visual indicator that there's unread mail in your inboxes. The Mail app icon displays a small red oval containing the number of unread e-mail messages in all of your inboxes (Figure 11-7).

Figure 11-7. *You've got mail! It looks like it's time to tap that mail icon and take a look at those 20 unread messages sitting in your various mailboxes.*

Launching the Mail App

Tap the Mail icon to launch the app. What you see is dependent on the number of e-mail accounts you have set up on your iPad and on whether the device is in portrait or landscape orientation. In portrait mode, a message is displayed. To list the inboxes (one per e-mail account), tap the Inbox button to display the Accounts list (Figure 11-8).

Figure 11-8. *The Accounts list shows all the e-mail accounts currently set up on your iPad, as well as the number of unread e-mails for each account. Note that the e-mail addresses in this and other images have been retouched for privacy.*

In landscape mode, there's enough room on the screen to display the Accounts list on the left side of the screen and a message on the right side (Figure 11-9). To view a list of mailboxes in any one of the accounts, tap the account description. If you have set that particular e-mail account for manual fetching of messages, the iPad will check the server for new messages at this point. There's also a small refresh icon in the bottom-left corner of the list of e-mail accounts and the list of mailboxes. Tapping this icon forces Mail to check the server immediately and retrieve any new messages that have arrived.

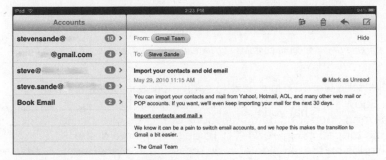

Figure 11-9. *Accounts are listed on the left side of the screen in this view of the Mail app, and a message appears on the right.*

For the Gmail account that we set up earlier, there is a large list of mailboxes—Inbox, Drafts (e-mails that have not been completed and sent), Sent Mail, Trash, a set of mailboxes specific to Gmail (All Mail, Spam, and Starred), and individual mailboxes automatically created for Personal, Receipts, Travel, and Work.

> **WARNING:** With IMAP accounts, sent mail can be saved on the server. With POP3 accounts, however, this may not be the case. If you find that sent messages are not being saved and you want to keep an archive of outgoing mail, use the blind carbon copy feature to send yourself a copy.

Reading Incoming Mail in the Inbox

To see the messages in the inbox, tap the Inbox icon. In the example inbox shown in Figure 11-10, there are three messages, two of which have not been read. The top of the inbox shows the number of unread messages in parentheses, and a blue dot appears next to the unread messages in the list.

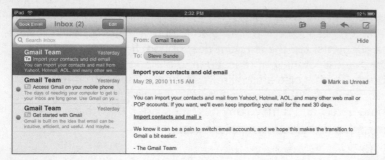

Figure 11-10. *The inbox for this example Gmail account contains two unread messages, and we're reading the third.*

Do you see the small box with the word *To* in it next to each message header? That appears only if you set the Show To/CC label as described earlier in this chapter. The Edit button at the top of the inbox performs batch deletions or moves of e-mails. For example, the Edit button was tapped in Figure 11-11. To delete all three of the messages, tap the empty circles on the left side of each message to mark them. Marked messages get "stacked" on the right side of the window. Tap the Delete button at the bottom of the window to throw the messages away. To delete individual messages in any mailbox outside of edit mode, swipe your finger left or right over the message. A red Delete button appears, and a tap sends the message to the trash.

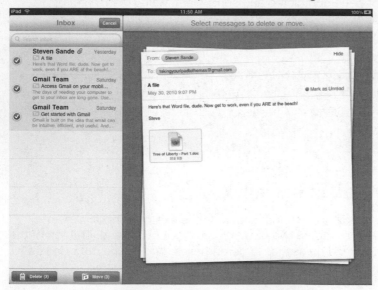

Figure 11-11. *To bulk-delete messages, tap the Edit button at the top of the message list; then tap the circles on the left side of the message list to mark the e-mails for deletion.*

Did you accidentally delete messages? In some situations you don't need to worry, since you may be able to retrieve them from the Trash mailbox. Open the Trash mailbox from the list of mailboxes for the account, tap the Edit button, mark the messages by tapping those empty circles, and then tap the Move button at the bottom of the window.

That displays the list of mailboxes so you can move them back to the inbox by tapping Inbox (Figure 11-12).

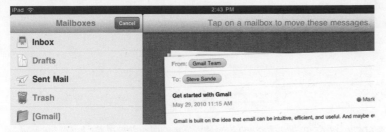

Figure 11-12. *Messages deleted by accident can be found in the Trash mailbox and then moved back to the inbox.*

To read a message in the inbox or any of the other mailboxes, just tap it. In landscape mode, it will appear in the right side of the window; in portrait mode, the message takes over the entire window. On the right side of the From line of the e-mail, you may see the word *Hide*. Tap this to hide any additional lines—To and Cc—that may be listed in the header of the message. Want to display them again? When To and Cc are hidden, the word *Details* appears, and a tap of the word brings those other address lines back into view.

Navigating Mail

There are several additional buttons at the top of every Mail window that are important to know about. In portrait orientation, up and down arrows on the top left side of the window let you navigate to the previous or next message. On the top right side of the window are buttons for moving the message to another mailboxes, deleting the message, replying or forwarding the message, or creating a new message.

The Move and Delete Buttons

Tapping the Move button displays the list of mailboxes; tap a mailbox to move the message to it. Tapping the Delete button moves the current message to the Trash mailbox, where either it will be deleted eventually or it will be retrieved by you if you've deleted it in error.

Reply/Reply All/Forward

When you tap the Reply/Forward arrow, a small pop-up menu appears with Reply and Forward buttons. Tapping Reply opens a new message addressed to the original sender, containing the content of the original message, and allowing you to write your reply at the top of the original message. The message subject is also repeated, with the word *Re:* listed at the beginning to let the original sender know you're sending a reply.

If a message was addressed to you and several other people, a third button appears—Reply All (Figure 11-13). Tapping this button sends the reply to the original sender and all of the other recipients of the e-mail as well.

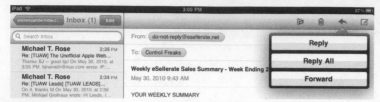

Figure 11-13. *You can reply to or forward any e-mail by tapping the Reply/Forward button at the top of the Mail message window.*

Finally, the Forward button forwards the message to third parties. The message appears in a new window with an empty address list, the subject is repeated with the word *Fwd:* to indicate to the recipient that you're forwarding someone else's e-mail to them, and then there's a place for you to write a short note to the new recipient of the message.

Receiving Attachments

Most people use e-mail to send documents or other files between computers. Let's say that somebody wants to send you a Microsoft Word .doc file so that you can make changes to it on your iPad. You'll need to know how to receive that attachment and then open it in the appropriate app (Pages) to make your changes.

When the e-mail arrives with the attachment, it appears in the inbox with a tiny paper clip icon denoting an attached. In this case, the file is a Word document that someone sent. Attachments usually won't be downloaded in order to reduce the amount of data being transferred to your iPad, in which case you can tap a download icon that looks like a downward-pointing arrow to transfer the document.

To determine what to do with the file, just tap and hold on the file attachment. A pop-up appears (Figure 11-14) with three buttons—Quick Look, Open in Pages (or whatever other appropriate app can open the document), and Open In. The names on the buttons will vary depending on the file type in the attachment.

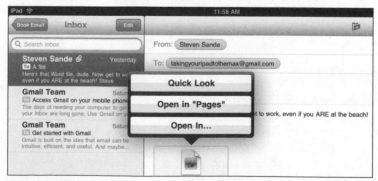

Figure 11-14. *To view or open an attached file that was sent to you, tap and hold the file icon until this pop-up appears; then select your action.*

Tapping Quick Look does exactly what it suggests; it gives you a quick look at the document in a reader. You can't make changes to the document or do anything else; you can just view it. Tapping Open in "Pages" saves the file onto the iPad, launches the Pages app, and then opens the document for editing. Finally, tapping Open In displays a pop-up listing all apps that can open the document on your iPad.

If you ever have problems getting Mail to open the attachment in the correct app, try opening the document in Quick Look, and then tap the Open In button in the upper-right corner of the Quick Look window. It lists all apps currently installed on your iPad capable of opening and editing files of that particular type.

Composing a New E-mail

The last button on the top right of the window composes new e-mail messages. The button icon looks like a pencil poised over a piece of paper, an apt picture since you're about to write a note to someone. Tapping the Compose Message button opens a blank message with an empty address list (To), an empty Subject line, and a content area showing only your signature (Figure 11-15).

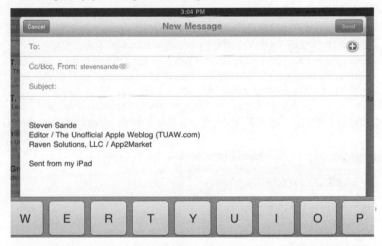

Figure 11-15. *Composing a new message in Mail. Your default signature and e-mail address are entered by Mail.*

To address an e-mail to someone, simply start typing the name. As you type, a pop-up appears with a list of all names from your contacts list or received e-mails that contain the letters you've typed. In the example in Figure 11-16, note that a list of people named Michael appears after typing in only the letters *Mic*. What this will actually look like for you is dependent on the names in your address book.

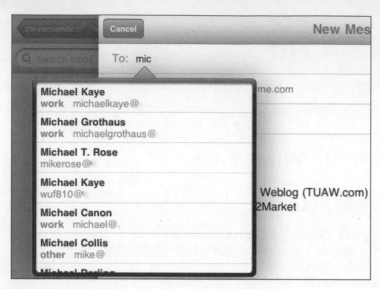

Figure 11-16. *As you type a name for the recipient of a mail message, a list of possible names and associated e-mail addresses appears.*

If you're addressing the e-mail to one person and they appear on the pop-up list, tap their name to add it to the To line of the e-mail. What if you want to send the e-mail to more than one person or to a group? Tap the circle at the right end of the To line containing a plus sign (+). That displays your contacts (Figure 11-17), and you can search for individuals by typing their names in the search box or by scrolling the list with a flick of your finger. To jump to a certain letter in the alphabet (for example, all people with last names beginning with *S*), tap the letter from the list on the right side of the pop-up.

Figure 11-17. *You can add as many contacts to your To list as you want by tapping the plus sign and then adding one name at a time. If you have a group you want to send an e-mail to, tap Groups and select the group name.*

As with the names that appeared in the search list, just tap a name to add it to the To list. To add a carbon copy or blind carbon copy recipient to your message, tap the Cc/Bcc, From line, and the line expands into three lines—Cc, Bcc, and From. Why does Apple hide these items? It's because most e-mails are sent from one person to another, with no need for carbon copy or blind carbon copy. If you need to send a cc or bcc, the recipient lines are easily accessible.

Your default e-mail address is listed in the From line, but if you want to have the e-mail sent from another e-mail account, just tap the From line, and a list of all of your e-mail accounts appears. Tap one of the accounts to select it for this e-mail message.

Next, you need to enter something into the Subject line. This is usually what your recipient sees first, so make it descriptive of the content of your e-mail. Finally, type your message into the body of the message. When you're ready to send the message, tap the Send button in the upper-right corner of the message. If you're currently connected to the Internet over a Wi-Fi or 3G connection, the message immediately attempts to move to the server. If you do not have an Internet connection, have quit Mail, or have shut off your iPad, the message gets placed in an Outbox mailbox. The next time the iPad connects to the Internet, any messages in Outbox mailboxes are sent.

Using Mail in Other Apps

You can send e-mail from many of the other apps, both those created by Apple and third parties, on your iPad. Generally, the app displays either an envelope icon or a Share icon, the latter appearing like a piece of paper with an arrow coming out of it. This section discusses some of the common Apple apps and how they integrate with Mail to let you share information with others.

Contacts

You can share address cards in Contacts through Mail. A Share button appears at the bottom of any address card. Instead of sending someone a laboriously typed list of a person's contact information, it's much easier to just tap the Share button and send them a `.vcf` (vCard file). The vCard contains every bit of contact information that you've captured for that person, including telephone numbers, addresses, e-mail addresses, URLs, and even a photo if one has been added to the contact.

Tapping Share opens a new, unaddressed message that contains the `.vcf` file for the person whose information is being shared (Figure 11-18). Address the message to someone, type in a subject line (**Dave's address information**, for instance), and then send the message.

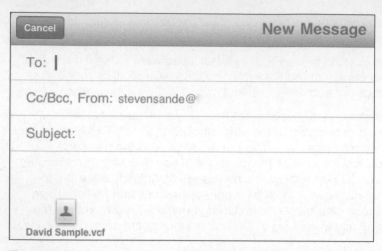

Figure 11-18. *An example of a mail message containing a vCard. To create this, just tap the Share button on any address card.*

Anyone receiving this e-mail on an iPad can tap the `.vcf` icon that signifies the file is attached to the message, and a small pop-up appears showing the information contained in the file (Figure 11-19). With a tap, the recipient can create a new contact with that person's information, or they can merge the information received with an existing contact in their address list.

Figure 11-19. *If you receive a vCard from someone, tap and hold on the icon to view the information it contains. You also have a choice of creating a new contact or adding this information to an existing contact.*

Likewise, the `.vcf` file, when clicked in an e-mail message on a Mac or Windows computer, will launch the appropriate application on the computer and ask the recipient whether they want to add the card to their address book.

To share contact information with others quickly and easily, send vCards through Mail.

Notes

As mentioned in the Notes section of Chapter 10, it's possible to send a note to yourself or others from this app.

Tap the envelope icon at the bottom of a page, and a new Mail message appears. The Subject line is filled in with the name of the note, the note is copied as text into the body of the message, and all you need to do is address the message and send it.

YouTube

There's nothing like finding a funny or thought-provoking video on YouTube and then sharing that clip with friends.

When you find a video in the iPad's YouTube app using the search function, a Share button appears just above the video sample on the page. Tap the Share button, and a new message (Figure 11-20) appears with the name of the video as the subject and a link to the video in the body of the message. Type in an address, and tap Send to let your friends share in the fun.

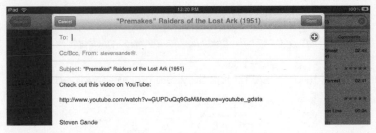

Figure 11-20. *Tapping the YouTube Share button creates a new message containing a link to the video you want to share.*

iTunes

iTunes also includes a quick link for telling friends about movies, music, TV shows, podcasts, or other items that you've found in the store. Tap the Tell a Friend link found in the upper-right corner of each listing in the iTunes Store to create a nicely formatted e-mail (Figure 11-21), complete with any images that accompany the store item, a button that links the recipient to the item in the store, ratings, and more.

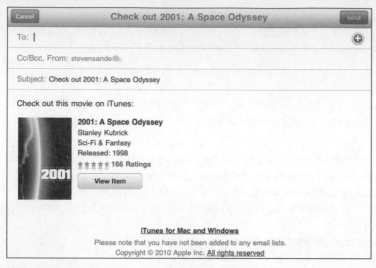

Figure 11-21. *From any listing in the iTunes Store, you can tell a friend about a movie, song, album, TV show, or other product.*

If the recipient doesn't have iTunes, there's even a link they can tap to download and install the program on their computer.

App Store

Once you own an iPad, it's tempting to let the world know about all the wonderful apps available for the device. Apple makes it easy to spread the word about fun or useful apps by including the same Tell a Friend link on every app description in the App Store. Like iTunes, the e-mail generated by the Tell a Friend link includes a picture of the app icon, the app rating, a button that links the recipient to the app in the App Store, and a link for downloading iTunes.

iBooks

If the other two stores on the iPad—iTunes and the App Store—include Tell a Friend links, then you might imagine that the iBookstore also provides a similar link. You're correct—for every book listing in the iBookstore, the Tell a Friend link appears in the same location (upper-right corner of the listing) that it occupies in iTunes and the App Store.

iWork for iPad

All three of the iWork for iPad apps—Keynote, Pages, and Numbers—include a Share button on the main page. The main page displays all the presentations, documents, or worksheets that you've created in one of the apps.

To share a file with a friend or co-worker, drag it to the center of the page, and then tap the Share button below the image of the document. A pop-up appears, with Send via Mail as the first of three actions you can choose.

Tap the Send via Mail button, and a dialog box appears asking which file format you want to convert the file to before sending. For Keynote, the choices are Keynote or PDF. For Numbers, you can select either Numbers or PDF. There are three file format choices for Pages—Pages, PDF, or Microsoft Word .doc format.

Once you've selected the file type, the document is formatted and then attached to a new e-mail message with the document name as the Subject line. Enter an address or two in the To line, tap the Send button, and your work moves on to another person.

Photos

There's nothing more fun than sharing photos with friends and family, and the Photos app on your iPad makes it simple to send one or more pictures to anyone with an e-mail address.

When viewing photos in any photo collection, album, or event, our familiar friend the Share button lurks in the upper-right corner of the window. Tapping the button adds Email, Copy, and Delete buttons to the upper-left corner of the window. To add up to five photos as attachments to an e-mail message, tap the photos you want to send, and a check mark appears on them (Figure 11-22). When you've selected the photos, tap the Send button to embed them in an e-mail.

Like many actions you can perform on an iPad, there's more than one way to send a photo in Mail. While you're browsing your photos, you may see an image that you want to share. Tap and hold the image until a Copy pop-up appears. When it does, tap the pop-up to copy the image. Paste that image into a Mail message, address it, and mail it to share the picture.

Figure 11-22. *Send photos through Mail by tapping the Share button and then marking the individual photos with a tap.*

Why can you send only five photos? It's all about the size of the images. Depending on the image resolution of the camera that takes the photos, it's not uncommon for photos to be many megabytes (MB) in size. Photos transferred to your iPad are downsampled to the maximum resolution of your iPad's display, which is 1024×768 pixels. That creates a file size of about 900KB. It doesn't sound like much, but five photos embedded in an e-mail message increases the file size to approximately 5MB.

To facilitate the sending of pictures from the iPad, Apple set a limit on the number of pictures. Just about any e-mail system will accept an incoming message with a 5MB file; double or triple that size, and many e-mail servers reject the message as being too large.

What if you have a lot of smaller images to mail to someone? Use the copy and paste method we described earlier to add as many photos as you want, but be cognizant of the fact that the recipient's mail system may reject your message if it is too large.

What happens to photos sent to your iPad in e-mail messages? When the messages appear in your inbox, you may see the photo or an icon that designates that the photo still needs to be downloaded to your iPad from the e-mail server.

Any photo sent to you can be either saved to Photos or copied for pasting into another app. To save or copy the photo, tap and hold it, and a pop-up appears with two buttons—Save Image and Copy. To save the image to Photos, tap Save Image. If you're going to paste the image directly into another document, tap Copy, which moves the image to the clipboard for pasting.

> **TIP:** Have you ever wondered how we got the wonderful screenshots for this book? To take a screenshot of whatever is on your iPad display, just press and hold the Home button and then push the On/Off Sleep/Wake button. Your screen "flashes," and a shutter sound tells you that the screenshot has been captured to your photo library.

Summary

As the primary conduit for electronic mail on your iPad, the Mail app is arguably one of the most important pieces of software on the device. Setting up Mail is easy, with the app handling much of the configuration work behind the scenes with a minimum of assistance required from the iPad owner.

In this chapter, we showed you how to set up the app and then use it to send or receive e-mail. We discussed how Mail works with many other applications on the iPad to provide a way to share information with others. These are important points to take away from this chapter:

- To use Mail, accounts must first be configured in the app. An easy way to move account information to the iPad from another computer is to sync Mail settings from iTunes on the computer.

- If you're setting up Mail accounts on the iPad, it's helpful to use Apple's Mail "cheat sheet" to capture all the settings necessary to successfully configure the accounts.

- When you receive an e-mail with attachments, tap and hold the attachment icon in the message to view or open the file on the iPad.

- Send vCard files from the Contacts app to quickly share contact information with others. vCard is a nearly universal file format that works well for Windows, Mac, and Linux users.

- All of the electronic storefronts on your iPad—the iTunes Store, iBookstore, and the App Store—include Tell a Friend links for sending friends detailed information about items in the store that you think deserve their attention.

- Only five photos at a time can be sent from the Photos application to avoid conflicts with message size limits on mail servers, but it's possible to work around this limit by copying and pasting photos into Mail.

Chapter 12

Working with Maps

The iPad has a powerful mapping application called Maps. It uses Google Maps to interactively find and display locations using map and satellite imagery. With Maps, you can get directions, view traffic, and more.

In this chapter, you'll discover how to navigate maps, bookmark locations, "walk down" a street in Street view, and even use your iPad as a compass. Maps isn't just a powerful app; it's a fun one as well. Let's get started.

Launch the app by tapping the Maps icon (see Figure 12-1). It looks like a small map that shows a cross section of Interstate 280. The pin on the icon just happens to be where Apple's headquarters is in Cupertino, California. This takes you into the Maps application, where you can view and explore geography from around the world.

Figure 12-1. *The Maps icon*

Maps Screen

Tap the icon to launch the Maps app. When you do, you'll be presented with your Maps screen (see Figure 12-2).

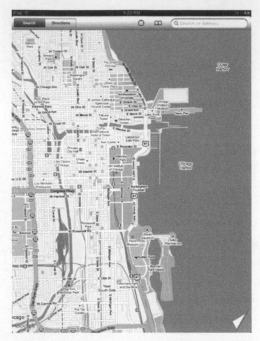

Figure 12-2. *The Maps screen. Note the page curl at the bottom right of the screen.*

At the top of the Maps screen, you'll see the Maps toolbar (see Figure 12-3).

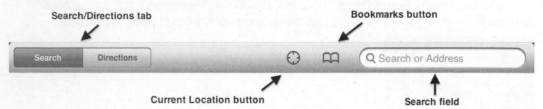

Figure 12-3. *The Maps toolbar*

The Maps screen, including the toolbar, shows the basic Maps interface, which consists of the following:

- *Search/Directions tab*: This tab allows you to switch between the search and direction functions of the Maps app. You can search for local business, attractions, and specific addresses and easily get directions to and from those locations.

- *Current Location*: This button, which looks like a circle with crosshairs, finds your current location on the map by using the iPad's built-in positioning tools. These built-in tools vary depending on which iPad you have. The iPad Wi-Fi + 3G uses both the Global Positioning System (GPS) and Skyhook Wi-Fi positioning to locate you. Skyhook Wi-Fi positioning uses known wireless hotspot locations to triangulate your current position. The iPad Wi-Fi only uses Skyhook Wi-Fi positioning because there is no GPS chip inside the iPad Wi-Fi.

- *Bookmarks:* The Bookmarks icon at the right side of the search field links to your saved locations. From the Bookmarks pop-up that appears when you tap the Bookmarks icon, you can edit your bookmarks, see recently viewed locations, or choose a location from your contacts list.

- *Search field:* Marked with a spyglass, the search field allows you to enter addresses and other queries. You can type an entire address (*1600 Pennsylvania Avenue, Washington, DC*) or search for contacts (*Bill Smith*), landmarks (*Golden Gate Bridge*), or even pizza places in any ZIP code across the country (*Pizza 11746*). When in Directions mode, the search field will turn into two search fields so you can enter beginning and end points.

- *Map:* The map itself takes up the rest of the screen. It's fully interactive. You can scroll by dragging your finger along the map, or you can zoom in and out using pinches and double-taps.

- *Page curl:* In the lower-right corner of the map (see Figure 12-2), you'll see the corner is curled up a bit. Tap the curl, or tap and hold and then drag the curl with your finger to reveal map settings, allowing you to change map views, get traffic conditions, and drop pins.

Navigating Maps

The iPad Maps app makes it so you can explore the world from the comfort of your couch. Like any other app, you navigate the map using gestures. You can also view the map in different modes.

Gestures

On maps you use gestures to zoom in, zoom out, pan, and scroll.

- *Zoom in:* You have two ways of zooming in. Either pinch the map with two fingers; or, using one finger, double-tap the location on the map that you want to zoom in on. Double-tap again to zoom in even closer.

- *Zoom out:* You can zoom out in two ways. Either reverse-pinch the map with two fingers or, using two fingers, double-tap the map. Double-tap with two fingers again to zoom even farther out.

- *Panning and scrolling:* Touch and drag the map up, down, left, or right to move the map around and view another location.

Changing Map Views

The default map view is Google's classic road map with orange, yellow, and white streets. But the Maps application also allows you to view the map in four additional views as well as with traffic overlay (see Figure 12-4).

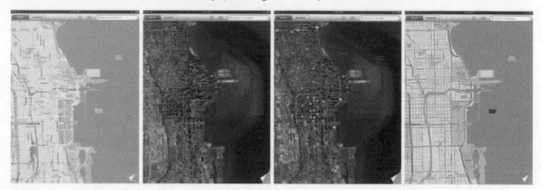

Figure 12-4. *Four map views, from left to right: Classic, Satellite, Hybrid, and Terrain.*

To access these features, tap or tap and drag the page curl at the bottom of the Maps screen. The map will curl up, and you'll be presented with the settings page (see Figure 12-5). Your settings include map views, overlays, and a special Drop Pin feature, which places, or *drops*, a pin anywhere on the map. These dropped pins let you easily mark a business, street corner, beach, or any other kind of location on a map.

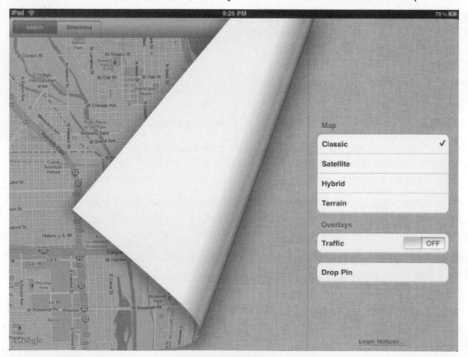

Figure 12-5. *The Maps setting page lies behind the page curl in the map.*

- *Classic*: This is the default map view. It uses Google's standard road map.

- *Satellite*: This view shows you the world using satellite imagery. It's perhaps the coolest map view because you can zoom in on streets and see little blips of people walking the day that the satellite imagery was taken. No labels appear in Satellite view.

- *Hybrid*: This view combines Classic and Satellite. You see the map in satellite imagery, but it has labels, roads, and borders overlaid on it.

- *Terrain*: This view shows you the terrain of given map. This view lets you see relief maps of terrain. The Terrain view also overlays roads, borders, and labels. This view is great if you're thinking of doing a cross-country cycle—you'll be able to see how hilly areas of your route are.

> **TIP:** The Classic view uses orange, yellow, and white to color streets. Orange indicates interstate highways. Yellow indicates state highways and county parkways. White indicates local and private streets.

- *Traffic*: Tap to turn Traffic ON. While on, the current traffic conditions will be overlaid on the map. To see current traffic conditions, you will need to be connected to a Wi-Fi or 3G network. We'll talk more about the Traffic feature later in this chapter.

- *Drop Pin*: Tapping this button causes the page to uncurl and drops a location pin in the center of the map. Use a dropped pin to easily mark a business, street corner, beach, or any other kind of location on a map. You can also drop a pin by touching and holding anywhere on the map. We'll talk more about dropping pins later in this chapter.

You'll notice we said that the Maps app allows you to view the map in Classic view as well as four additional views—so five views total. The fifth view is called Street view, and you access it from search results or a dropped pin. We'll talk more about Street view later in this chapter.

Finding Locations

The Maps app gives you multiple ways to find locations. You can search for locations using the search field, automatically find your current location using the iPad's built-in GPS or Skyhook location services, or even just zoom in and browse the map like a bird flying overhead.

Depending what you are looking for, some types of search are better than others. For example, if you are looking for your favorite spot on a beach, chances are it doesn't have an address or name, so your best bet is to navigate to the beach and then zoom in and scroll around in Satellite view until you find that favorite spot.

Search

You'll find most of your locations through the search function in the toolbar at the upper right of your screen (see Figures 12-2 and 12-3). Tap the search field, and a Recents pop-up and keyboard appears (see Figure 12-6). Remember that if you have a hardware keyboard synced to your iPad, the software keyboard will not appear on the screen.

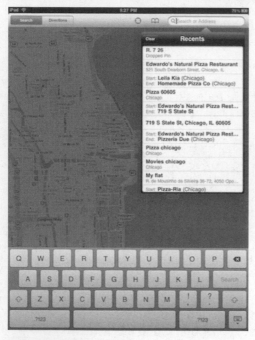

Figure 12-6. *Searching Maps*

There are many ways to search for a location. You can type an entire address (*1600 Pennsylvania Avenue, Washington, DC*) or search for contacts on your iPad by typing in their name (*Bill Smith*), landmarks (*Eiffel Tower*), or even pizza places in your local ZIP code (*Pizza 60605*).

The Recents pop-up shows you all your recent searches, including recent directions (see Figure 12-7). Tap any of the Recents result to be taken to its location. Tap the Clear button in the Recents pop-up window to clear the Recents results list. Clearing the Recents list ensures that no one else who uses your iPad will be able to see the locations you have searched for. For example, if you looked up directions to a special restaurant that you are taking your wife to for her birthday, you don't want her seeing it. Clearing the Resents list ensures she won't. Be careful not to clear the list if you are going to frequently be pulling up the same directions, however. Though the Maps app can save any kind of location, whether or not it has an address, it does not have the ability to permanently save direction routes. Those routes will remain in the Recents list—for quick access—until you clear it, however.

Figure 12-7. *The search field with the Recents list*

Enter your search query, and one or more red pin will fall onto the map. Imagine you're taking a trip next week to Chicago. As you'll see in Figure 12-8, we searched for *Pizza Chicago*. Several red pins populate the map, all representing pizza places.

Figure 12-8. *Search results pins on the map*

When you touch one of the red pins, you get the pin's information bar (see Figure 12-9). The information bar tells you the name of the establishment (a pizzeria, in this case) and displays an icon on either side. Those icons represent the information window and Street view.

Figure 12-9. *A search result pin's information bar shows the name of the establishment with a Street View icon on the left and an information icon on the right.*

You can also view your search results as a list. After the pins fall onto the map, a gray circle with three lines appears in the search field next to your queried search term. Tap the circle, and your results will be presented in a drop-down list (see Figure 12-10). You can then keep tapping names in the list and see their locations bounce to life on the map.

Figure 12-10. *The search results list*

Information Window

Tap the white and blue *i* on the pin's information bar to make the information window slide open. The information window (see Figure 12-11) displays information for the establishment, such as its phone number, web page, and physical address, and gives you several options on how you can use this location further on your iPad.

Figure 12-11. *The information window*

- *Image*: Depending on the establishment, you may see a thumbnail icon of the establishment's Street view in the information window. You can tap this thumbnail to be taken to Street view. More on that in a bit.

- *Directions To Here*: Tap here to be taken to the directions toolbar. The address of the establishment will be populated in the second (end destination) directions field. We'll talk more about directions later in this chapter.

- *Directions From Here*: Tap here to be taken to the directions toolbar. The address of the establishment will be populated in the first (origin destination) directions field.

- *Phone*: The establishment's phone number. Touch and hold to copy the number to the clipboard.

- *Home page*: The establishment's web address. Tap it to close Maps and be taken to the web address in Safari.

- *Address*: The establishment's address. Touch and hold to copy the address to the clipboard.

- *Add to Contacts*: Tapping this button will add the name of the establishment, the phone number, the web address, and the physical address to a contact. You get the options Create New Contact and Add to Existing Contact.

  If you choose Create New Contact, a new contact window will slide up (see Figure 12-12) in the information window, populating contact fields with information and also allowing you to add more information to the contact. Tap Done to save the new contact.

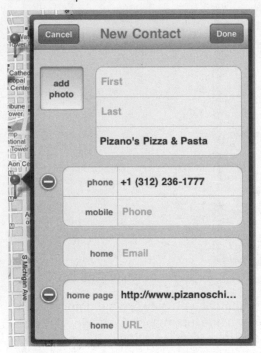

Figure 12-12. *The New Contact windows lets you add a search result's information to your address book from within the Maps app.*

  If you choose Add to Existing Contact, a list of all your contacts from your address book will slide up in the information window. Tap the contact you want to add the information to. The information will be added, and the contacts list will slide away.

- *Share Location*: Tapping this button will allow you to e-mail a link of the establishment's name, add a Google Maps link, and attach a vCard (a virtual business card the receiver can choose to add to an address book).

- *Add to Bookmarks*: Tapping this button will allow you to save the location to your Maps bookmarks. You'll be able to name the bookmark, so you can change "Edwardo's Natural Pizza Restaurant" to "My favorite pizza joint." We'll talk more about bookmarks in a moment.

Tap anywhere on the map to close the information window.

Street View

Street view is the fifth way to view maps that we mentioned earlier. Street view uses Google technology to display 360° panoramic views of the location you are. To enter Street view, tap the white and orange Street View icon in the pin's information bar (see Figure 12-9), or tap the picture thumbnail in the information window (see Figure 12-11). Your map will begin to zoom in on the pin and then tilt up and present you with a street-level panoramic view (see Figure 12-13).

Figure 12-13. *Street view fills the entire screen. Tap the white arrow on the road to move forward down the street. Tap the map navigation icon to return to map view.*

Google has had Street view available on the Web for some time, but using it on the iPad brings it to a whole different level. The fact that you can touch and drag and pinch and zoom around the street gives Street view an immediacy it's never had.

While in Street view, drag your finger around to experience the 360° panoramic views. Pinch or double-tap the screen to zoom in. Reverse-pinch to zoom back out. To "walk" down the street, find the big white arrows at the end of a street label and tap them. You'll then move that direction.

The small circular navigation icon sites at the bottom right of a Street view map. It shows you the direction you are looking in. Tap the icon to return to your last map view location.

Street view isn't available in all cities yet, but it is in most major North American and European ones. Street view is a wonderful tool because it lets you check out what a place or area looks like in advance. Thinking of moving to a new area of town? You can virtually scroll down the street in Street view to see whether you like the looks of it before you take the time and trouble to start searching for houses in the neighborhood.

Current Location

Curious about where you are in the world? The Maps app allows you to find your current location with a tap of a button. The current location button is in the toolbar at the top of the screen (see Figure 12-3). It looks like a circle with crosshairs. Tap it to jump to your current location on the map.

Current Location works by using the iPad's built-in positioning tools. These built-in tools vary depending on which iPad you have. The iPad Wi-Fi + 3G uses both GPS and Skyhook Wi-Fi positioning to locate you. The iPad Wi-Fi only uses Skyhook Wi-Fi positioning, because there is no GPS chip inside the iPad Wi-Fi.

GPS uses satellite location technology to pinpoint your location with an accuracy of up to 16 feet (5 meters). Skyhook Wi-Fi positioning uses known wireless hotspot locations to triangulate your current position with an accuracy of 60 to 100 feet (20 to 30 meters).

As mentioned earlier, if you have an iPad Wi-Fi + 3G, it will use both technologies to pinpoint your location. Even though GPS has a much more accurate range, there are some areas where Skyhook has an advantage over GPS, namely, in urban locations. Tall buildings can obscure GPS satellite signals, so Skyhook's wireless network triangulation has an advantage there.

Your current location is signified by a blue dot, as shown in Figure 12-14. If the Maps app can't determine your exact location, a blue circle appears around the dot. The circle can range in size—its size depends on how precisely your location can be determined. What the circle means is you are somewhere in that location. The smaller the circle, the more precise the current location marker.

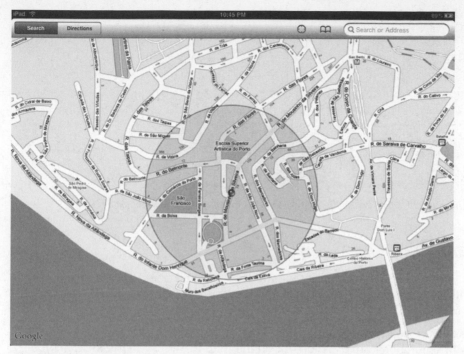

Figure 12-14. *The blue dot surrounded by the circle represents your approximate location.*

NOTE: Location Services must be turned on for your iPad to find your current location. To turn on Location Services, go to Settings ➤ General ➤ Location Services ➤ ON.

When you are in Current Location mode, the Current Location icon in the toolbar turns blue. After you've found your current location, if you drag the map around, you can simply tap the current location button again to have the map center back on it.

You can tap the blue current location dot on the map to open the Current Location information bar (see Figure 12-15). The address of the current location will be displayed. Tap the *i* button to get the information window for the location, including the ability to get directions to/from the location, bookmark it, add it to contacts, or e-mail the location. Tap the Street View button to enter Street view (if available in the area).

Figure 12-15. *The current location information bar displays the address of your current location.*

Digital Compass

Not only can your iPad find your current location, but when it does, you can use it as a compass. With your current location found, tap the blue Current Location button in the toolbar to activate the Digital Compass mode.

The current location icon changes to a compass icon in the toolbar (see Figure 12-16), and a headlight emanates from the blue dot on the map to show you the location you are facing (see Figure 12-17). The map will rotate as you do, so the top of the map will always show what's ahead of you, and the bottom will show what's behind. A compass will appear in the top right of the screen to show you which way north is.

Figure 12-16. *The Current Location button (left) turns into the Digital Compass button (right) when you tap it again.*

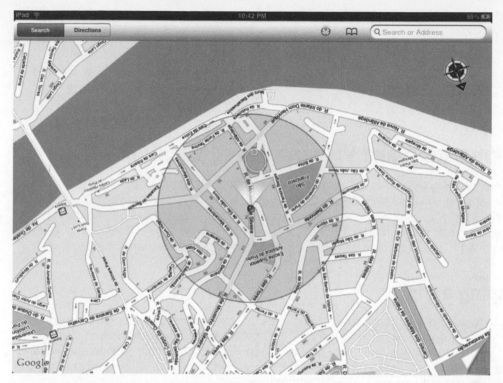

Figure 12-17. *Digital Compass mode. This is the same image as in Figure 12-14 but with the Digital Compass turned on. Notice how the map is pointing the other direction? That's because the iPad is facing that direction, which in this case is south. Note the compass pointing north in the upper-right corner and the "headlight" emanating from the blue current location dot.*

The first time you use Digital Compass mode, you'll need to calibrate the compass. A gray icon will appear on the screen telling you to move your iPad in a figure eight (see Figure 12-18). Doing so will complete the calibration. Lots of metal and magnets (like from a car's speaker system) affect compasses. You may need to calibrate the compass from time to time, but the iPad will tell you when calibration is needed.

Figure 12-18. *The digital compass calibration notice*

> **TIP:** The Current Location and Digital Compass features are cool, but both require Location Services to be on, which requires extra battery power. If you aren't using either, turn Location Services off to conserve battery power. To turn off Location Services, select Settings ➤ General ➤ Location Services ➤ OFF.

Bookmarking and Viewing Saved Locations

There are two ways you can bookmark locations you've navigated to in Maps: dropping a pin or tapping the Add to Bookmarks button in the location's information window. Dropping a pin allows you to mark any location on a map, regardless of whether it has a physical address; you can then add the pin's location to your saved bookmarks. Once you've saved locations, you can view them all in the handy Bookmarks menu.

Dropping a Pin

Navigate to a point of interest on the map without doing a search for something. In the example in Figure 12-19, we found a location by Chicago's Shedd Aquarium that has beautiful views of the sunrise over Lake Michigan. To drop a pin, all you have to do is press and hold your finger on the map where you want to drop it. After a second or two, a purple pin will fall and stick in the map.

Figure 12-19. *A dropped pin and its information bar with the approximate address*

The pin's information bar will appear with the approximate address of the pin as well as the usual icons for Street view and the information window. If the pin's location isn't exactly where you want it, you can tap and hold the purple pin's head and drag it to the location you want. Remove your finger to sink the pin into the map.

Tap the *i* button to get the information window for the pin's location (see Figure 12-20), including the ability to get directions to/from the location, bookmark it, add it to contacts, or e-mail the location; or you can tap the Street View button to enter Street view (if available in the area).

Figure 12-20. *A dropped pin's information window lets you find directions, add the location to contacts and bookmarks, or share the location.*

You can also drop a pin in the center of the map by accessing the Maps settings page behind the page curl in the lower-right corner (see Figure 12-6). Tap or tap and drag the page curl at the bottom of the Maps screen, and tap the Drop Pin button. The settings page will uncurl, and a pin will drop in the center of the map. You can then tap and drag the pin to move it to anywhere you want on the map.

Dropping pins might seem like a nice but unnecessary feature at first. Why, if you can search maps with the apps powerful search features, would you manually add locations? Again, dropped pins are great because they allow you to mark locations that do not have a fixed address, like a good trail in the mountains, the site of your first kiss (for the romantic among you), or even the location of your favorite bench in Central Park.

Bookmarking

So far in this chapter we've shown you several ways to bookmark locations, whether it be by a dropped pin or the information windows of a business, friend, or address you looked up. But where are all those bookmarks you've saved? In the Bookmarks window, of course!

Tap the Bookmarks icon in the Maps title bar (see Figure 12-3). It looks like a book folded open. The Bookmarks window will appear. The Bookmarks window presents three views: Bookmarks, Recents, and Contacts (see Figure 12-21).

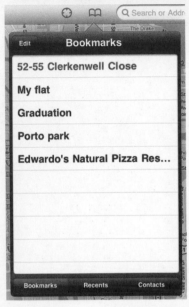

Figure 12-21. *The Bookmarks window displays your bookmarked locations, recent locations, and contact's locations.*

- *Bookmarks*: This lists all the bookmarks you've saved in the Maps app. Tap any bookmark to jump to it on the map. Tap the Edit button to delete a bookmark, move it up or down the Bookmarks list, or change the name of the bookmark.

- *Recents*: This lists all the recent search queries, driving directions, and dropped pins you've made (see Figure 12-22). Tap any item on the list to jump to it on the map. Tap the Clear button to remove all items from the list. Remember, clearing your Recents list will ensure that people who use your iPad can't spy on locations you've searched for. Be aware, however, that it will also clear your direction routes. Routes can't be bookmarked, so the only way to quickly access them is through the Recents window. If you clear the window, you'll need to perform your route searches from scratch.

- *Contacts*: This list shows you all the contacts who you have addresses for (see Figure 12-22). Tap any contact on the list to jump to their address on the map. If a contact has more than one address, you'll be asked to choose which address to navigate to. Tap the Groups button to navigate through your contact groups.

Figure 12-22. *The Recents and Contacts Bookmarks windows*

TIP: To close any pop-up window, such as the Bookmarks window or a search results list, tap anywhere on the map. The pop-up window will fade away.

Directions and Traffic

The iPad Maps app lets you search for directions and view current traffic conditions. Like the Maps app itself, directions and traffic require an Internet connection. If you have an iPad Wi-Fi + 3G, this won't be an issue if you're using it to find directions while on the road. If you have an iPad Wi-Fi only, you'll need to look up the directions before you leave home.

Directions

To get directions, tap the Directions tab in the Maps toolbar (see Figure 12-3). You'll notice that the search field becomes a double field to enter your start and end locations (see Figure 12-23). The Maps app will put your current location, if available, as the starting location. If you don't want to use your current location as the starting address, tap it in the first search field, and tap the *X* to remove it or choose another location from the Recents pop-up list that appears.

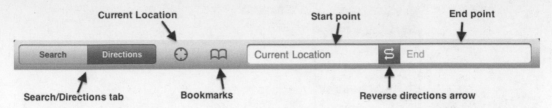

Figure 12-23. *The Maps toolbar changed to directions input when you tap the directions button.*

> **NOTE:** You can also begin a directions search from any pin's information window.

To enter an address from one of your contacts, tap the Bookmarks icon, and then choose a contact. You'll be asked to choose Directions to Here or Directions From Here. Choose the one you want, and the contact's address will be populated in the appropriate directions field. To reverse the start and end points, tap the curvy S arrow to switch the points (and get reverse directions). The reverse directions feature is nice because sometimes the route you came isn't the quickest route back. Reverse directions will show you whether another route home is quicker.

When you have selected both a start point and an end point, a blue line will appear on the map showing you the route you are to take (see Figure 12-24). A green pin represents your starting location on the map, and a red pin indicates your end location. You'll also notice that a blue directions bar has appeared at the bottom of the screen (see Figure 12-25). The directions bar lets you choose between driving (car icon), public transit (bus icon), or walking (person icon) directions. These different modes of transportation may give you direct direction routes on the map between the same two locations. This is because people aren't allowed to walk on highways, and cars aren't allowed to drive on pedestrian streets and on certain bus routes, depending on the city you live in.

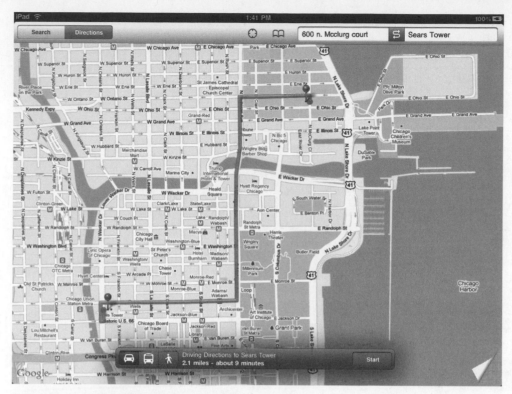

Figure 12-24. *The map with the directions route*

Figure 12-25. *The directions bar allows you to switch between driving, public transit, and walking directions.*

Driving or Walking Directions

Tap either the driving or walking icon. You'll see the length of the route and the estimated time it will take to get there. If traffic data is available, the estimated journey time will adjust accordingly.

To navigate through the directions step-by-step, tap the blue Start button. The directions bar will change to the one in Figure 12-26. Tap the icon of the three dots with lines trailing them to see the directions displayed in a list format (see Figure 12-27). Tap any step in the list to be taken to that part of the route on the map. To return to the directions bar, tap the blue icon in the top-left corner of the directions list window.

Figure 12-26. *Tap the left or right arrow to move through the directions step-by-step.*

If you'd like to navigate through the directions step-by-step in the map, tap the right-pointing arrow on the bar. Each subsequent tap will bring you forward one step in the route. To move back a step, tap the left arrow.

Figure 12-27. *Directions presented in a list format. Note the map displays a circle to show you what step of the route you are on.*

Public Transit Directions

Tap the public transit button. In the blue directions bar, you'll see the estimated time it will take to get there. If traffic data is available, the estimated journey time will adjust accordingly.

Tap the clock icon to display a pop-up list of departure times and schedules (see Figure 12-28). Tap Depart to choose a date and time. The Depart field defaults to the current date and time unless you change it. Below the depart time, you'll see a list of alternate schedules. Select one, and then tap the Done button.

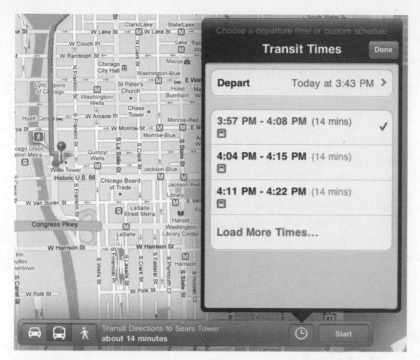

Figure 12-28. *The directions bar shows public transit routes. The clock icon allows you to select between different transit schedules.*

To navigate through the directions step-by-step, tap the blue Start button. The directions bar will change to the one in Figure 12-29. Tap the icon of the three dots with lines trailing them to see the directions displayed in a list format. Tap any step in the list to be taken to that part of the route on the map. To return to the directions bar, tap the blue icon in the top-left corner of the directions list window.

Figure 12-29. *Tap the left or right arrow to move through the public transit route step-by-step.*

If you'd like to navigate through the directions step-by-step in the map, tap the right-pointing arrow on the bar. Each subsequent tap will bring you forward one step in the route. To move back a step, tap the left arrow.

NOTE: We've mentioned it before, but unfortunately, you can't bookmark routes. That's a pity because it would be nice to be able to quickly pull up traffic conditions on your favorite routes. Ideally Apple will add this feature in the future.

Traffic

The Maps app can display traffic conditions that help you when planning an immediate journey. To turn on traffic conditions, tap or tap and drag the page curl at the bottom of the Maps screen and switch Traffic to ON (see Figure 12-6). Back on the map, you'll notice that green, yellow, and red lines have appeared over some of the roads (see Figure 12-30).

Just how on Earth does the Maps app know what the current traffic conditions are? Most major U.S. cities have sensors embedded in the highways and major roads. These sensors feed data back, in real time, to the Department of Transportation (DOT). The DOT uses this information to update digital traffic signs that report local traffic conditions (like those bright Broadway-like signs that hang from overpasses on major metro highways that tell you how long it will take to get to a certain exit). The DOT also shares this data, which Google collects and uses to display near real-time traffic maps.

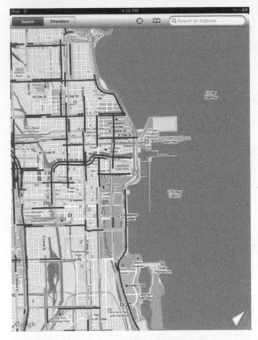

Figure 12-30. *Traffic overlays on the map*

Green lines indicate traffic is flowing at least 50 mph. Yellow ones mean that traffic is flowing between 25 and 50 mph. Red highways mean that traffic is moving below 25 mph. A gray route indicates that traffic data is not available for that street or highway.

The traffic feature is limited to certain regions, mostly major metropolitan areas in the United States, France, Britain, Australia, and Canada, but new cities and new countries are frequently added. If you don't see traffic conditions, try zooming out on the map. If you still don't see any, they aren't available in your area yet.

Maps in Other Apps

You aren't limited to using maps on the iPad in only the Maps app. Several iPad apps allow you to navigate and search maps on their own, including using maps for other things. Here are just a few.

Flixster

Flixster is a popular iPad app that allows you to look up movies in your area. Among its many features, the app shows you a list of theaters near you—based on your current location—and shows you the location of the theater on the app's built-in Google map. It's free in the App Store.

The Weather Channel

The Weather Channel app is a versatile app that shows you all the weather information you can dream of. It also uses built-in Google map that displays overlays including Doppler Radar, cloud coverage, temperatures, rain, and UV index maps (see Figure 12-31). It's free in the App Store.

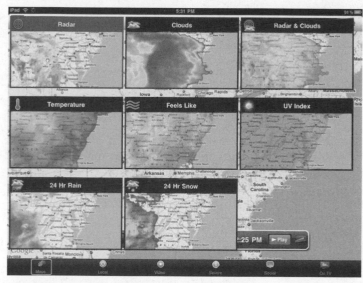

Figure 12-31. *The Weather Channel's map overlays*

Ndrive US HD

Ndrive is a powerful navigation app for the iPad. It uses its own built-on mapping software and stores map data on your iPad so you can use it without an Internet connection. Plan routes, get step-by-step directions, and locate more than 1.5 million points of interest. It's $4.99 in the App Store.

UpNext 3D Cities

UpNext gives you maps of New York City, Washington D.C., and San Francisco, among others, in 3D. Swipe and zoom on the 3D maps, and touch a building to find out what businesses are inside (see Figure 12-32). It's an amazing app and shows you where the future of personal mapping apps is going. It's free in the App Store.

Figure 12-32. *Touchable 3D buildings in UpNext 3D Cities*

Summary

Maps is the world in your pocket. With it, you can now find directions to your favorite pizza joint, get an instant fix on your current location, or check out what the tops of the Pyramids of Giza look like without leaving your living room. You've learned how to use maps to find public transport times and routes, to get current traffic conditions, or just to virtually stroll down the street of a neighborhood you are thinking of moving to. Here are some tips to take away with you:

- When a person or business is in your contacts list, save yourself some time. Don't type in the entire address. Just enter a few letters of the name, and select the contact.

- Tap individual items on the directions list to jump to that part of your route.

- The Recents list (in Bookmarks) shows both recent locations *and* recent directions.

- URLs that link to Google Maps automatically open in the Maps application, whether they are tapped in Safari or in Mail.

- Street view is fun, and it's useful if you want to explore an area of your city—or almost any major city in the world—you've never visited.

- Plenty of other apps support map usage on the iPad. Some use Google Maps, and some use their own mapping software. Check out the recommendations in this chapter, or search *maps* or *navigation* in the App Store for a plethora of apps that take advantage of interactive maps.

Chapter 13

Touching Your Digital Photos

With the iPad's Photos application (launched from its icon, shown in Figure 13-1), you can free your photos from your home computer and pass them around the room like you used to do with photos of old. Hand your iPad to your friends, and they can swipe through your photos in their hands without the need to huddle around a desktop computer. In this chapter, you'll discover how to navigate your photo collections, share them with friends and family, and use the iPad as a digital picture frame.

Figure 13-1. *The Photos app icon*

Getting Photos onto Your iPad

Before you can view your photos on the iPad, you first need to put them on it. There are four ways you can do this: syncing photos from your computer, importing photos from a digital camera directly into the iPad, saving photos from e-mailed messages, and saving images found on web pages.

Syncing Photos from Your Computer

We discussed syncing photos to your iPad in Chapter 2, but let's touch upon it briefly again. iTunes can synchronize your iPad with pictures stored on your computer. This allows you to bring your photo collection with you and share it using the iPad's unique touch-based interface. Who needs to carry around thick and heavy physical photo albums when you have an iPad with its thin body and vibrant display?

To get started, connect your iPad to your computer, and launch iTunes. Select your iPad from the source list (the blue column on the left side of the iTunes window), and open the Photos tab. Select the "Sync photos" box, and then choose the location of the photos you want to sync. Your choices depend on your operating system.

On the computer, your options will be Adobe Photoshop Elements 3.0 or newer or any folder on your computer, such as My Pictures. On the Mac, your options will be iPhoto 4.0.3 or newer, Aperture 3.0.2 or newer, or any folder on your computer.

After you choose where to sync your photos from, select whether to sync your entire photo collection (a good choice for relatively small libraries) or individual albums (better for large libraries that might not fit on the iPad's limited storage space). In the latter case, pick only those albums you want to copy to your iPad.

If you are using a Mac and iPhoto or Aperture, you'll have the option to sync faces (iPhoto '09 or newer), events (iPhoto '08 or newer), and albums (see Figure 2-38). Faces are smart photo albums that contain all the photos that have a selected individual's face in them. It does this by using iPhoto's built-in facial recognition software. Events are another type of smart album that groups photos together that were taken on the same day. This helps eliminate clutter and keeps your photo library organized.

To finish, click Apply to save your changes, and then sync.

Importing Photos from a Digital Camera or iPhone

You can also import photos to your iPad directly from any camera that can connect via USB or that uses a SD card. To do this, you will need to purchase the iPad Camera Connection Kit ($29 at the Apple Store). The kit includes two adapters—one for connecting a camera through a USB 2.0 cable, the other for reading SD memory cards (see Figure 13-2).

The iPad supports standard photo formats, including JPEG, GIF, TIFF, PNG, and RAW. You can connect most cameras to your iPad through the USB adapter in the iPad Camera Connection Kit, including an iPhone so you can do direct iPhone to iPad photo transfers. You can even connect the popular line of Flip cameras to the iPad, but because of USB power issues, you will need to connect the Flip camera to an external power source before you connect it via USB to your iPad.

You can also import video clips taken by your camera through the iPad Camera Connection Kit if those video clips are in one of the video formats the iPad supports. Supported iPad video formats are M4V, MP4, MOV, MPEG-4, and H.264. The iPad does not support many popular video formats such as AVI and WMV, but there are countless applications that let you convert AVI and WMV files to iPad-compatible formats. Google *WMV to iPad* or *AVI to iPad* to see all the software that offers conversion capabilities.

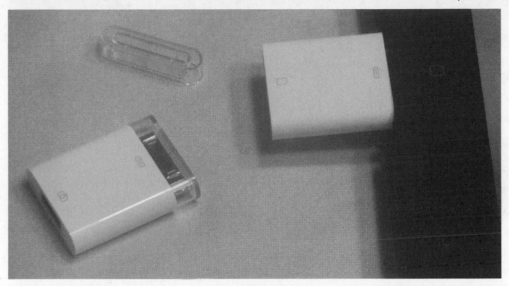

Figure 13-2. *The iPad Camera Connection Kit features a USB adapter and an SD card reader.*

To import photos, plug in either the USB adapter or the SD card adapter into the iPad. If you are using the USB adapter, connect your digital camera to it via the USB cable the camera came with, and switch the camera into transfer mode (see your camera's manual for details). If you are importing photos you took from your iPhone's camera, plug the iPhone into the USB adapter via the iPhone's Dock Connector to USB cable. Make sure the iPhone is turned on. If you are importing using the SD card adapter, plug the adapter into the iPad, and insert the SD card into it.

Once your camera or SD card is attached, unlock your iPad by sliding the unlock bar on the bottom of the lock screen. The Photos application will automatically appear and display all the photos available for importing. You now have two options: import all the photos by tapping the Import All button (see Figure 13-3) or import only certain photos.

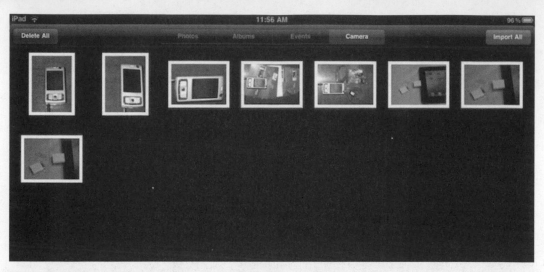

Figure 13-3. *Import all your photographs by tapping the Import All button in the top-right corner.*

To import just some photos, tap each photo, and a check mark will appear on it (see Figure 13-4). When you are done selecting all the photos you want to import, tap Import and select Import again.

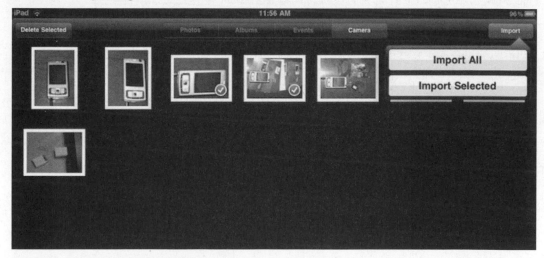

Figure 13-4. *Importing some of your photographs*

After a successful import, you will be able to choose whether to keep or delete the photos from the device you imported them from (see Figure 13-5).

Figure 13-5. *Choose to save or delete the imported photos on the external device.*

The newly imported photos will show up in an album called Last Import (see Figure 13-6) and in a new event, which contains the last imported photos. If you have imported photos previously, you'll see an album called All Imported.

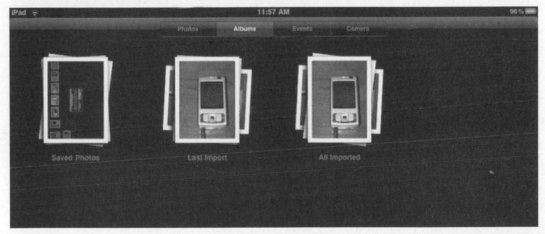

Figure 13-6. *Photos imported directly to the iPad from a digital camera or SD card will show up in the Last Import album.*

Once you have transferred your photos, you can disconnect the camera connection adapter from the iPad. To import the photos from the iPad to your computer, connect your iPad and open iPhoto on a Mac or Adobe Elements on a Windows computer.

Using a USB Thumb Drive to Transfer Photos to the iPad

You may find yourself in a situation where you quickly want to add some photos from your computer to the iPad but don't want to have to go through an entire synchronization procedure or change the iPad's settings to import other folders of photos. Wouldn't it be great if you could quickly import images to the iPad using a USB thumb drive?

Good news! You can *unofficially* use the iPad Camera Connection Kit to attach some types of USB thumb drives for quick and easy transfer of photos from your computer to the iPad. To do this, you have to trick your iPad into thinking your thumb drive is a camera.

DCIM (Digital Camera Images) is a universal standard used by camera manufacturers to organize photos on your camera by a defined file system and structure including the file naming specification, file formats, and metadata information. Before the iPad connects to your camera or SD card, it looks for a DCIM folder on the device that tells it that the device uses DCIM standards and thus is OK to import the photos the folder contains.

A camera's SD card automatically creates a folder labeled DCIM when you take the first picture. Since there's not much difference between an SD card and a USB thumb drive (both are just forms of solid-state storage), you can simply create a DCIM folder on the thumb drive to trick your iPad into thinking it's a camera.

The easiest way to do this is to create a new folder on your desktop and name it "DCIM." Drag that folder to the USB thumb drive. Once the folder is on the thumb drive, find and drag whatever photos you want from your computer into the DCIM folder on your thumb drive. After the photos are copied, plug the thumb drive into the USB adapter in the iPad Camera Connection Kit, and the iPad will see the photos in the DCIM folder and think it's talking to a camera, thus allowing you to import those pictures from the thumb drive into the iPad Photos app.

Saving Photos from Mail and Safari

You can also store photos on your iPad without importing them from your computer or camera. If someone e-mails you a photo, in the iPad's Mail app you'll see the photos appear in the body of the e-mail message. Tap and hold your finger on any photo, and you'll see a pop-up appear that allows you to save that one photo or all the photos contained in the e-mail (see Figure 13-7). The photo or photos you've selected to save will appear in an album labeled Saved Photos in the iPad's Photos app.

Similarly, in the iPad's Safari web browser, you can tap and hold your finger on any photo in a web page and select the Save Image pop-up that appears (see Figure 13-7). That photo will be saved to a Saved Photos album in the iPad's Photos app.

Figure 13-7. *Saving photos from an e-mail (left) or a web page (right)*

> **NOTE:** Many third-party apps (such as web browsers and magazines) also allow you to save images to your iPad. Some apps may have their own, unique way of saving images, but most should be fairly similar to the way you save images in Mail or Safari.

Navigating Your Photos

This is where the fun begins. When you touch your digital photos for the first time, you feel like you've finally stepped into the 21st century—that promised utopian future where technology merges with our fondest memories and we can go back and relive and explore them like never before. When you start pinching, dragging, and expanding your photos and albums, you'll feel like a child again who has just been given his first bag of marbles and spread them on the ground and then stares wide-eyed at the colors and shapes that he can control before him.

To launch the Photos app, tap its icon on the Home screen. Once launched, the Photos app displays thumbnails of the beginning of your photos in your Photos library, as shown in Figure 13-8.

Figure 13-8. *The Photos app*

Running along the top of the app, right above the thumbnail photos, you'll see the menu bar (see Figure 13-9). This bar allows you to switch between the different ways your photos are organized. To select a view, tap its tab in the menu bar.

Figure 13-9. *There are different ways your photos are organized on the iPad.*

- *Photos*: This is the first view you see when you launch the Photo app. On the Photos tab (see Figure 13-8), your pictures aren't grouped into any kind of albums at all. They are displayed in a sequential order by date taken. If you have lots of photos synced on your iPad, scrolling through this list can take quite a while.

- *Albums*: This view displays your photos in their albums as you've arranged them on your computer (see Figure 13-10). You will also see a Saved Photos album if you've saved images from the Web or that you've received in an e-mail on your iPad. Also, as mentioned earlier, if you've imported photos directly to the iPad from a digital camera, you will see them in a Last Import album.

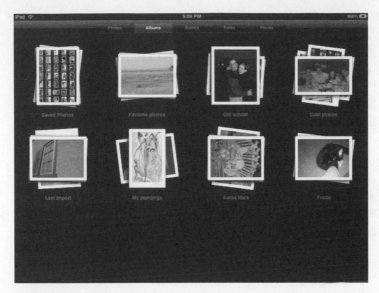

Figure 13-10. *Album view*

NOTE: Did you know you can take screen shots of your iPad? A *screen shot*, or a *screen capture*, is an image taken of whatever appears on the iPad's screen at the moment you are taking it. To take a screen shot, press and hold the power button on the iPad, and then press and release the Home button while still holding the power button. The iPad's screen will flash white, and you'll hear a shutter click sound effect. Once you hear the sound, you can let go of the power button. The captured screen shot will appear in the Saved Photos album. You can use screen shots to save images of entire web pages or show off that high score in a video game. Most of the images in this book were taken using the iPad's screen capture function.

■ *Events*: This view displays your photos in events (see Figure 13-11). Events are used in Aperture 2 and iPhoto '08 and newer as a way to automatically arrange your photos according to the date they were taken. This helps people automatically keep large photo libraries in easy-to-navigate shape. The Events tab is a Mac-only feature. You will not see this tab if you are using a Windows computer to sync your iPad.

Figure 13-11. *Events view*

- *Faces*: This view displays your photos grouped into an individual's "face" album (see Figure 13-12). If you are using iPhoto '09 or Aperture 3 on a Mac, the programs have facial recognition software built in. The Mac software automatically creates albums of individuals and groups all the photos they appear in. It's an amazingly fun way to see all the photos a certain friend or family member is in. Faces also works to some extent on cats and dogs. You will not see this tab if you are using a Windows computer to sync your iPad with; Faces is a Mac-only feature.

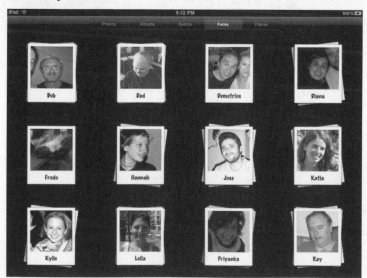

Figure 13-12. *Faces view*

■ *Places*: Many cameras today feature *geotagging*, which codes the photo with the location coordinates where it was taken. What the Places tab does is take your photo's coordinates and display them on a Google map (see Figure 13-13). This is arguably the coolest feature of Photos on iPad because it lets you navigate your photos on a map that you can view from a global level to a street level. It's an especially cool feature for travelers: you can see at a glance where you have been and just how much of the world is left to explore.

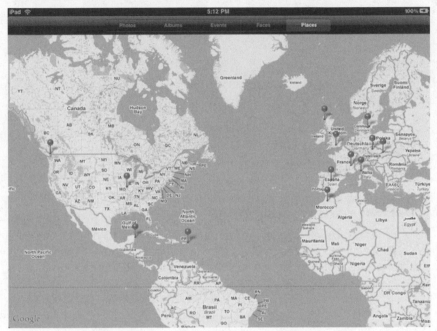

Figure 13-13. *Places view*

Red pins appear on the map that signify the geographic location of your photos. You can pinch and zoom on the map to get closer. As you do, you may see more pins appear on the map (see Figure 13-14).

Figure 13-14. *Note that more pins appear as you zoom in to an area of the map signifying greater accuracy of the photo's coordinates.*

Tap a pin to see an album pop-up appear (see Figure 13-15). You can then explore all the photos that were taken in that location. Places requires an Internet connection to display the Google map.

Figure 13-15. *Tap a pin to see an album thumbnail of every photo that was taken at that location.*

As you can now see, the iPad's photo app organizes your photos into five views for easy navigation. It is important to note that you may not see all the views on your iPad. The view categories you see depend on whether you are using a Mac or Windows computer, whether you have chosen to sync albums from each category view, and whether your photos are tagged with geocoordinates.

As long as you have one photo on your iPad, you'll always see the Photos tab. Most likely you will see the album tab too, especially if you've imported photos from a digital camera onto the iPad (a Last Import album is automatically created) or if you've saved an image you received in an e-mail or saw on the Web (a Saved Photos album is automatically created). To see other albums, events, or faces, you'll need to sync them from your computer. You don't need to do anything to sync Places; its tab will appear automatically if you have any photos tagged with geocoordinates.

Touching and Viewing Your Albums and Photos

Now you know how to navigate your photo collections, you'll learn how to touch and view them. Remember all the gestures covered in Chapter 4? When viewing a collection of albums or a single image full-screen, the iPad allows you to interact with that album or photo using a number of these gestures.

Touching and Viewing Albums

For this section, an *album* will refer to a regular album, an event, or a faces album, since interacting with these are all the same. As you can see in Figure 13-11, there are a series of event albums. An album appears as a pile of some of the photos that are contained in the album. To open the album, you have two options to expand, or open, the photo album:

- Tapping the album once will cause the photos in it to spread out and expand.

- Starting with two fingers together on an album, slowly spread them apart in a reverse pinch motion, and you'll see the album's photos start to spread out (see Figure 13-16). Remove your fingers to expand the album fully.

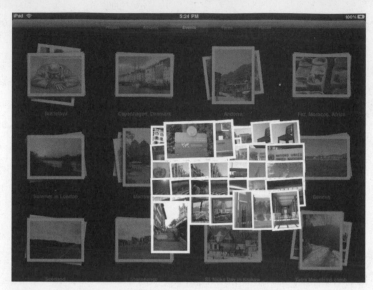

Figure 13-16. *An album being expanded by a reverse pinch*

You'll notice the menu bar at the top of the screen has changed once you are in an album (see Figure 13-17). It now displays the name of the album, with a back button that takes you to the category view you were previously in, as well as showing a Slide Show button and a Share button, which allows you to present your photos and share them with others (we'll talk about both of those a little later).

Figure 13-17. *Photos inside an album*

To exit the album, tap the back button (which will be named after the category the album is in; in Figure 13-17, the album *Montreux* is contained in the Events category—*Events* being the back button in this example) or pinch the photos of the album together. They will collapse on each other, and you'll find yourself back on the album screen.

While on the Places tab, the red pins on the map act as albums containing all the photos taken there. Tap the pin to be presented with an album thumbnail (see Figure 13-17); then tap the thumbnail, or reverse-pinch it, to expand the photos of that location onto the screen (see Figure 13-18).

Figure 13-18. *Expanding a series of photos taken in the same location in Places view*

Touching and Viewing Photos

When in an album, you will see thumbnails of the photos it contains (see Figure 13-17). To view a photo full-screen, you have two options to expand, or open, the photo:

- Tapping the photo once will cause the photo to fill the screen.

- Starting with two fingers together on a photo, slowly spread them apart in a reverse pinch motion, and you'll see the photo start to grow. Remove your fingers to expand the photo fully to fill the screen.

Once you display a photo full screen, you have several ways to interact with it:

- Pinching allows you to zoom into and out of the photo.

- Double-tap to zoom into the photo. Double-tap again to zoom out.

- When your image is displayed at the normal zoomed-out size, drag to the left or right to move to the previous or next image in the album. When zoomed into an image, dragging the photo pans across it.

Tap any image once to open the image overlay, as shown in Figure 13-19. The image overlay features a menu bar at the top of the screen and a scrubber bar at the bottom.

Figure 13-19. *Viewing a photo. Note the image overlay bars.*

The image overlay menu bar at the top of the screen shows you the number of the selected image out of the total number of images in the album, the back button to return to the album, and a Slide Show button and a Share button (discussed next). Slide your finger across the photo thumbnails in the scrubber bar at the bottom of the screen to quickly scan through your images (see Figure 13-20).

While viewing a photo in the Saved Photos album, you'll notice a garbage pail icon next to the Share button. This garbage pail icon shows up only in the menu bar of images in the Saved Photos album. Tapping this button will delete the selected photo. We talk more about deleting photos later in this chapter.

Figure 13-20. *The scrubber bar*

While viewing individual photos, flip your iPad onto its side to have your photo reorient itself. If the photo was shot using landscape orientation, it fits itself to the wider view.

You can tap a full-screen image once with two fingers to return to album view.

Viewing Your Photos as Slide Show

When viewing the contents of any album or a single image in any album, you'll see the Slide Show and Share buttons in the upper-left corner of the screen (see Figure 13-21). As the name suggests, the Slide Show button displays the contents of a photo album, one image after another. We'll discuss the Share button after the Slide Show button.

Figure 13-21. *The Slideshow and Share buttons display in the right of the menu bar when viewing a single photo or the contents of any album.*

Slide shows are an awesome way to share your photos with your friends and family. Remember, however, that our images are associated with our personal memories, so they are always going to be more pleasant for us to watch than for others. All you have to do is remember a time you were stuck looking at someone else's photos and the seconds ticked by as if they were hours. To keep slide shows exciting for your viewers, keep a few things in mind:

- *Shorter is better.* The average shot (a clip of video displayed between cutting away to another shot) in a movie or TV show is less than two seconds nowadays. Back in the 1950s, the average shot was 30 seconds long. Watch an episode of *Friends* and then an episode of *I Love Lucy*, and you'll see exactly what we mean. *Lucy* seems to trudge along so slowly by today's standards. As the world—and media—got faster, our attention spans shrunk. This applies to viewing still images too. People can take in a lot from an image in just two or three seconds. If they are forced to look at an image any longer, they start to get bored. Keep the time a single image is displayed short. Also, keep the entire length of the slide show short. When you watch a movie trailer in the cinema, their time is exactly two minutes and twenty seconds, which a perfect amount to whet the appetite, show people the best shots, and leave them feeling fulfilled but not exhausted.

- *Music always helps:* Playing the appropriate kind of song in the background of a slide show really adds a lot of ambience and power to a slide show. Music is a powerful tool for conveying the emotion and sense of place and situation. In film school, one of the authors had an editing class where we watched clips from the now classic horror film *Halloween*. We watched a clip, as it was shown in theaters—with the soundtrack score, dialogue, and sound effects—that showed Michael Myers chasing his victim with a big butcher's knife. Pretty scary stuff. Then we watched the same clip with the dialogue and sound effects only—the soundtrack's score was removed. The clip went from being scary to being almost comical. Music adds more to your images than you realize.

- *Transitions help too.* A transition is the effect that occurs when moving from one image to the next. It adds some visual flair to the change of images. Photos' slide shows allow you to choose between five transitions. Use them as eye candy to keep your audience entertained.

- *Use your TV*: If you are having a party, a great way to show off your photos without wrangling up all your guests and forcing them to sit and watch is to project your slide show on a TV and set it to repeat. That way, your slide show is constantly playing in the background, and your guests can continue to catch glimpses of it as they mingle. Images on slide shows playing in the background are great conversation starters and allow you to play much longer slide shows and display individual images for longer, since you don't have to worry about a captive audience. If you are going to play your slide shows in the background, you can choose to show several thousand images for as long as five or ten seconds each; that way, the entire show could run for hours, and it won't get boring or tedious.

To begin a slide show, tap the Slideshow button. A drop-down menu will appear that shows you your slide show options (see Figure 13-22).

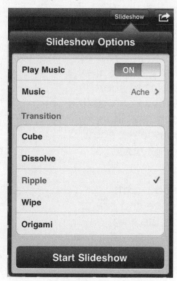

Figure 13-22. *The Slideshow Options drop-down menu*

- *Play Music*: If switched to ON, this will play music in the background while the slide show runs.

- *Music*: Tap here to navigate through all the songs in your iPad's music library. Once you find the song you want, tap it to select it.

- *Transition*: You have the option of selecting one of five transitions to display between images: Cube, Dissolve, Ripple, Wipe, or Origami.

- *Start Slideshow*: Tap this button to start the slide show. The images overlays disappear, and the slide show plays. To stop the slide show at any time, touch the screen. This stops the slide show and places you in the full-screen photo display. To start the slide show again, tap the Slideshow button and tap Start Slideshow.

Slide shows display each slide for a set period of time, which you can set. To export your slide show to a TV screen, you'll need to purchase a special cable from Apple that connects your iPad to your TV. Apple offers three different cables, which are discussed in Chapter 7.

To customize how your iPad displays its slide shows, go to your Home screen, and navigate to Settings ➤ Photos. As shown in Figure 13-23, this settings screen allows you to specify exactly how you want your slide shows to display:

Figure 13-23. *The Slideshow settings*

- *Play Each Slide For:* Here, you can set the slide duration. Your choices are 2 seconds, 3 seconds (the default, which works really well for most people), 5 seconds, 10 seconds (which starts to get boring fast), and 20 seconds (which is probably recognized officially by Amnesty International as torture for most humans; seriously, don't do this to your friends and family).

- *Repeat:* Set this to ON to make your slide show loop.

- *Shuffle:* Show your pictures in a random order by switching Shuffle from OFF to ON. When Shuffle is disabled, your pictures display in album order.

Sharing Your Photos

You have a number of ways to share photos you have on your iPad. To access all the ways you can share your photos, bring up a photo full-screen and tap the Share button, which looks like an arrow breaking free from a small box (see Figure 13-21). You'll be presented with a drop-down menu of sharing options (see Figure 13-24):

Figure 13-24. *The Sharing drop-down menu*

- *Email Photo:* Tap this to see an e-mail compose window appear on the screen. You'll notice the photo has been copied into the body of the e-mail already (see Figure 13-25). Enter the recipient's e-mail, a subject, and body text; then tap Send, and your photo is on its way!

Figure 13-25. *The new message compose screen appears with the photo in the body of the e-mail.*

Alternatively, you can e-mail up to five photos at a time from within the Photos app. While in an album, tap the Share button, and you'll see the album menu renamed to Select Photos. Tap up to five photos that you want to send, and then tap the Email button in the upper-left corner (see Figure 13-26). An e-mail compose window will appear on the screen with the photos in the body of the message. Note that although you are limited to e-mailing five photos at a time from the Photos app, you can actually copy as many as you want and then open the Mail app, compose a new message, and paste them all in the body of the e-mail.

Figure 13-26. *You can e-mail up to five photos at a time from within the Photos app.*

■ *Send to MobileMe:* MobileMe is Apple's e-mail service that also allows you to publish and share your photos online. The Send to MobileMe option lets you upload your photos to your MobileMe Gallery online right from your iPad. Tap Send to MobileMe. A window will appear asking you to name the photo and write a description if you want (see Figure 13-27). Select the MobileMe Gallery album you want to publish the photo to; then tap Publish.

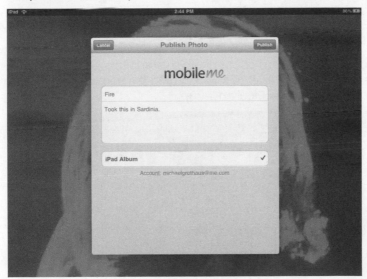

Figure 13-27. *Uploading a photo to a MobileMe gallery*

A pop-up will appear when the photo has been finished uploading, and you'll be able to tap View on MobileMe, which takes you to your MobileMe web gallery in Safari or Tell a Friend, which opens the Mail app and composes an e-mail with the link to the photo in the body of the message.

To use these MobileMe features, you must have a MobileMe account. See www.me.com for details.

- *Assign to Contact*: This option allows you to assign a photo to an address book contact. Tap Assign to Contact, and then select the contact's address book entry from the drop-down menu (see Figure 13-28).

Figure 13-28. *Select the contact to add the photo to.*

Move and scale the thumbnail of the photo that appears between the opaque bars on top and bottom to zoom in onto the contact's face; then tap the Use button (see Figure 13-29).

Figure 13-29. *Move and scale the contact's photo.*

The next time you view the contact in the iPad's Contacts app, the image you selected for them will appear next to their name. This image will sync with their contact information in Address Book and Entourage on a Mac and Outlook on a Windows computer.

■ *Use as Wallpaper*. Tap this button to use the selected image as wallpaper on your iPad. From the menu bar (see Figure 13-30), you'll be able to select whether you want to use the image for the iPad's lock screen, the Home screen, or both. This isn't the only way to set your iPad's wallpaper options. We'll talk about the other way in a bit.

Figure 13-30. *The wallpaper menu bar options let you select which screen you want to use the photo as wallpaper for.*

■ *Copy Photo*. Tap Copy Photo to copy the image. This saves the image to your clipboard for use in pasting into other things (such as an e-mail or document) later.

You can also copy multiple photos at a time. When viewing an album, tap the Share button. You'll see the album menu renamed as Select Photos. Tap as many photos as you want to copy. A check mark will appear on each selected photo (see Figure 13-26). After you have selected all your photos, tap the Copy button in the upper-left corner. These photos can then be batch copied into an e-mail or other applications.

Deleting Your Photos

Apple made it so you can only delete photos on your iPad that are part of the Saved Photos album. This album contains any photos you have saved from the Web or an e-mail on the iPad. Apple disabled deletion of photos from your other albums synced to your iPad because it didn't want users accidentally deleting photos they had stored on their computer.

To delete the photos, navigate to your Saved Photos album and tap the Share button. Tap the photos you want to delete, and a check mark will appear on them; then tap the red Delete button (see Figure 13-31). Alternatively, while displaying a photo full-screen in your Saved Photos album, you'll notice a trash can icon next to the Share button (see Figure 13-32). Tapping this button will cause a Delete Photo confirmation pop-up to appear. Tap Delete Photo to delete the selected photo from your iPad.

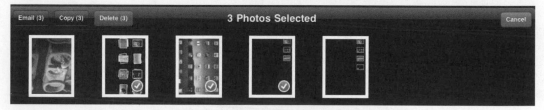

Figure 13-31. *You can only delete photos on the iPad from the Saved Photos album.*

Figure 13-32. *The trash can icon in the upper-right corner of a photo in the Saved Photos album*

To delete other photos on your iPad, you must delete them on your computer first and then resync the iPad.

Picture Frame

On the iPad's lock screen (the screen that appears when you turn on your iPad or wake it from sleep) to the right of the Slide to Unlock bar, you'll notice there is a small icon of a flower inside a box (see Figure 13-33). This is the Picture Frame button. Tap this to turn your iPad into an awesome digital picture frame. The picture frame turns your iPad into an interactive piece of furniture in your office or living room and is a great way to still "use" the iPad while you're doing other things. You can buy one of the many stands that supports the iPad to make best use of the Picture Frame feature.

Figure 13-33. *The iPad's lock screen with Picture Frame button in the lower-right*

To start the picture frame, lock the iPad by briefly pressing the power button. Press the power button or Home button on the iPad again to be taken to the lock screen. To the right of the Slide to Unlock bar, you'll see an icon of a flower in a box (see Figure 13-33). Tap this icon to enter picture frame mode. The icon will change to a blue color, and the screen will fill with a photo, displaying one after the next. To pause the slide show, tap the screen. The current image will pause in the background as the lock screen fades into view. To disable Picture Frame, tap the blue picture frame icon, and you will return to the lock screen with its selected wallpaper displayed.

You have several options for the Picture Frame feature, which can be configured from within the iPad's Settings app. Navigate to your iPad Home screen, and tap the Settings icon. Select Picture Frame (see Figure 13-34).

Figure 13-34. *Picture Frame settings*

■ *Transitions*: Choose between Dissolve and Origami to flow from one photo to the next.

■ *Zoom in on Faces*: When this is set to ON, photos that display in the picture frame will focus on faces in the picture. It knows which faces you like because of the Faces feature built into the Photos app. If more than one face is in a picture, it will choose one at random to focus on. Face zooming is only an option when transitions are set to dissolve.

■ *Shuffle*: When set to ON, your photos will show in a random order.

The Picture Frame feature will display all the photos from your Photos app by default. You can select to show only photos from certain albums, faces, or events by selecting their category and then selecting the one you want to show.

Changing the Wallpaper Without Using the Photos App

We showed you how to set your wallpaper from a photo in the Photos app, but you can also set it from within the iPad's Settings app. To do this, navigate to your iPad Home screen, and tap the Settings icon. Select Brightness & Wallpaper. You'll see two images, one representing your iPad's lock screen and the other its Home screen (Figure 13-35). The pictures you see on each image show you the wallpaper you have selected for each one currently.

Figure 13-35. *The Brightness & Wallpaper settings*

Tap the images to be taken to the wallpaper selection screen (Figure 13-36). Here you'll see a list of every album in your Photos app and also a new album labeled Wallpaper.

Figure 13-36. *You can select from Apple's included wallpapers or use any photo you have on your iPad as wallpaper.*

Wallpaper includes images Apple included on the iPad to be used as wallpaper. Select an image from any album, and you'll get a full-screen preview of it. Then tap Set Lock Screen, Set Home Screen, or Set Both to use the image for the background of the lock screen, Home screen, or both the lock screen and Home screen (see Figure 13-30). If you choose to use the image just for, say, the lock screen, you can go back and select another image for the Home screen.

Summary

This chapter introduced you to the iPad's Photos app and showed you how to navigate your photo collections, share them with friends and family, change the iPad's wallpaper and even use your iPad as a digital picture frame. Once you view your digital photos on the iPad, you might find that you'll never want to navigate and view them on a computer monitor or laptop screen again.

Here are some final thoughts for this chapter:

- The iPad's Photos application offers some of the most instantly appealing ways to show off the power of your iPad. You can scroll through your albums, zoom in and out with a pinch or double-tap, and flip the unit on its side. These features all deliver the iPad "wow" factor.

- You can import photos directly from a camera onto the iPad. This is a huge help for professional photographers who might be out in the field shooting. They can load their images on the iPad and instantly see what they look like on a bigger screen. They can even zoom in to see more detail.

- Consider investing in an inexpensive business card holder and a cheap speaker. They make watching slide shows on your iPad a lot easier, especially for more than one person at a time. A video-out cable from Apple increases the fun by sending the slide shows to a TV screen.

Chapter 14

On the Go with iWork

In this book, we've discussed apps that can help you get organized, let you communicate with others, or enjoy media in the form of music, books, videos, and photos. Now we're going to talk about three apps that turn your iPad into a powerful work platform.

The three apps are Pages, Numbers, and Keynote, together known as iWork for iPad. These Apple-produced apps can be purchased in the App Store for $9.99 each, and they provide much of the functionality that productive workers need while they're on the go. With that, we'll add a caveat: for serious work, you should consider using your iPad to remotely control your "real" work computer. Apps such as LogMeIn Ignition and iTeleport make this possible, although a detailed explanation of their configuration and use is not included in this book. In this chapter, we'll cover the basics of each app only, because a detailed dig into iWork could easily be the subject of another book.

Buy and Install iWork for iPad

of the apps built into your iPad, iWork for iPad apps must be purchased on your iPad. In Chapter 8, we told you about the App Store app and how our iPad to assist you in browsing, purchasing, and installing iPad software.

ed to purchase all three of the apps if you don't need some of the For instance, if you just need a good word processing app and don't do t requires spreadsheets or presentations, you can just buy Pages. night just want to purchase Keynote, and budget managers could just pick

me things you may choose to use each app for.

Pages:

- Writing letters
- Creating or updating a résumé
- Developing a project proposal

- Writing a term paper

- Making creative posters, greeting cards, invitations, or flyers

Numbers:

- Creating checklists

- Making comparisons of mortgages or other loans

- Developing a budget

- Creating expense reports and invoices

- Logging business and personal auto mileage

- Drawing charts and graphs from data

Keynote:

- Developing business presentations

- Creating class presentations by both students and instructors

- Making strikingly attractive personal slide shows

- Using your iPad as a teleprompter for giving speeches

Launch the App Store app, and then type the word **pages** into the search box in the upper-right corner of the App Store. Tap the Search button on your keyboard, and a list of apps with *pages* in their names appear. Under iPad Apps, look for Pages (listed in the productivity category), and then tap the price button. That button turns into a green Install App button. Tap it, and you'll be asked to enter your Apple ID. Pages downloads to your iPad and then automatically installs itself. The same process works with both Numbers and Keynote.

These apps are big—more than 20MB each—so be sure to have your iPad connected to a Wi-Fi network prior to installation. If you try to install any of the iWork apps while connected to a 3G network, a message will ask you to either install while you're on a Wi-Fi network or install the app through iTunes on your computer. Our recommendation is to purchase and install the iWork for iPad apps through iTunes on your computer.

Pages

Pages is more than a word processing app for iPad—it can be used to create sophisticated page layouts with graphics, tables, charts, and numerous text styles. The Mac version of Pages evolved over its lifetime to become a powerful writing and desktop publishing tool, but the iPad version was born with many of the same capabilities. The app is optimized for use with the touch interface of the iPad, making it a joy to use.

In this section, we'll familiarize you with the user interface and some of the functionality of Pages.

Creating a New Document

Launching Pages for the first time, you're greeted with a document with the title Tap to Get Started with Pages. It's more than just a pretty set of pages; it's an interactive tutorial into many of the features of the app. It coaxes you to use common iPad interface gestures to move, rotate, scale and delete images, restyle text, and add objects to your documents.

The My Documents page, the first thing you see in Pages, looks like a piece of gray cloth on which all of your documents are nicely laid out side by side. To open a previously created document, tap it once.

To start with a blank piece of paper or perhaps a template, you can either tap the New Document button in the upper-left corner of the Pages window or tap the plus sign (+) icon in the middle of the bottom of the window. Tapping the plus sign below an existing document in the My Documents window gives you a choice of creating a new document from scratch or duplicating the existing document.

If you tap either of the New Document buttons, the first thing you see is a Choose a Template screen with a number of useful document types (Figure 14-1). You can choose to start with a wide-open piece of paper or a well-designed document template. Templates help when you want to create a professional-looking document quickly or when you're faced with writer's block and need some ideas to launch your imagination.

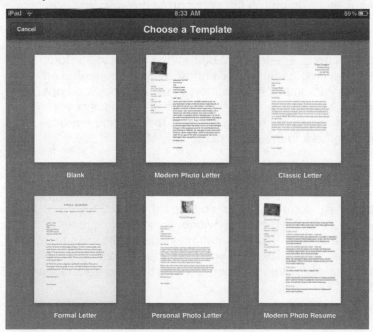

Figure 14-1. *Creating a new document in Pages for iPad provides the option of starting with a blank page or using a professionally designed template.*

For the purposes of this book, we'll start with a blank page. Tap the blank page in the upper left of the Choose a Template window, and you're ready to start writing. Before you begin, we'll explain a bit about what's on the top of the Pages window (Figure 14-2).

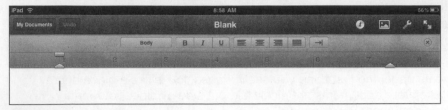

Figure 14-2. *The Pages Style ruler*

The Pages Style Ruler

Apple named the ruler-like user interface element shown in Figure 14-2 the *Style ruler*, because it provides both a way to style your text and a ruler for aligning page elements. You can make the Style ruler disappear from your page by tapping the circled *X* in the upper-right corner, and you can make it reappear by double-tapping the barely visible edge of the ruler at the top of the screen.

The Style ruler is different from the toolbar just above it. The toolbar includes a button for returning to My Documents, an Undo button (for reverting to previous versions of a document), and a set of buttons on the right side that we'll describe in a moment. Unlike the Style ruler, the toolbar is always visible.

The ruler features a number of buttons. The leftmost button (the one marked Body) applies styles to any currently selected paragraph. To apply a style, double-tap any text in a paragraph, and then tap the Paragraph Styles button. A scrolling pop-up appears with a list of common paragraph styles—title, subtitle, headings of various sizes, subheadings, body text, bulleted text, captions, headers and footers, and more. Selecting one of those styles applies it to the entire paragraph of text.

Undo/Redo

Did you just accidentally apply the incorrect style to a paragraph of text? No problem. Tap the Undo button on the toolbar at the top of the window, and the text reverts to the original style. If you later decide that you really meant to make a specific change, tap the Undo button again. A pop-up may appear allowing you to choose to redo an action. Unlike many other iPad apps, Pages does not support shaking the iPad from side to side to undo/redo.

The next set of buttons—B, I, and U—apply common styles to characters. B stands for bold, I for italic, and U for underlines. To select a word, double-tap it. When you select a word, it's highlighted with a light blue background and gains a pair of selection handles, one at each end (Figure 14-3).

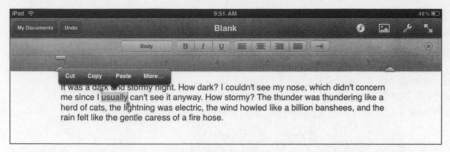

Figure 14-3. *Double-tapping any word in a Pages document selects it, adds selection handles to either side to expand the selection, and displays a pop-up menu of actions.*

Expand your selection by dragging the handles left or right, or select an entire paragraph by triple-tapping it. A pop-up also appears, showing actions that can be applied to the text. The most widely used actions—Cut, Copy, and Paste—appear in the pop-up. Tapping the More button provides several more actions—Copy Style, Replace, and Definition.

Cut, Copy, Paste, and Copy Style

Cut, Copy, and Paste work just like they do in any word processing program on a Mac or Windows computer. It's possible to cut a word or phrase out and paste it somewhere else or to copy text to paste in another location. Copy Style copies the existing style of the text. For example, if you create your own style for a word by using bold and underlining it, you can apply bold and underlining to any other text by copying the style of the word and then pasting the style (which appears when you've copied a style) to another selected word or phrase.

Replace

Replace assumes that you've misspelled a word and displays possible replacements to apply. Tapping one of the replacement words inserts it in place of the existing word. Definition provides a one-tap dictionary lookup. When you select Definition, a pop-up appears with the dictionary definition of the word (Figure 14-4).

low dark? I couldn't see my nose, which didn't concern
nyway. How stormy? The thunder was thundering like a
ectric, the wind howled like a billion banshees, and the
a fire hose.

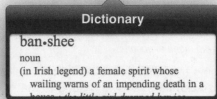

Figure 14-4. *Definition provides a way to determine the meaning of any word without needing to quit Pages and move to another app.*

Justifying Text

Moving down the Style ruler, you come upon a set of icons covered with lines. From left to right, these are left-justify, center, right-justify, or fully-justify text. The final button, the one that looks like an arrow pointing at a wall, applies tabs or breaks (Figure 14-5).

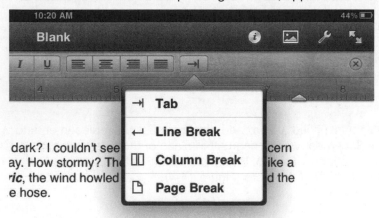

Figure 14-5. *The final button on the Style ruler is used to apply tabs, line breaks, column breaks, and page breaks.*

Applying a tab to the beginning of a line of text can be used to indent the text by half-inch increments. A line break ends the existing line of text and moves the insertion point (where new text appears) down a line. Column breaks work only when you have set up the document with more than one column, in which case applying a column break moves text located after the insertion point to the next column. Finally, a page break starts writing text on a new page.

NOTE: If you're using an external Bluetooth or USB keyboard or the Apple Keyboard Dock, you can use the Tab key in place of the tab button. Other buttons on the top of the keyboard provide varying functions, including setting sound volume and increasing or decreasing the brightness of the iPad display.

If you'd like to set tabs at various points on the ruler, just tap the ruler and then drag the tab to the appropriate point. Now when you press the tab button several times in succession, it will jump between the tab points that you have set. A right tab, meaning that text is moved to the right of the tab point, is set by default. Double-tapping a tab once turns it into a center tab (text centered around the tab point), and double-tapping a tab twice converts a tab into a left tab (text aligned to the left of the tab).

The Style ruler also displays adjustable margins and a first-line indent tool. The small upward-pointing arrows (Figure 14-6) indicate the margins, which default to 1 inch from each side of a traditional 8.5" × 11" sheet of paper. Those margins can be moved left or right depending on your needs. The first line of a paragraph can be indented by dragging the indent tool (the small rectangular block above the left margin indicator on a new page) to the right.

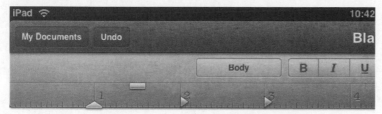

Figure 14-6. *Indent the first line of a paragraph by dragging the indent tool (the rectangular tool at 1.5 inch) to the right. Several right tabs are visible in this image as well.*

Renaming a Pages Document

Moving back to My Documents by tapping the My Documents button, you can rename the "Blank" document by tapping the name that shows up beneath the image of the document. Type a new name, and then tap Done to save the name (Figure 14-7).

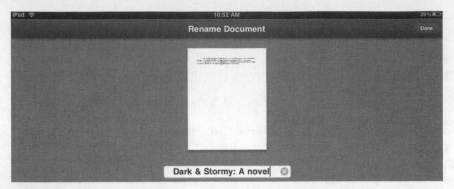

Figure 14-7. *Renaming your document helps identify it uniquely in the My Documents view in Pages.*

The Pages Toolbar

Now let's look at some of the other tools on the toolbar above the Style ruler. As we mentioned earlier, the Undo button lets you correct mistakes. In fact, it can correct a lot mistakes—each time you tap Undo, another earlier action you took in Pages is undone.

Info

Migrating across the toolbar past the document name, you come to a small round icon that looks a lot like the international sign for information—a lowercase *i*. Apple calls this the Info button, and depending on what is currently selected on your iPad, text or an object, it provides different capabilities.

For text, the Info button gives you the choices of Style, List, and Layout (Figure 14-8).

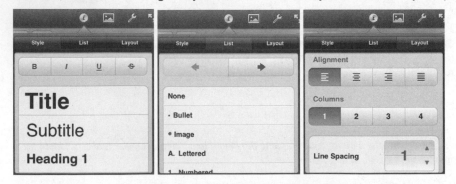

Figure 14-8. *The Info button is your portal for changing style, list, and layout settings.*

The Style tab reiterates the text styles you saw earlier; it allows bolding, italicizing, underlining, or striking through text and also (at the very bottom; they're not visible in Figure 14-8) text options such as size, color, and font. The List tab sets lists as bulleted, lettered, numbered, or bulleted with an image. Use the large arrows to increase or decrease the indentation of list items in formatted outlines. The Layout tab is another way to apply alignment to a document, set it up with up to four columns, or adjust the line spacing.

For objects (images, charts, tables, or shapes), the Info button changes to show the Style and Arrange tabs (Figure 14-9).

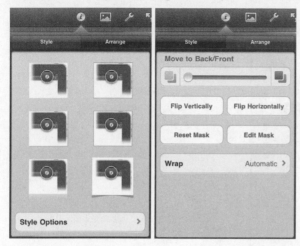

Figure 14-9. *Objects can be styled or arranged using the Info button.*

When applied to an object, the Style tab adds a variety of frames, shadows, and reflections to provide a sense of depth to the object. The Style tab provides a number of options, including turning an image border on or off, scaling the border, changing the line type from whole to dashed, and choosing from a dozen different frames. The Arrange tab moves an object backward or forward compared to other objects, allows you to flip an object vertically and horizontally, allows you to do some in-document cropping of images with masks, and allows you to set how text wraps around the object.

When we discuss Numbers, you'll learn about some other uses of the Info button, such as for setting options for charts and shapes.

Insert

The Insert button looks like a little drawing of a landscape. It inserts media from your Photos library, tables, charts, or shapes into your document (Figure 14-10).

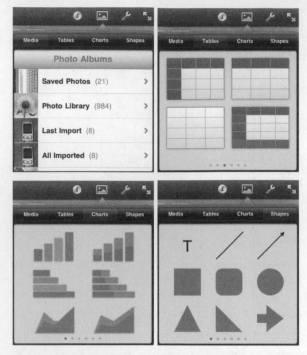

Figure 14-10. *Use the Insert button to add images, tables, charts, or shapes to your Pages document.*

The Media tab adds pictures in the Photos app to your document. Tables provides a number of attractive and colorfully shaded preformatted tables for displaying tabular information in your document. With Charts, there's a choice of bar, column, area, line, scatter, and pie charts in various shades to add to your document. Double-tapping a chart you've inserted displays a simple spreadsheet for editing the charted information. Finally, if you need to add a box, a cartoon balloon, a line, or geometric shapes to your Pages document, just tap Shapes.

Once you've added a table, a chart, or a shape to a document, tapping that element and then tapping the Info button displays a pop-up that makes changing options for that element a snap. We'll describe the table and chart options in more detail when we talk about Numbers.

Tools

The little wrench-like icon that's next on the toolbar is the Tools button (Figure 14-11). It's used to change settings that apply to the document as a whole.

Figure 14-11. *The Tools button in Pages provides features that apply to a complete document, not just a word or paragraph.*

Tapping the Document Setup button displays a blueprint-like layout of the document on which you can tap and edit headers and footers or move the document margins. Do you need to find and replace a word or phrase in a document? Find searches your entire document for a set of characters, replaces them (if you've chosen the find and replace option), and can even match case or complete words if you need a more finely tuned search (Figure 14-12).

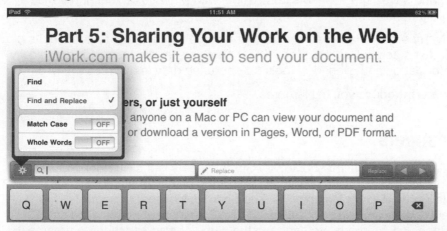

Figure 14-12. *The Find function under the Tools button in Pages is a powerful tool for making global replacements throughout a document.*

The next button under Tools, Go to Help, starts up Safari and points you to Apple's online help for the iWork for iPad suite. There's a surprising amount of information contained in the online help, so if you get stuck using a certain feature in Pages, Keynote, or Numbers, be sure to check it out.

Another Tools button turns edge guides on or off. What are edge guides? If you have more than one object on a page, dragging one of them will display alignment guides so you can see when the center or edges of the objects line up. Turning edge guides off means that only the center guides appear when moving objects.

The last tool enables or disables the real-time spelling checker. As you type in a Page document, words that might be misspelled appear with a red dotted underline. Tapping the word displays any possible replacements, and tapping one of those inserts the replacement word. If you find the constant reminders to be annoying, disable the spelling check.

Coming to the final icon on the toolbar, one that looks like a pair of arrows pointing diagonally, you find the control that can give you a full page without the toolbar, Style ruler, or anything else. This is most useful when you're reading a document and want to see as much of it as possible.

With this description of the many tools available to you in Pages, you can now begin to work with the app and discover how powerful this iPad word processor and page layout tool can really be.

Numbers

Once you're familiar with Pages on the iPad, it's easy to understand how to use Numbers. For people who need to organize data and numbers, the Numbers app creates, opens, and saves spreadsheets compatible with Microsoft Excel or the Mac version of Numbers.

Not only does Numbers for iPad contain a lot of the same spreadsheet features of its big brothers on Windows computers and Macs, but it contains charting tools for graphically representing information and even form tools for capturing data in a spreadsheet.

Follow along as we introduce you to Numbers.

My Spreadsheets

Does Figure 14-13 look familiar? It should. My Spreadsheets is the Numbers equivalent of My Documents in Pages. In fact, everything about the user interface in My Spreadsheets is identical to My Documents. The Sharing, New or Duplicate Spreadsheet, and Delete icons below the image of a spreadsheet perform the same tasks as their Pages counterparts; you can tap the name of a spreadsheet to rename it, and there's a New Spreadsheet button.

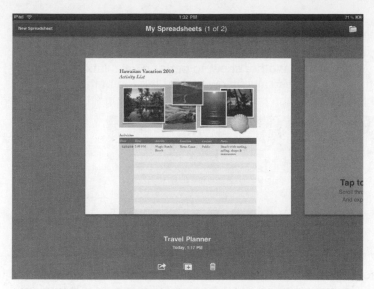

Figure 14-13. *My Spreadsheets is analogous to My Documents in Pages. It's used to create new spreadsheets, rename them, delete them, and share them with others.*

The New Spreadsheet button opens to a window that's the Numbers version of the New Document window. As with Pages, you can either select a blank spreadsheet or choose from a number of templates thoughtfully provided by Apple.

The Numbers templates (Figure 14-14) range from simple checklists to mortgage calculators and from weight loss and running logs to class attendance sheets. Although not everyone may need a GPA calculator, it's available. Many of the templates exist to give you a taste of the range of tasks you can perform with Numbers.

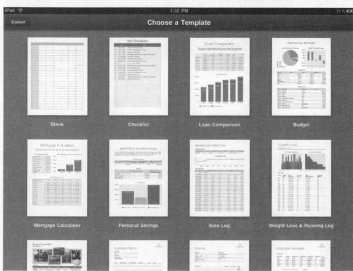

Figure 14-14. *Apple includes 16 templates with Numbers, many of which can be used to perform useful calculations.*

One unique Numbers user interface feature is the concept of tabs. As shown in Figure 14-15, tabs define different sheets or forms for a spreadsheet. As an example, a Numbers spreadsheet could consist of one sheet to describe how to use the spreadsheet, a form to capture data, and another sheet to perform calculations on the data you captured. Each of those pages displays its own tab at the top of the spreadsheet, making navigation between the pages as simple as tapping a tab.

Review your spreadsheet

 Tap the Full Screen button to see more of your spreadsheet. Touch and hold a cell, then drag across a range of cells to see a data

Figure 14-15. *Use tabs to name individual sheets or forms in a Numbers spreadsheet file.*

If you're familiar with Microsoft Excel, just think of tabs as sheets and the group of sheets as an Excel workbook. To add a new tab, just tap the rightmost tab. It's marked with a plus sign, and tapping it displays a pop-up with two buttons—New Sheet and New Form. Any tab can be renamed by double-tapping the existing name and then typing a new name.

As in Pages, there's a very helpful Getting Started document that is a thinly disguised interactive Numbers tutorial. For iPad owners just getting started with Numbers, it's well worth the time and effort to go through the Getting Started pages.

Adding Elements to a Spreadsheet

A blank spreadsheet isn't very useful. Although even the "Blank" template contains a generic table that you can begin to type numbers or text into, tapping a tab creates a totally blank sheet. Where are the rows and columns you're used to? In Numbers, you need to add a table to the sheet to begin using it. As you'll recall, the Insert button in Pages let you add media, tables, charts, and shapes to a blank page. That's exactly what the Insert button does in Numbers as well. The Tables tab is slightly different, but Media, Charts, and Shapes tabs are identical to their siblings in Pages in that they provide a way to add pictures, create charts, or draw shapes on a page.

In Figure 14-16, we've added a simple five-column table to a blank sheet. As you can see, the first column contains a check box for each row, while the rest of the columns are blank. The table has a name—Table 1—and some things that look like scrollbars to the top and left of the table.

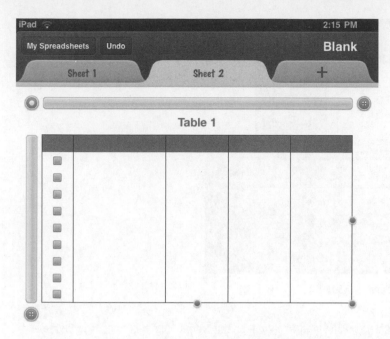

Figure 14-16. *A blank table added to a blank sheet in Numbers*

See those little things at the end of the scrollbars that look like buttons on a shirt? Dragging one of those to the right or down adds another column or row to the table. Dragging a button up or to the left removes a row or column from the table. To move the entire table around on the sheet, drag the button in the upper-left corner of the table.

The dark dots on the right and bottom edges of the table stretch the table when dragged, increasing the width of all the columns and rows without adding any new columns or rows. Likewise, you can make the table smaller by dragging those "handles" up or to the left.

Although we won't go through the details of the many spreadsheet functions that you can choose from in Numbers, let's talk about how you enter information into spreadsheet cells. Double-tapping a cell on the spreadsheet highlights it with a dark blue border, and a data entry field appears on the screen along with an appropriate keyboard (Figure 14-17). On the far left you'll see a button with "42" on it, which indicates that you use this button to enter numbers into the cell. The numbers can be formatted as plain numbers, as currency (using the dollar sign button on the data entry keyboard below), as a percentage (using the percent sign button), as a star ranking from 1 to 5 (using the star button), or as a check box (0 or 1, using the check box button). Buttons on the right side of the keyboard take you to the next cell to the right or to the next cell down for quick navigation around the spreadsheet.

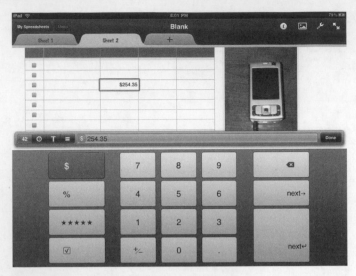

Figure 14-17. *The numeric data entry keyboard*

SUBTLE JOKE ALERT! Are you wondering why the numeric entry button has "42" on it? In the classic science fiction series *The Hitchhiker's Guide to the Galaxy*, 42 is the answer to the ultimate question of life, the universe, and everything. We're speculating that someone on the Numbers development team is a sci-fi fan.

Use the next button, which looks like a clock, to enter dates, times, or durations into spreadsheet cells. The keyboard looks different as a result (Figure 14-18), featuring the months of the year on the keypad and buttons for denoting whether you're entering a date and/or time or a duration. What's the difference between a date or time and a duration? A date is a specific date, for example June 10, 2010, and a time is a specific time, like 4:32:06 p.m. A duration is a length of time that can be measured between two time points. One of our writers has a lifetime measured with a duration of 52 years, 9 months, 19 days, 1 hour, and 22 minutes.

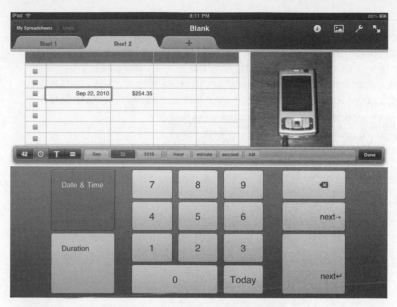

Figure 14-18. *The date, time, and duration entry keyboard*

Moving further down the data entry field there is a button with the letter *T* on it. Use this button to enter text into a cell. A standard text keyboard appears (Figure 14-19) after tapping the button.

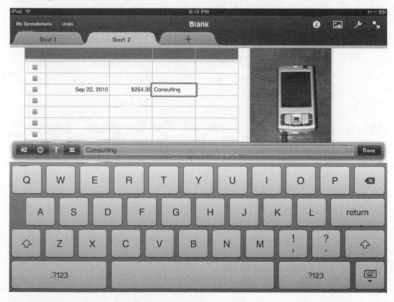

Figure 14-19. *The text entry keyboard*

The last button has an equal sign (=) on it. This button displays the formula entry keyboard (Figure 14-20) when pressed. A formula operating on data contained in cells, using functions entered through the functions key, is typed into the data entry field and applied to the cell by tapping the check mark button at the end of the field. The keyboard also contains a set of mathematical operators (parentheses, plus, minus, multiply, divide, exponents, and logical operators) for use in spreadsheet formulas.

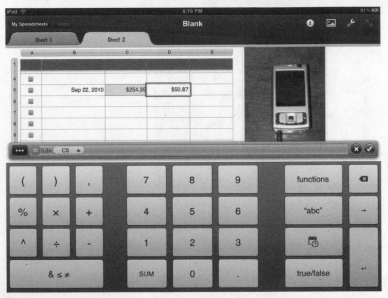

Figure 14-20. *The formula entry keyboard is used to enter both simple and complex formulas into spreadsheet cells.*

The Info Button

Remember the Info button in Pages? Numbers has one, too. Tapping the Info button when selecting a table displays a pop-up for changing table settings (Figure 14-21).

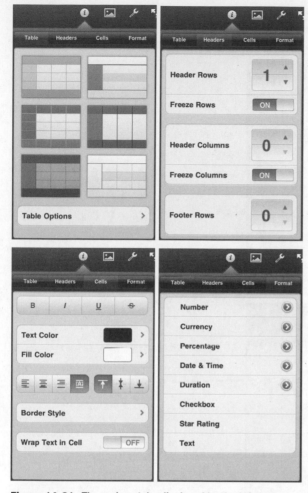

Figure 14-21. *The various tabs displayed by the Info button when a table is selected.*

The first tab, Table, applies a choice of different shading colors and types to a table from a palette of six prepackaged types. The Table Options button on this tab provides options for disabling the table name, deleting the border of the table, shading alternating rows in the table, turning off lines in the table grid, and changing the font and text size for any text or numbers in the table.

The Headers tab adds header rows, header columns, and footers to a table. You can choose to freeze header rows and columns so that they're always visible, even when you have scrolled the table down or to the right.

The Cells tab applies formatting to text cells on the table and is very useful for configuring header rows. The last tab, Format, applies special formats to cells or ranges of cells in the table. A cell can be formatted as a number, currency, a percentage, a date and/or time, a duration, a check box, a star rating (1 to 5 stars), or text.

Tapping the Info button while an image is selected causes the same two tabs (Style and Arrange) to appear that we described in the earlier section about Pages. When a chart is selected, tapping the Info button displays an entirely different pop-up (Figure 14-22).

Figure 14-22. *Access chart options by tapping a chart first and then the Info button.*

The Chart tab provides some preset options for the color of your chart. Tapping the Chart Options button at the bottom of this tab displays controls for enabling or disabling the chart tile, legend, and border; changing the text size and font; turning value labels on and off; or changing the type of chart.

The X-Axis tab is available only when your chart displays both x- and y-axes—it wouldn't make sense on a pie chart. It controls the visibility of category labels and series names; allows you to orient the labels along the x-axis of your chart horizontally, diagonally, or vertically; allows you to add gridlines or tick marks for the axis; and lets you enable or disable an axis title.

The Y-Axis tab is similar to the X-Axis tab but controls the options for the vertical axis of your chart. The Arrange tab moves your chart forward or backward in relation to other objects on the same page.

When you tap shapes that have been added to your sheets, the Info button provides an entirely different set of tabs (Figure 14-23).

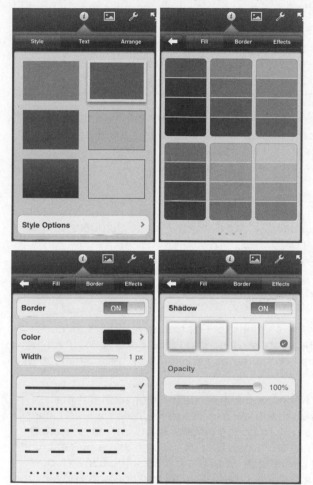

Figure 14-23. *The Info button displays a different set of tabs when a shape is selected. Note that these same tabs appear in Pages and Keynote when a shape is selected and the Info button is tapped.*

The first tab, Style, displays a palette of colors for the shape and a button marked Style Options. When tapped, another set of tabs appears. Fill provides a number of color and grayscale fills, Border enables or disables a border around the shape, and Effects creates a shadow and determines the opacity of the shape. Believe it or not, you can actually use a transparent color shape as a "filter" for exciting image effects.

For example, suppose you'd like to add a colored highlight to a photo to call out a certain object in the picture. Creating a red oval shape, setting it to be transparent, and then dragging it over the object in the photo makes a functional and professional-looking highlight.

The two other tabs that accompany Style are Text and Arrange. The Text tab adds text styles to text typed into the shape, while Arrange once again places the shape in front of or behind other objects on the page.

The familiar wrench icon in the toolbar of Numbers acts as your gateway to Tools. Choices for Tools are fewer than in Pages, with only Find, Go To Help, Edge Guides, and Check Spelling showing up. As with Pages, there's a full-page mode in Numbers enabled by tapping the arrows icon on the far right end of the Numbers toolbar.

Remember, you can't really hurt anything by creating a new spreadsheet and playing with Numbers. It's a great way to become familiar with the app, and you'd be surprised what you can learn just by creating fun or useful spreadsheets.

Keynote

By this point in the book, you may have become familiar with Pages, Numbers, and all of the many common features available in those two apps. Now you'll learn about Keynote, which is the presentation app of the iWork for iPad suite. Keynote is the only iWork app that can be used with the various video-out cables for the iPad for the purpose of projecting your presentation, so it is a powerful tool for teachers, businesspeople, and anyone else who needs to get their message across to groups of people.

This part of the chapter is shorter than the sections for Pages and Numbers, because we are assuming that you have read the sections describing those two apps. If you have not, you may want to review the information for Pages and Numbers because much of it is relevant to using Keynote.

Before we get too far into the topic of Keynote, it should be mentioned that not all imported PowerPoint or Keynote presentations will transfer to Keynote for iPad cleanly. Images may scale improperly, text sizes might be too large or small on your imported document, and transitions and builds are often lost. Do not assume that a presentation that has been moved to your iPad will be perfect—be sure to check the converted presentation on the iPad before "going public." Finally, the importation and conversion of large presentations is very time-consuming.

My Presentations

Launching Keynote by tapping it, the first thing you see is My Presentations (Figure 14-24). This is analogous to My Documents in Pages and My Spreadsheets in Numbers. Also like its siblings in iWork for iPad, Keynote comes with a Getting Started presentation document that is useful in learning how the app works. It's interactive, teaching you how to work with Keynote as you follow the instructions provided in the presentation.

Figure 14-24. *The My Presentations window is very much like the My Documents window in Pages and My Spreadsheets in Numbers.*

When you tap the New Presentation button in the upper-left corner of the My Presentations window, you're asked to choose a theme (Figure 14-25). Apple provides a dozen themes that range from plain white to fancy.

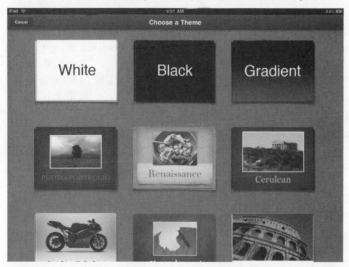

Figure 14-25. *Pick a theme from one of the dozen professionally designed themes built into Keynote for iPad.*

Tapping any one of the themes displays the first slide in your presentation deck, which by default is a title slide. Figure 14-26 shows the title slide and toolbar for the Renaissance theme.

Figure 14-26. *The default title slide for the Renaissance theme. Both the text and the image are placeholders that you replace with your title, subtitle, and image.*

Editing and Adding Slides

Although the risotto on the slide looks appetizing, that's probably not what you have in mind for your presentation. That's OK, since that image is just a placeholder, just like the "Double-tap to edit" text is waiting for you to edit it. To change the title slide image, tap the small circular image icon that is in the corner, and the familiar Photo Albums list is displayed. Select an image from your photos, and it takes the place of the placeholder.

The image placeholder may be smaller than your image, so your image is masked—part of it is made transparent so that it appears that the image is cropped. If you want to change the way the photo is masked, double-tap it, and the entire image appears (Figure 14-27). Use your finger to slide the image up or down, or scale the image using the slider control. When things look the way you want them, tap the Done button.

Figure 14-27. *Masking an image is useful in making sure that your audience is focused on the most important details of your image.*

Editing the text placeholders is done the same way. Double-tap them; the placeholder text disappears, and a standard iPad keyboard appears. Type in your new title and subtitle to make your title slide shine.

Unless you plan on giving a very short presentation, you're going to want to add more slides. That's what the plus sign at the bottom of the left sidebar is for. Tap the button, and a pop-up palette of slides appears (Figure 14-28). All of them have been designed to match the colors, fonts, and general look and feel of your title slide.

Figure 14-28. *The Add a Slide pop-up presents a graphical representation of eight different slide types. Tap any one of the slide images to add a new slide to your presentation, and then edit the slide to your requirements.*

Some of the slides show bulleted text, some are blank or nearly so, others are designed to display images, and several slides show text and images side by side. Tap the appropriate slide type for your next slide, and it is added to the slide show under the title slide.

Like your title slide, the other slide types all contain placeholders. Double-tap text to edit it, and tap the image icon on an image to replace the placeholder image with your own picture. You don't have to add an image; since the tools in Keynote are similar to those in Pages and Numbers, the Insert button can provide you with a way to add tables, charts, and shapes as well. You edit and configure all of these objects using the same tools discussed earlier in the chapter.

Not only does the Insert button appear in the Keynote toolbar, but the Info button is here as well, and it works the same way that it does in the other two iWork apps. Our familiar friend the Tools button is also present, and it provides the Find, Go to Help, Guides, and Check Spelling tools as well as a new item, Slide Numbers, which enables the placement of small numbers on the bottom of each slide in a presentation deck.

Two other unique buttons appear in the Keynote toolbar. At the far right end of the toolbar is the Play button. When it is tapped, the toolbar and sidebar disappear, and your presentation is displayed in full-screen. If one of the video-out cables is attached to the iPad, the window goes black, and a special control pad appears in the center of the window.

To navigate your presentation as it is playing, you can tap the screen to advance through slides or bullet points, or you can swipe your finger left to advance to the next slide. If you need to go back to the previous slide, swipe your finger right. When using the video-out cable to project your presentation, holding down your finger on the iPad screen creates a virtual "laser pointer" that is useful in highlighting items on the projection screen. Should you need to exit your presentation at any point while it is playing, double-tap the screen.

> **WARNING:** The virtual laser pointer in Keynote for iPad isn't that great. If you take your finger off of the iPad for just a second, you lose your laser pointer. Since the display just shows a black screen with previous and next arrows, there's no easy way to "aim" the pointer.

The Animation Button

The other button that is unique to Keynote is the Animation button, which looks like a diamond and is found in the middle of the pack of buttons at the right end of the Keynote toolbar. The Animation button is used to add animated slide transitions to your slide show, something that can really increase the impact of your presentation. The type of transitions available to you as a Keynote user vary by theme.

To add a transition to a slide, tap the slide in the sidebar to select it, and then tap the Animation button. A black arrow, initially marked with the word *None*, appears and is pointing at the slide you're adding the transition to. Tap the blue circle on the arrow, and a Transitions pop-up appears (Figure 14-29). This scrolling list contains a number of different animated transition effects, all of which add life to otherwise dull presentations. To see how a specific transition works with your slide, tap the name of the transition, and it is demonstrated for you.

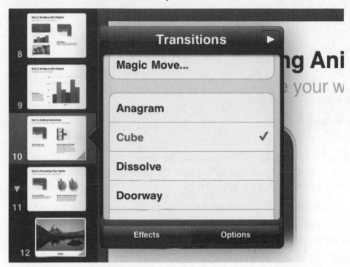

Figure 14-29. *The Transitions pop-up contains a comprehensive list of eye-catching animations to use in transitioning between slides.*

The Options button (Figure 14-30) on the Transitions pop-up sets options such as direction, speed, delay, and when to start the transition. Each transition effect is bit different, so each has its own options to set. Once you've changed option settings, you can see how the changes affect your transition by pressing the small Play button in the upper right of the Transitions pop-up.

Figure 14-30. *Each effect has a separate set of option controls to customize the speed, delay, direction, and other factors. For the Cube effect selected in Figure 14-29, the speed at which the transition plays and the direction in which the cube spins are the only variables that you can change.*

If you're familiar with setting up presentations in either Microsoft PowerPoint or the Mac version of Keynote, then you know that slide transitions aren't the only animations available to spice up your presentations. Animated builds, which add movement to slides by moving or spinning graphics or adding text bullets one at a time, can also rivet the attention of your audience.

To add a build effect to an object (graphic or text) on a slide, tap the Animation button, and then tap the object or text. A double-sided pop-up appears (Figure 14-31) for adding a build-in (a transition where text or a graphic is being added to the slide) or build-out (a transition to remove text or graphic from the slide).

Figure 14-31. *The build pop-up. Tap the plus button on the left to create a text build to add one bullet at a time, and tap the button on the right side to create a build that removes the build when moving to a new slide or object.*

Tapping the plus sign on the pop-up allows you to select the effect and change options. Two other buttons on the Build pop-up weren't on the Transitions pop-up—Delivery and Order. Delivery is usually available only for bulleted text, and it determines whether the text appears all at once or one bullet at a time. If you're using multiple builds on your slide, Order allows you to set the order in which the builds appear.

Although slide transitions and builds can be useful in creating an attractive presentation, be sure not to overuse them to the point of distracting from the goal of your slides— providing information to an audience.

Importing Documents from a Computer

Many times, you may want to work on documents that you already created on your computer or that someone else sent to you through e-mail. In Chapter 11, we showed you how to open attachments that have been sent to you in Mail, so e-mailing documents to your iPad is one way that to work on them while mobile.

Another method is to transfer the documents to your iPad by using iTunes on your computer. With your computer and iPad connected by the Dock Connector to USB cable, launch iTunes on the computer. When the iPad appears in the Devices list in the left sidebar in the iTunes window, click it, and then click the Apps tab.

Scrolling past the list of apps on your iPad toward the bottom of the Apps tab, you'll find an area with the title File Sharing. There's a list of apps that can transfer documents between the iPad and computer, and the iWork apps that you've installed on your iPad will be in that list (Figure 14-32).

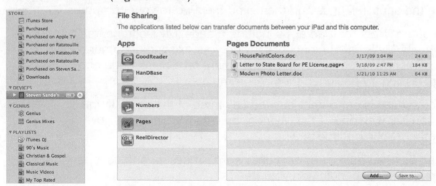

Figure 14-32. *You can transfer files to the iWorks applications from iTunes on your computer.*

To transfer documents from your computer, click the appropriate app name on the left, and then click the Add button on the right side. A standard file Open dialog for your computer appears, and then you can select one or more documents to transfer. Once the document files have been added to the list on the right side, clicking the Sync button in iTunes transfers the documents to your iPad.

Within any of the iWork apps, pressing the folder icon in the top-right corner of the My Documents, My Spreadsheets, or My Presentations window displays the documents stored on your iPad, and tapping the filename opens the file in the app.

A number of iPad file manager apps like Air Sharing Pro and GoodReader provide another way to move files to your iPad. These apps connect to MobileMe's iDisk, Dropbox, and other servers; allow you to view the files on the server; and then download and open them in iWork for iPad. With iPad printing support built into Air Sharing Pro, it makes a wonderful companion to iWork.

Moving documents out of iWorks is not as simple, because there is no common file store for these file managers to retrieve files from. In many cases, the only choices you may have for exporting documents are through e-mail (Chapter 11), saving the documents to iWork.com (Apple's online repository for sharing iWork documents), or using iTunes as described earlier.

Summary

The iWork for iPad trio of Pages, Numbers, and Keynote is a powerful set of apps for creating documents for work or pleasure while you're on the go. These optional Apple apps work well with their Mac counterparts and, to a more limited degree, Microsoft Office.

In this chapter, we've provided a look at the user interface and major capabilities of Pages, Numbers, and Keynote. Although a more detailed discussion of each app could easily fill another book, we've given you the information you'll need to get started using iWork for iPad. Some important points to remember from this chapter include the following:

- Pages, Numbers, and Keynote do not come with your iPad. To purchase the apps for $9.99 each and then install them, use the App Store app on your iPad while you're connected to a Wi-Fi network or purchase the apps in iTunes and then sync the iPad to your computer.

- All three of the iWork for iPad apps include a page (My Documents/My Spreadsheets/My Presentations) displaying your existing documents, and you can choose to create a new document on a blank page or with a professionally designed theme or template.

- The user interface is consistent between all three of the apps. If you become familiar with one of the iWork apps, you'll understand how to use the other two in no time at all.

- Pages can be used both as a traditional word processor and as a page layout application depending on your needs.

- Numbers tabs are similar to sheets in an Excel workbook. Each tab can have one or more table (spreadsheet) on it, as well as media (images), charts, and shapes.

- Add transitions and builds to your Keynote presentations to make them more interesting and vibrant to your audience.

- Transferring documents from your computer to your iPad is a great way to work on the go. You can transfer them by e-mail, through iTunes, or through a growing number of file management utilities.

Chapter 15

Other Great Ways to Use Your iPad

Throughout this book, we've shown you how to use your iPad to listen to your music and watch movies, write e-mails and documents, navigate with maps, and show off your photos, but all that (and it's a lot!) is just the start.

In this chapter, we show you just some of the many other ways you can use your iPad in everyday life, including as a helper in the kitchen, as a teaching tool, as a gaming device, as an artist's canvas, and more!

The iPad as a Game Machine

The iPad is a great device when you just want to kick back and unwind. You can listen to music, watch your favorite TV shows, and flick through photos of your last vacation with ease. Another way to unwind on the iPad is by playing games.

Whether you're into card games, adventure epics, or sports, there's a game for you. As a matter of fact, as of the time of this writing, there are more than 4,000 dedicated iPad games available in the App Store, and that's not including the 90,000+ iPhone games that play on the iPad as well.

Here we spotlight just some of the types of games you can play on the iPad.

Pinball HD

Pinball HD (Figure 15-1) harkens back to the times when games existed in three dimensions in the physical world and not on a computer screen. You'll quickly forget that you aren't playing on an actual pinball machine, however, because the level of realism in Pinball HD is amazing. You can choose from three pinball tables including the Wild West, a jungle, and the deep ocean. The app is a steal at $2.99.

Figure 15-1. *Pinball HD*

Air Hockey

Air Hockey (Figure 15-2) is another iPad game that harkens back to the day of nondigital games. What's so cool about this game is that you can play your friend on the same iPad. Because the iPad is a Multi-Touch device, it recognizes multiple inputs, not just from your finger either. Launch the app, choose a side, and show your friend who rules with the air puck. Best of all, it's only $0.99.

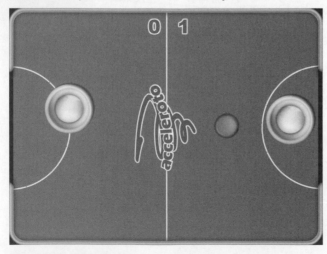

Figure 15-2. *Air Hockey*

iFish Pond HD

This isn't a game in the traditional sense. Oh, you interact with it as much as you would any game, but iFish Pond HD (Figure 15-3) can be fun even if you don't touch it. The game gives you a virtual fishpond on your iPad screen. Tap the water, and watch it ripple. See the colorful fish scurry away from your fingers, only to slowly come back to the calm of the pond. Add dragonflies, frogs, and pond lilies as you like; then sit back and enjoy the tranquility of nature on your iPad. It's $2.99.

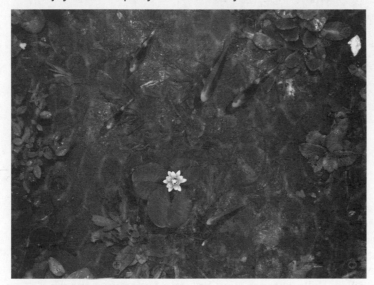

Figure 15-3. *iFish Pond HD*

Vector Runner HD

This game (Figure 15-4) pays homage to the early arcade games of the 1980s. You race your "car" along a track filled with wire-frame obstacles. As you race along, you pick up speed, which makes avoiding the obstacles harder and harder. There's a ton of racing games in the App Store that would make you think you were behind the wheel of a real car, but this game, with its simple 2D graphics, proves that games don't need to be highly detailed or complex to be fun. It's $2.99.

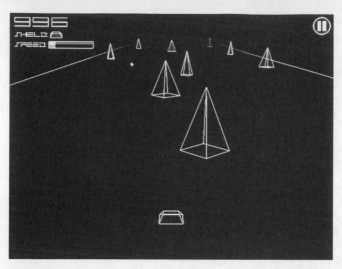

Figure 15-4. *Vector Runner HD*

Mirror's Edge

Major game developers are releasing games for the iPad in droves. One of the biggest game developers in the world, Electronic Arts, has a host of games out already. Mirror's Edge (Figure 15-5) was originally released for the Xbox 360 and PlayStation 3, and Electronic Arts has successfully ported it to the iPad, which goes to show just how powerful of a gaming device it can be. You play Faith, a "runner" who must get secret information past totalitarian police. With using nothing but your fingers and the iPad's built-in tilt sensors, you pilot Faith through her world by making her flip, slide, jump, and run. It's one fun game and is just a hint of the kind of action games you can expect to see coming to the iPad in the future. It costs $12.99.

Figure 15-5. *EA's Mirror's Edge*

The iPad as a News and Weather Center

The iPad is an awesome device that puts the Internet in your hands. You'll always be able to open the Safari web browser and check out any news site in the world. However, web sites are different from physical newspapers. They have a different layout, and you interact with them differently. Many major newspapers make apps for the iPad so you can navigate the news in the format you are used to in their physical counterparts. In addition, there are specific weather apps for the iPad that show you the weather forecast in a nicer and faster way than if you looked it up on the Web. Here we'll touch on just some of the news and weather apps available for the iPad.

News Apps

It seems that there's a new news app added to the App Store every day. We've sorted through the clutter and present to you with four of our favorites. There are many more out there—some very good—so browse through the App Store to find others that deliver the latest headlines to your iPad as well.

Bloomberg Finance

Bloomberg is one of the most trusted names in financial news, and Bloomberg for iPad (Figure 15-6) gives you that information in an elegant and interactive package so you can keep up with up-to-the-minute news on financial markets around the world. Bloomberg offers news, stock quotes, company descriptions, market leaders/laggers, price charts, market trends analysis, and more. You can create a list portfolio of stocks to track and monitor market currencies. What's more, you can even download the latest Bloomberg audio podcast from within the Bloomberg app itself and listen to them on the go. It's free in the App Store.

Figure 15-6. *Bloomberg for iPad*

NYT Editors' Choice

The *New York Times* is often referred to as the "newspaper of record" because of its long history of reporting on "All the news that's fit to print." When you browse the NYT Editors' Choice app (Figure 15-7) on your iPad, you feel as if you're holding the actual paper in your hand. Tap an article to see it displayed in typical newspaper-column view. Even the "paper" the articles are on look as if it's the real paper of the *New York Times*.

The Editors' Choice application offers a selection of latest news, opinion, and features from the paper's Latest News, Opinion, Business, and Tech sections. You can scroll through an article's photos and even view in-article videos. Best of all, the app stores articles locally on your iPad, so you don't need to be connected to the Internet to read them once you've downloaded the content. It's free in the App Store.

Figure 15-7. *NYT Editors' Choice*

BBC News

The BBC News app (Figure 15-8) takes the best of the BBC's web site and news channels and rolls it into one beautifully designed iPad app. Scroll through the latest news in Top Stories, Technology, Business, Science & Environment, Regional, and more than a dozen other categories. Listen to live BBC radio from within the app with the tap of a button; watch short video news clips; share articles easily via e-mail, Facebook, and Twitter; and even read news articles in other languages including Russian, Chinese, Arabic, and Portuguese. It's free in the App Store.

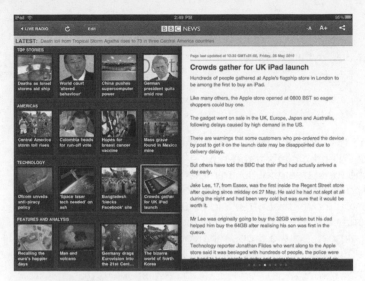

Figure 15-8. *BBC News*

USA Today for iPad

USA Today has done an excellent job at making its iPad app (Figure 15-9) look like the real paper—right down to the serrated newspaper edges that border the top of the screen. Browse and read stories from the News, Money, Sports, and Life sections; see local and national weather forecasts; and keep up-to-date on all the latest sports scores. The Day in Pictures section of the app is particularly interesting. It lets you swipe through the day's best photos in news, sports, and entertainment. You can also play the images as a slide show. It's free in the App Store.

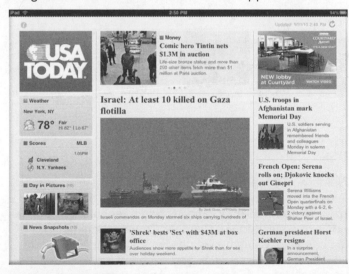

Figure 15-9. USA Today

Weather Apps

Just like with news apps, there are myriad weather apps for the iPad, but these are two of our favorites.

Weather HD

Weather HD (Figure 15-10) isn't the most full-fledged weather app, but it is the most beautiful. Browse through your selected city's three-hour and seven-day forecasts while being captivated by some of the most beautiful 3D animated landscapes representing the current weather outside. The Weather HD app shows you just how beautiful your iPad screen can be. Watch as you move through a field of lush green grass and tall wind turbines or fly through the clouds with a glorious moon rising in the distance. Raining outside? You'll swear you can almost feel the drops mist your face as Weather HD glides you through a green countryside as dots of rain float in the air. It's a steal at $0.99 in the App Store.

Figure 15-10. *Weather HD*

The Weather Channel Max+

Although it lacks the beauty of Weather HD, the Weather Channel's official iPad app more than makes up for it in features. The Weather Channel Max for iPad (Figure 15-11) delivers in-depth weather reports for current, 36-hour, and 10-day forecasts. Watch the latest weather-related news stories and a selection of Weather Channel original programming right in the app. You can even navigate weather maps by pinching and zooming. See Doppler radar, cloud coverage, Feels Like, and even UV Index maps. It's the weather of the world in your lap. Best of all, it's free in the App Store.

Figure 15-11. *The Weather Channel Max+*

The iPad as an Artist's Canvas

As you've seen, the iPad isn't just a tool to consume data; you can also use it to create a number of things including documents, spreadsheets, and presentations. But the iPad's creation abilities aren't limited to those who work in the business world. The iPad is a wonderful artist's tool. It's quite literally a blank canvas that you can use to create masterpieces Picasso would be envious of. Although there are several iPad artist apps, here are two that are our favorites.

Brushes

Brushes got its start on the iPhone and has since moved to the next level on the iPad (Figure 15-12). Brushes is a powerful tool for creating original works of art using your iPad's Multi-Touch display. Drag and swipe your fingers to create brush strokes on a blank canvas. Use the advanced color picker, myriad brushes, layers, the eyedropper tool, undo and redo controls, and more to create whatever your mind can conceive. Think creating artworks on the iPad isn't for "serious" artists? Artist Jorge Colombo famously created the June 1, 2009, cover of *The New Yorker* entirely using Brushes...for the iPhone. Now imagine what he—and you—could do with a digital canvas the size of the iPad's screen. The app costs $7.99, but think of home much money you're going to save by not having to buy replacement canvases and paints.

Figure 15-12. *It looks like it was drawn by a 2 year old, but it was actually created by one of the authors in about 30 seconds. Try your own hand at creating art on the iPad with Brushes.*

Adobe Ideas

If Brushes is a canvas, Adobe Ideas is a sketchpad (Figure 15-13). Using the tips of your fingers, sketch that latest idea you have for the dress that is going to take New York and Milan by storm, test designs for next year's most popular new superhero, or even use it as a white board for coffee-table meetings in Starbucks. A nice feature of this app is you can export any image you create as a PDF and e-mail it to yourself or others for editing in Adobe's professional apps like Illustrator and Photoshop or for viewing with any PDF viewer. Adobe Ideas is free in the App Store.

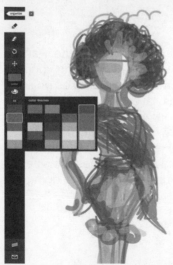

Figure 15-13. *Adobe Ideas lets you get your ideas down on paper...er, Multi-Touch screen.*

The iPad as a Phone

When the iPad was first unveiled, some people joked that it was nothing more than a big iPhone. As you can now tell, they couldn't have been more wrong. However, you can actually use your iPad as a phone. All you need to do is download the free Skype app (Figure 15-14) from the App Store, and you can make calls from your iPad to any phone in the world.

Figure 15-14. *Skype's iPhone app running on the iPad*

We want to note that, at the time of this writing, Skype has not released an iPad app. However, because most iPhone apps run on the iPad, you can download and use Skype for IPhone on the iPad without any problems. To use the app, you'll need a free Skype account, which you can set up at www.skype.com. You'll also need to be connected to a Wi-Fi network since Skype uses VoIP (calls made over Internet lines) to make phone calls.

Once you log in to the Skype app on your iPad, you can make free iPad-to-computer calls with other Skype users. If you buy Skype credit, you can make iPad-to-landline or cell phone calls. One of the writers uses Skype on his iPad in London to call his mother on her house phone in the United States because it is much cheaper than regular international rates or even buying a calling card. So, the iPad is not just an oversized iPhone, but it can make calls like the iPhone can.

The iPad as a Kitchen Helper

It may sound strange, but the iPad is very much at home in the kitchen. Whether you're using it as an electronic cookbook, surfing the Web while waiting for water to boil, or listening to music while you cook, the iPad is the perfect kitchen computer. You'll want to make sure that your iPad isn't near liquids or heat, but if you treat it with the respect of a beloved cookbook, you're probably fine.

Since you'll be chopping veggies and slicing meat, using a case with a built-in stand to keep the iPad in an upright position is a good idea. It takes up less counter space that way, and with a quick glance at the screen, you can find out what ingredient you need to add next to your recipe. Apple's iPad Case works very well to place your iPad in the proper position. We also suggest setting Auto-Lock (Settings ➤ General ➤ Auto-Lock) to Never so that you're not constantly having to turn the iPad back on. With those hints in mind, let's explore some kitchen-friendly apps.

Epicurious

If you're not sure about using your iPad in the kitchen, then Epicurious (Figure 15-15) is the perfect app to install to try your device as a kitchen helper. The free app calls upon recipes from *Bon Appétit* and *Gourmet* magazines, a broad spectrum of cookbooks, and the Epicurious web site to provide tens of thousands of recipes, all of which are rated by users. The list of featured recipes changes by season, and holiday specials are always useful for family get-togethers.

Figure 15-15. *The free Epicurious app turns your iPad into an intelligent cookbook with recipes for every occasion.*

The Epicurious app provides a way to change the font size, so if you want to set your iPad a bit farther away from your stove, you should still be able to read the screen from across the kitchen. There's also a bright orange pointer that you can drag down the recipe page so you'll never lose your place.

Each recipe has a shopping list icon; tapping that icon pushes the ingredients to a shopping list. Once you're ready to go to the store, it creates a combined shopping list that can be e-mailed to your iPhone, since you probably won't want to carry your iPad around the grocery store. The app has one downside; you can't easily share your favorites and recipes between devices or people.

BigOven

Another electronic cookbook to spice up your iPad is BigOven (Figure 15-16). BigOven comes in both a free Lite version and a full $9.99 version. The app searches more than 170,000 recipes in the BigOven.com database by name, by keyword (such as *rutabaga*), and even by what leftovers you have around the house.

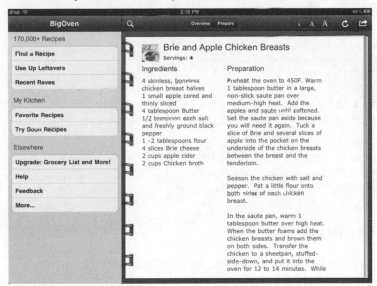

Figure 15-16. *BigOven is another wonderful resource for the iPad-toting chef. The ability to search for recipes that use up your leftovers is priceless. The free version is ad-supported.*

The recipes display in both an overview format and a prepare format. The latter lists ingredients in one column and preparation instructions in the other. BigOven is one recipe app that works better in portrait orientation, so you'll need to find a way to prop your iPad up (hint: the iPad Dock works just fine).

The full version of the app includes powerful syncing functions to make your grocery list and other information available on your iPad, on your iPhone, and on the Web.

My Recipe Book

Sometimes recipes don't come from an electronic source but are provided to you in the normal manner, such as scrawled on a note card by your Aunt Minnie in her indecipherable handwriting. Once you get a chance to sit down with her to translate the recipe, consider entering it into My Recipe Book (Figure 15-17).

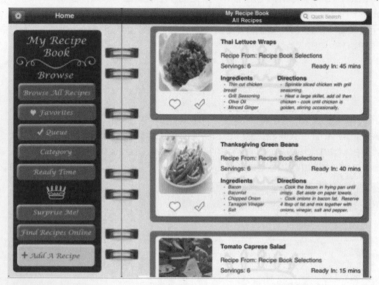

Figure 15-17. *Finally, My Recipe Book provides a place to organize all of those handwritten recipe cards you've been collecting over the years.*

This $2.99 app is just the thing for organizing recipes that would otherwise clutter up a recipe box or get stuffed into a kitchen drawer. My Recipe Book includes a way to search by preparation time and even includes a kitchen timer.

Serving Sizer Pro for iPad

Have you ever become so good at making a particular recipe that you're "volunteered" to cook it for thirty people instead of four? Serving Sizer Pro for iPad (Figure 15-18) can help.

Figure 15-18. *Serving Sizer Pro for iPad is a great tool for upsizing or downscaling recipes for various size groups.*

After entering a recipe into Serving Sizer Pro for iPad for a set number of servings, the $4.99 app not only keeps your recipe but can scale it to any number of portions.

Wine Ratings Guide for iPad

There is an old French proverb that says "Un jour sans vin est comme un jour sans soleil," which means a day without wine is like a day without sunshine. For people of many countries, wine is a welcome accompaniment to meals, and there's nothing better than a really good bottle of wine with a special meal.

The Wine Ratings Guide for iPad ($3.99) provides names of good wines, ratings, a photo of the label on the bottle, recommendations on food pairing, a flavor profile, and the price. The $3.99 app is probably the best wine app for iOS, although the iPad version hasn't been written to truly take advantage of the display size of the device.

The iPad as a Teaching Tool

Teachers, presenters, and people who need to get a point across to an audience have a compact and low-cost tool available in the iPad. Rather than needing a dedicated Windows computer or Mac to drive a projector, teachers can use an iPad with inexpensive software to produce professional, good-looking presentations or course materials.

Keynote

We talked about Keynote in Chapter 14, so we won't belabor the point in this section. It's just important to understand that Keynote for iPad can display both Keynote for Mac and PowerPoint presentations on a computer projector.

Many presentations created on Macs or Windows computers work perfectly when transferred to the iPad. Be sure to test those presentations and any video-out savvy apps in advance before you have a live audience, and make sure that all transitions, builds, and fonts transfer to the iPad properly.

Sadun's Whiteboard

There's only one flaw with using an iPad as a teaching tool, or should we say there *was* one flaw? There was no way to just write on a slide or display a web site and have it displayed through the Dock Connector to VGA cable.

The technical editor of this book, Erica Sadun, wrote the aptly named Sadun's Whiteboard (Figure 15-19) app to resolve this issue. The $0.99 app starts off displaying a plain white background on which you can use black, red, blue, and green markers to draw or write on a virtual white board. Sadun's Whiteboard supports video-out, so everything you put on the white board is displayed on an attached computer projector.

Figure 15-19. *Sadun's Whiteboard is an inexpensive electronic white board that is perfect for teachers or presenters who need to display handwritten notes or marks on a virtual white board, on a web page, or on a Keynote presentation.*

If that's not enough functionality for you, Sadun's Whiteboard also displays your Keynote slides, and you can "write" on them. It also has a built-in web browser, perfect for demonstrating sites or web apps, and once again, you can mark up the sites with your virtual markers.

The Education Category in the App Store

Finally, if you're a teacher or just a parent who wants to give your child an advantage in school, take some time to search the large and growing list of education apps for iPad.

Launch the App Store on your iPad, tap the Categories button at the bottom of the page, and then tap the Education button.

What is displayed (Figure 15-20) is every educational iPad app written for iPad. When we were writing this book, there were already 786 apps in the Education category in the App Store.

Figure 15-20. *The Education category in the App Store has something for everyone, from preschoolers to graduate students. Many apps are available for free.*

Depending on the topic and type of app, you may be able to download many education apps for free.

iTunes University

Although it's not iPad-specific, we would be remiss in discussing educational content for iPad without discussing iTunes University (Figure 15-21). Accessible from the iTunes U button at the bottom of the iTunes app is a vast collection of free video courseware made available by prestigious organizations throughout the world.

Figure 15-21. *iTunes University provides a wealth of free courseware about almost any topic.*

The videos range in topics from farming to astrodynamics and range from content for kindergartners to graduate students. iTunes University is the perfect destination for anyone who desires to further their knowledge.

The iPad as a Travel Computer

Whether you travel for business or pleasure, your iPad is a lightweight and unobtrusive traveling companion. If you're used to lugging a laptop and all of the sundry accessories (power supply, extra battery pack or two, Ethernet cable, and the laptop case) on your trips, you'll be surprised at how useful and powerful the iPad is as a fully functional travel computer.

Business travelers are usually interested in being able to track and book travel, communicating with people at home or back at the office, and determining whether weather is going to affect their travel plans. For leisure travelers, those requirements are usually the same, with the addition of being able to edit or retouch photos and video. Let's take a look at a handful of iPad apps that are perfect for travelers.

FlightTrack Pro

FlightTrack (Figure 15-22) is a handy app for determining the status of most flights, domestic or international, and in its free version displays beautiful maps showing the location of a flight in progress, departure and arrival times, and other important information.

Figure 15-22. *The free FlightTrack app for iPad is a fascinating tool for tracking the status of your flight. The $9.99 FlightTrack Pro app adds a significant amount of functionality, including synchronization with TripIt.com itineraries.*

Upgrade to the $9.99 Pro version, and you add a whole new level of functionality. FlightTrack Pro synchronizes itineraries with the TripIt.com travel planning service, so your flight information is automatically entered into the app. If you have multiple flight segments planned for a trip, FlightTrack Pro tracks all your flights on one screen for easy updates on flight status.

If a flight is delayed or canceled, a notification is pushed to your iPad even when the app isn't open. For those canceled flights, FlightTrack Pro finds alternate flights with a tap. Even when you're on a plane and have your device in airplane mode, FlightTrack Pro's maps will still work, showing your location on a detailed map. Weather information is available at a glance, with live radar maps showing any storms along your flight path.

Kayak Flights for iPad

Kayak.com's motto is "Search one and done," meaning that one search will find the best possible airfare between two airports. Although you can't actually book the flights that are found in an exhaustive yet fast search, the free Kayak app (Figure 15-23) provides a toll-free number and a web site link so you *can* book the flights. In many cases, you're even provided with the number of seats left at a certain price on a particular flight.

Figure 14-23. *Rather than making you search a lot of airline web sites for the best air fare deals, the Kayak Flights for iPad app does it all for you. Enter the departure and arrival airports, add a few details, and within seconds you have the lowest possible fares.*

If you need a hotel or rental car, Kayak Flights links you to the Kayak Web site.

Urbanspoon for iPad

Man does not live on airline food alone, so the traveler needs restaurants to survive on the road. Urbanspoon (Figure 14-24) is a popular free app for finding popular and good restaurants in almost every cuisine.

Figure 15-24. *The Urbanspoon app is a fun way of exploring restaurants in your local area or in any major city, all from the screen of your iPad.*

The app lists every restaurant in an urban area; in locations such as New York City, it's not uncommon to see 25,000 restaurants highlighted. To help you make a decision, there's a Popular button to narrow down the list to only those restaurants that have gained success through positive reviews and diner feedback. Urbanspoon also provides a way to narrow your search to individual neighborhoods, cuisines, and cost.

A fun thing to do is to use the Spin button to have Urbanspoon randomly pick out a restaurant for you. Once you've decided whether the restaurant is actually a place you really want to try, tap the map for an address and phone number, the menu of the restaurant, and more reviews and information.

Don't be stuck with room service food when you're traveling; find out where the locals eat with Urbanspoon, and go enjoy yourself.

Built-in iPad VPN Support

Business travelers who need a secure Internet connection back to the services available in their offices often rely on virtual private networks (VPNs). A way to describe VPNs is that they create a secure, encrypted tunnel between your iPad (possibly sitting in a hotel room on an open Wi-Fi network) and your office.

Your network or IT support group has probably created a VPN portal for your company. You'll need to know the following information in order to configure your iPad:

- Type of VPN: L2TP, PPTP, IPSec
- Server address
- Account name
- Whether or not you using an RSA SecurID fob
- Password (if not using RSA SecurID)
- Secret
- Proxy server information (if required)
- For PPTP: encryption level
- For IPSec: group name, and whether a certificate being used

Once you have this information in hand, go to Settings ➤ General ➤ Network ➤ VPN. Add a VPN configuration, and enter the information in the appropriate places before saving the VPN configuration.

To connect to the VPN, make sure that you have a working Internet connection, and then turn on VPN and select your configured network. The iPad negotiates a secure connection, and you're free to work on your office network as if you were actually sitting there instead of next to the pool.

Getting the VPN configuration set up properly can be difficult, so ask your IT department for assistance if you run into any problems.

Photography/Videography Apps: PhotoGene, Masque, ReelDirector

It's common to see travelers using small digital cameras or iPhones to take pictures and video while they're visiting faraway places.

Your iPad can serve as a portable digital backup tool and editing suite. Use the iPad Camera Connection Kit to transfer your digital photos or video to the Photos app, and your digital imagery is backed up to another device. Next, you can use one of these apps to retouch or edit your work before sharing it with friends back home.

Photogene (Figure 15-25; $1.99) is a powerful iPad tool for making your good photos even better. Pull an image from your photo library, and Photogene's tools let you crop or rotate it, adjust the resolution of the photo, add preset filters, adjust colors, remove red-eye from pictures of people, and even add frames and annotations.

Figure 15-25. *Photogene's palette of preset effects and filters is useful in making good photos shine.*

Once you're done creating your photographic masterpiece, Photogene makes it easy to share the photo through Twitter, Facebook, and e-mail. Your retouched photos can be saved to your photo library for posterity and eventual syncing to your Windows or Mac computer.

Another photo-editing and enhancement app is Masque (Figure 15-26, $5.99). It also takes your work from the photo library but performs some different functions. For example, you can apply gradient effects to your photos and stack filters to create completely unique images.

Figure 15-26. *The Masque toolset is different from Photogene's, and the two apps complement each other.*

Nexvio's ReelDirector (Figure 15-27; $3.99) is an easy-to-use video-editing suite for iPad. Although you won't want to edit your next feature-length documentary on the iPad, ReelDirector is perfectly suited for making short movies to share with family and friends.

Figure 15-27. *Whether you're editing a video presentation for a business meeting or just compiling clips for a family video, ReelDirector is an iPad-based film studio in an app.*

To use ReelDirector, load video from a camera or iPhone into the photo library using the Camera Connection Kit. In ReelDirector, create a new project, and begin adding film clips to it. Move the clips around on the timeline, trim or split them, and then add transitions, soundtrack, and titles, or zoom and pan on a clip.

When the edited product is done, ReelDirector renders the video into a playable movie incorporating all the elements you added. The finished product is sharable through e-mail, although the relatively large size of most movies means that you'll probably want to sync them to your Windows computer or Mac instead. The app also includes compression tools for creating lower-quality movies with smaller file sizes.

Remote Desktop Computing

An iPad is a tech support guru's dream. Being lightweight and unobtrusive, it's easy to carry around while fixing technical issues. Several apps can help you support local or remote users without needing to be tied to a desktop or laptop computer.

The first two tools discussed in this section are used for remote support of Mac or Windows users. In both cases, the app has a counterpart running on the target machine that you want to control.

iTeleport

iTeleport (Figure 15-28; $24.99) is an excellent example of what is known as a *virtual node controller* (VNC) client. Using a piece of software (iTeleport Connect) on a Mac, Linux, or Windows computer, an iPad can take over control of a remote machine.

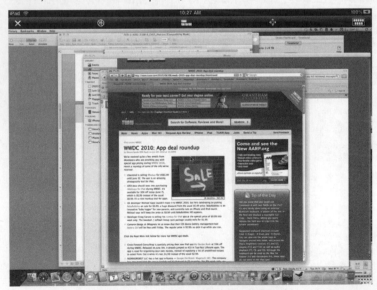

Figure 15-28. *iTeleport's remote control functions are fast and very usable for supporting Mac, Linux, or Windows computers.*

Special buttons at the top of the iTeleport window control how the touch screen acts as a mouse on the remote machine, set up special keys, provide access to the function keys on the top of most keyboards, and display the iPad's virtual keyboard for text entry.

LogMeIn Ignition

LogMeIn Ignition (Figure 15-29; $29.99) is another remote-control app. It's a product of LogMeIn, a company specializing in secure control of computers of any type. For large IT shops using LogMeIn, LogMeIn Ignition provides a way for support personnel to take over control of remote machines for troubleshooting purposes.

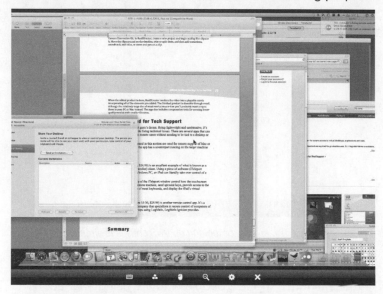

Figure 15-29. *LogMeIn Ignition is better suited for larger organizations with more computers to control.*

Between iTeleport and LogMeIn Ignition, the former is best used in situations where there are few computers to control, while LogMeIn Ignition is better suited for individuals who don't want to hassle with complex configuration or who must have access to a large number of computers.

As with iTeleport, your finger acts as a mouse on the remote machine, and you can use the familiar two-finger zoom gesture to look at details on the screen.

NetTools

Many times computer problems are not the fault of the computer. Instead, the network is causing issues. For that reason, most tech support personnel become very familiar with tools that allow them to troubleshoot network problems.

NetTools (Figure 15-30; $3.99) places three of the most popular network tools—Ping, Traceroute, and DNS—on your iPad. Ping is used to determine whether another device is actually visible on a network, Traceroute looks at the various network hops between your iPad and another machine, and DNS provides information about the Domain Name Service (DNS) server corresponding to an Internet address.

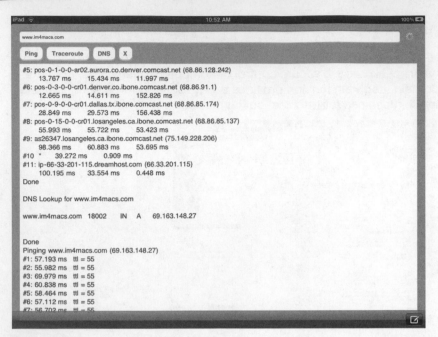

Figure 15-30. *Pinging networked devices, running a Traceroute, or looking up DNS entries is simple with NetTools. Any of the test results can be copied for e-mailing.*

Although it's not the most powerful network toolkit on the market, NetTools has just enough functionality to make it useful for IT support people who are using an iPad.

Summary

In this chapter, we discussed a variety of use cases for iPad owners. Whether you're a gamer, a traveler, an artist, a foodie, or an IT geek, or you just like to see what's going on in your world, there's probably an app for you.

Don't just stop here—your iPad is an incredible tool and toy that changes with every app. Make a quick look at the App Store part of your everyday routine, and you'll find more delightful and useful apps to enjoy. These are some of the key points to remember from this chapter:

- There are more than 4,000 iPad-specific games, and your iPad can also run more than 90,000 iPhone games.

- Free or inexpensive news and weather apps are easily available for your iPad, and they often rival or surpass their web-based counterparts in capability and speed.

- Your iPad isn't a phone, but it can make VoIP calls using the free Skype iPhone app that also works on iPad.

- iPads are the perfect kitchen helper. Just be sure to protect your iPad from heat and liquids.

- The Dock Connector to VGA cable is a useful accessory for iPad-toting educators.

- Travelers no longer need to worry about carrying the bulk and weight of a laptop computer and its accessories with them. iPad apps provide laptop-type functionality in a smaller form factor.

Index

D

L

O

P

W

You Need the Companion eBook

Your purchase of this book entitles you to buy the companion PDF-version eBook for only $10. Take the weightless companion with you anywhere.

We believe this Apress title will prove so indispensable that you'll want to carry it with you everywhere, which is why we are offering the companion eBook (in PDF format) for $10 to customers who purchase this book now. Convenient and fully searchable, the PDF version of any content-rich, page-heavy Apress book makes a valuable addition to your programming library. You can easily find and copy code—or perform examples by quickly toggling between instructions and the application. Even simultaneously tackling a donut, diet soda, and complex code becomes simplified with hands-free eBooks!

Once you purchase your book, getting the $10 companion eBook is simple:

1. Visit **www.apress.com/promo/tendollars/**.

2. Complete a basic registration form to receive a randomly generated question about this title.

3. Answer the question correctly in 60 seconds, and you will receive a promotional code to redeem for the $10.00 eBook.

233 Spring Street, New York, NY 10013

Offer valid through 11/10.